11.95

Snake River Of Hells Canyon

JOHNNY CARREY, CORT CONLEY, ACE BARTON

FIRST EDITION
Limited to 3000 Copies

ᵍ
BACKEDDY BOOKS
P.O. Box 301
Cambridge, Idaho 83610

By Johnny Carrey and Cort Conley
The Middle Fork and the Sheepeater War (Backeddy Books, 1977)

River of No Return (Backeddy Books, 1978)

Library of Congress Cataloging in Publication Data

Carrey, John 1914-
    Snake River of Hells Canyon

    Bibliography: p.
    Includes Index.
      1. Snake River.   2. Hells Canyon
      I. Conley, Jim Cort, 1944–   Joint author.
      II. Barton, Ace, 1925–   Joint author.
      III. Title.
    F752.S7C37   979.6'1   79-55450
    ISBN-0-9603566-0-6

Some of them have left behind a name
that is remembered to their praise;
but of others there is no memory,
for it perished when they perished
and they are as though they had never lived,
they and their children after them.

Ecclesiasticus 44:8-9

Dedicated to the founders
of the
Hells Canyon Preservation Council
who valued a river more than a reservoir —
and to Gerald Tucker
who knew that without history
there is no story.

Contents

Acknowledgements

On opposite rims of Grand Canyon, about 10 miles apart, live Kaibab and Abert Squirrels. Other than separate habitats, the only feature which differentiates the two animals is the Kaibab's white tail — the Abert has a dark tail. Centuries ago a few Aberts may have crossed the Colorado River and developed the coloration change. In a similar sense, the homesteaders living on opposite sides of Hells Canyon have histories separated by the river. The gorge remains a formidable obstacle for the aural historian who attempts to trace and record canyon stories. Idaho information was accessible to the authors, while Oregonians furnished significant help from across the river. Without their assistance, this book would have been as incomplete as a bobtail flush.

"There is no book so poor that it would not be a prodigy if wholly wrought out by a single mind, without the aid of prior investigators," said Samuel Johnson. This book is certainly no prodigy — materials were gathered from many sources. Considerable effort was expended researching names and facts, but man's recollection is a frail thread. "Clouded fact and memory fuse." In some cases we were forced to choose between conflicting stories, accepting that which seemed most plausible or cross-checked reliably. We did this without intending any disrespect for our informants. Rebecca West remarked that "It is a pity every human being does not at an early stage of his life have to write a historical work. He would then realize that the human race is in quite a jam about truth." If a reader recognizes error or has additional information we would be grateful for communication. Someday it may be possible to print a revised edition.

Obviously even so modest a work as this could only have been accomplished with the aid of many people. We wish to express gratitude and sincere thanks to: Mike and Kathy Doolittle, without whose kindness and generosity to their "writer in residence" this book would not have been written, to Pearl Carrey for her support and patience, to Earl Perry and Robert Conley for editorial assistance, to Dr. Merle Wells, who generously allowed verbatim use of his definitive articles on the steamboats *Colonel Wright*, *Shoshone* and *Norma* (edited for brevity, and supplemented where relevant with material from Dryden's *Marine History of the Pacific Northwest*) and also to: Gerald and Lucile Tucker, Jim and Murrille Wilson, Jim Camp, Grace Bartlett, Emma Davis, Minni Wilson, Daisy Spivy, Edna and Paul Butler, Hazel Wilson, Harold Smith, Kirk and Pat Spain, Julie Sliker, Frank Sotin, Earl Hibbs, Allen Wilson, Mary and Ralph Stickney, Jo Soules, Dick Rivers, Mrs. Lew Brundige, Vera Garrett, Harry and Nita Robinson, Bud Wilson, Len and Grace Jordan, Ron McCormick, Janet Friedman, Frank Hunsacker, Katherine Wyatt Sewell, Afton Rogers, Hazel Platt, Dick Sterling, Florence Smith, Amos Burg, Fred Himelwright, Winifred Lindsay, Jim Davis, Ora Robinette, Florence McGrady, Mel Smith, Otis "Dock" Marston, Willis Johnson, Jim Huntley, Margaret Allen, Boyd Norton, Dr. Earl Hamilton, Dan and Viola Cole, Ralph Page, Ray Holt, Mona Lanning, Doris and Bert Babcock, Hugh Beggs, Margaret Peterson, Georgie White, Helen and Joe Elliott, Mabel Ray, Don Harris, Jim Campbell, Dixie Wilmarth, Jim Zanelli, Floyd Harvey, Jerry Hughes and Carole Finley, Dean Snell, Bob and Jan Sevy, George Mancini and Karen Hopfenbeck, Chuck and Patti Bartholomew, Pearl Jones, Don Hatch, Nina Hawkins, Marcia and Bob Beckwith, Jim Collord, Gomer Condit and Bob Brown of Idaho Power Company, Catherine Evenson, Gary Swift, Larry Hill (photographs), Marjorie Gerberding, George Billingsley, Duane, Marney and Carole Garrett of Garrett Photography in Boise, Norm Riddle, Wesley Heitman, Paul Filer, Wade Hall, Elmer Earl, Susan Seyls, C. Leo Hitchcock (flowers), Dr. Haruo Aoki, Idaho Historical Society, Oregon Historical Society, Montana Historical Society, Smithsonian Institution, University of Oregon Library, Washington State University Library, Lora Dillon of the Luna House Historical Society, Lewiston, the Weiser Chamber of Commerce, Wallowa County Chieftain, Lewiston Morning Tribune, Grangeville Free Press, Cambridge News-Reporter, and High Country News.

Foreword

"History is what time leaves in an old man's eyes," observed William McIllvanney. The authors have attempted to record some events left in the eyes and minds of older people, and this book represents the completion of a trilogy dealing with historic aspects of three Idaho rivers. The effort was motivated by a desire to retrieve and perpetuate stories which are associated with riparian locations. Idaho rivers are remarkable and so are their stories — though not necessarily in this telling.

Stephen Spender wrote, "History is the ship carrying living memories to the future." Since embarking upon this task, many invaluable passengers have left the voyage — and in some cases, we arrived at our destination too late. While the ship's hold is not as full as it might have been had others been more concerned, we still believe the cargo was worth conveying.

In dealing with place names in Hells Canyon the writers have used those found on U.S. Geodetic Survey maps. Such maps often initiate and perpetuate errors, but attempting to change them here would be ineffectual, if not futile. The Forest Service was responsible for a parcel of changes and one might as well argue with the shadow of death as to insist on the original names at this late date. Changes can be justified in some cases because they eliminated duplication. Forest Service lookouts on fire towers had to direct supression crews to specific locations with a minimum of confusion.

In using the maps which accompany the text, it should be noted that mile 1 is Hells Canyon Dam — so computation of distance from the dam requires deduction of one mile from the map mileage. (The Army Corps of Engineer navigation markers on the river are numbered with digits preceded by the letters RM. Those numbers indicate the distance in river miles to the Snake's confluence with the Columbia River at

Pasco, Washington.) Locations described as being on the right or left side of the river are given facing downstream.

Special mention of the area's principle managing agency is necessary. The Forest Service has been faulted in the past for serious omissions and commissions regarding its responsibility for historic assets on National Forest lands. No single government agency has destroyed more buildings — often deliberately — which given time would have had irreplaceable value. It is encouraging to be able to commend the Hells Canyon National Recreation Area planning team, under the direction of Ron McCormick, for a substantial and admirable program aimed at the identification, evaluation and protection of sites which exist in Hells Canyon. About $200,000 has been spent on this effort since it was initiated in 1976. The program could serve as a model for other National Forest areas.

More than 200 sites of native American occupation have been identified along the river. Such sites are largely ignored in this guide because of damage which might be done to them. The same approach has been taken with pictograph locations because extensive "overpainting" has already occurred

A famous archaeologist, Sir Leonard Woolley, said, "All excavation is destruction." He was right. On the other hand, his profession has provided us with a great deal of knowledge. Archaeologists labor to interpret from a site as much as possible about the culture of those who lived on it and then convey that information to the public for a better understanding of human development and its relation to our own culture. This is only possible where artifacts can be studied in context. Once artifacts are removed from their original location, information which could have been interpreted is lost forever.

There are federal and state laws against disturbing such antiquities. Immense damage has already been done — particularly within the last five years. The cross-cultural patterns which existed in Hells Canyon give the location considerable significance to archaeologists. Unfortunately, the sites may serve not as examples of a previous culture, but of the actions of one segment in our present culture which places profit and personal possession above knowledge and human respect.

VICINITY MAP

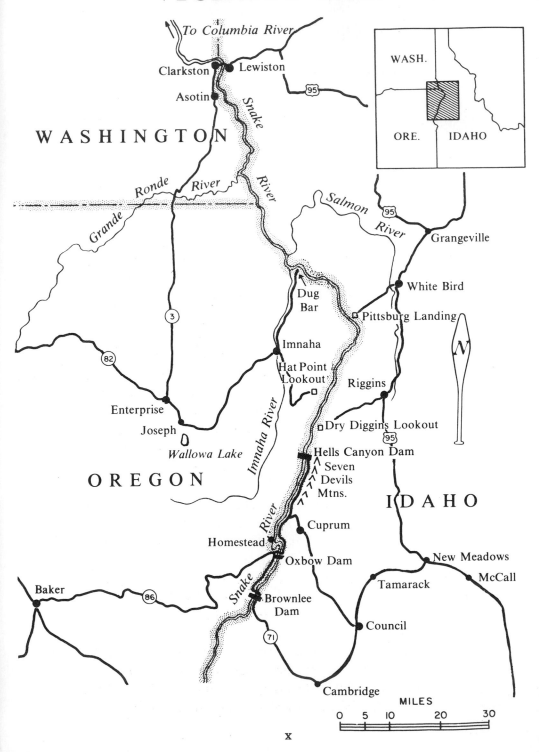

To Columbia River

Clarkston
Lewiston
Asotin
95

WASH.
ORE. IDAHO

WASHINGTON

Grande
Ronde
River

Snake
River

Salmon
River

95

Grangeville

Dug
Bar

White Bird

Pittsburg Landing

3

Imnaha

Hat Point
Lookout

Riggins

82

Imnaha River

N

Enterprise

Joseph

Wallowa Lake

Dry Diggins Lookout

95

Hells Canyon Dam
Seven
Devils
Mtns.

OREGON

IDAHO

Snake
River

Cuprum

Homestead

Oxbow Dam

New Meadows

McCall

Baker

86

Snake
River

Brownlee
Dam

71

Tamarack

Council

Cambridge

MILES
0   5   10   20   30

X

The Snake Uncoiled:
An Introduction

"The last thing we discover in writing a book is to know what to put at the beginning."
— Pascal

On the Pacific slopes of the Continental Divide in south central Yellowstone Park, the Snake River is born. Snow melting in the Rockies of western Wyoming flows westerly to the base of the Teton Mountains, then shifts southwest in a graceful scythe across the plains of southern Idaho. In the course of its thousand mile journey, the Snake exacts fluvial tribute from 40 rivers in six states. Where the river forms the border between Idaho and Oregon it has cut, rim to river, the deepest gorge in North America.

The geology of the canyon is complex. About 250 million years ago, flow rocks and sediments were deposited in the shallow waters of a lake or inland sea. When the volcanic action ceased, the area was gently folded and elevated above water level, perhaps as a result of continental shift. Much of the land was eroded and again covered with a sea — about 200 million years ago, according to fossil evidence. Layers of mud and limey sediment accumulated for 30 million years. Then the Seven Devils region emerged from the sea and has been subjected to erosion ever since.

About 15 million years ago, the eroded granitic rocks of the Seven Devils area were covered by massive lava flows which formed the Columbia River basalts. The landscape was reduced to a monotonously flat surface with scattered lakes and marshes. Two periods of deformation in the last five million years formed the Seven Devils and Cuddy Mountain uplifts. The uplifts probably blocked the old Snake River (which may have flowed through northern California to the sea) and formed Lake Idaho.

Geologists hypothesize that a south-cutting stream breached the northern lip of the lake near the Oxbow about a million years ago, causing the lake to drain down a tributary of the ancient Salmon River. Rapid downcutting formed the present Snake River drainage.

1

There were two stages of alpine glaciation during this period, which affected Council Mountain and Long Valley, just east of the Seven Devils. Glacial gravels slightly above the highest lake level (3,500 feet) suggest that Lake Idaho's spillover occurred a bit prior to the last glacial period. The oversteepened creek mouths and the deeply incised canyon of the Snake are indications of a young and vigorous river.

In historic times, the lands edging the upper and middle reaches of the river were occupied by the Shoshone. Because they painted snake heads on sticks to terrify their enemies, and possibly because a sinuous movement of the hand was used as sign language to signify their tribe, Indian neighbors and early trappers spoke of the Shoshone as the "Snakes." Flowing through Snake country, the river acquired that tribal name. The Shoshone referred to the Snake River as "piahuna" or "pabahuna" and the Nez Perce called it "piku:nen" or "himequin-imewe:lepe."

The derivation of Hells Canyon's sobriquet is more difficult to ascertain than that of the river which carved this canyon. Most old-timers knew the gorge as Box Canyon or Snake River Canyon. The first reference to Hells Canyon which the writer has been able to locate appears in an 1895 edition of *McCurdy's Marine History of the Pacific Northwest*. In discussing the voyage of the steamboat *Norma* (at the mouth of Deep Creek, just below the site of Hells Canyon Dam) the author writes: "She then bounded off, swinging into midstream, and, like a racehorse, shot into Hell Canon, where the river winds like a serpent and the wall rocks tower to such a height that they almost shut out the sun." The name was twice used by the Mazama hiking club of Portland in their 1931 bulletin, though Forest Service maps in 1935 still labeled the area Box Canyon. It was not until the early 1950's that Hells Canyon became a popularly accepted descriptive term for the gorge — primarily because of several articles by Oregon's Senator Neuberger which used the present name.

Miners, stockmen and settlers began establishing land claims in Hells Canyon in the 1870's and 80's. The mining laws made it possible for some individuals to reside in the canyon on a small piece of ground with minimum expense. Anyone may enter federal land, except areas closed by law or administrative action, to seek minerals. By staking a claim of about 20 acres, and diligently searching for minerals, one could hold the claim indefinitely, as long as he did annual assessment work amounting to $100. Title to the land could be obtained if the mineral discovery made was sufficient to warrant an ordinarily prudent man

2

investing further of his time and money to develop a commercial mine.

In 1861, Abraham Lincoln had addressed Congress with the following words:

> The prudent, penniless beginner in the world labors for wages awhile, saves a surplus with which to buy tools or land for himself and at length hires a new beginner to help him. This is the just and generous and prosperous system which opens the way to all — gives hopes to all, and consequent energy and progress and improvement to all . . . I am in favor of settling the wild lands into small parcels so that every poor man may have a home."

A year later, President Lincoln signed the Homestead Act. It has been called the "greatest democratic measure of all history." It was this legislation, and laws which expanded it, that brought settlers to Hells Canyon.

The Homestead law provided that the head of a family (any age), a widow, or a single man over the age of 21, who was a U.S. citizen or had filed a declaration of intent to become a citizen could stake a homestead not exceeding 160 acres on the surveyed public domain. Title to the homestead could be acquired by continuous residence, improvements of five years, and payment of a fee of $34 on the Pacific Coast and $26 in the other states. After six months actual residence, and suitable improvements, the claimant might commute his homestead entry into full title simply by paying $1.25 per acre. Any improvement of an acre or more was sufficient for commutation. Filing final entry was called "proof" or "proving up" and the title received was known as a "patent." Lands acquired under the act were exempted from liability for debts incurred prior to issuance of a patent. An affidavit was required from each entrant swearing that the application was "for his or her exclusive use and benefit . . . for the purpose of actual settlement and cultivation." A person was allowed only one homestead entry.

Congress attempted to resolve the growing conflict between stockmen and settlers in 1877 by passing the Desert Land Act. Under this act, a settler might purchase 640 acres if he would irrigate it within three years after filing. He could acquire title by proof of compliance with the law and payment of $1.25 per acre. Again, each person was allowed a single entry. The act was useful to Hells Canyon settlers because with ditch irrigation they could acquire enough land to get a foothold in the livestock business in a region too arid for ranches limited to 160 acres of grazing ground.

An act passed in 1880 provided that any settler on surveyed or

3

unsurveyed land, who intended to claim it under the Homestead Act, was to be allowed a period of time to file his homestead application and to perfect his entry. This right dated back to the time of entry and was known as a "preemption right."

The Forest Homestead Act of June 11, 1906, allowed forest reserve lands valuable for agriculture to be opened under the homestead laws. This legislation allowed the boundaries of the 160 acres to follow the contours of the land, rather than the inflexible corners of the township survey system. "June 11 homesteaders" often controlled fertile strips in sidestream canyons or along the river.

In 1909, the Enlarged Homestead Act gave settlers permission to take 320 acres, provided one fourth of the land was cultivated. No irrigable, timber, or mineral land could be entered under the new law. Because conditions were different in Idaho, the settler could live anywhere within 20 miles of his claim, as long as he cultivated half of it.

The Homestead Act has been humorously characterized as an attempt by the government to "bet you 160 acres of land that you couldn't live on it five years without starving to death." Yet it is interesting to note that 70 percent of all successful homesteading was done in the Twentieth Century. More than a quarter of the total federal acreage available was transferred to private ownership in a 10-year period during and after World War I. There were 60,221 final homestead entries in Idaho, utilizing almost 10 million acres. These entries peaked in 1913.

Though miners and stockmen left their imprint on the Canyon of Hell, it was the homesteader who made the most significant contribution. Most of their holdings have been reacquired by the Forest Service for the National Recreation Area, coming full circle like the seasons. But evidence of their efforts still speckles the canyon. In looking at homestead sites it is well to keep in mind the scarcity of two resources: wood and water. Wood for buildings, fence posts, and fuel had to be packed to its destination. Unless creek water could be ditched around the skirt of a hill to feed cabin, garden, and hay, a bar was uninhabitable. These factors set limits to the land. Today the canyon visitor sees sagging fences, hay fields overgrown, and a few cabins that recall Agee's description: "a human shelter, a strangely lined nest, a creature of killed pine stitched together with nails into about as rude a garment against the hostilities of heaven as a human family may wear." At the same time, we need remember that the demands upon their lives were relieved by ample fish and game, good range, and surroundings of undeniable beauty.

4

Tempting the Snake:
Captains and Boatmen

"History is the essence of innumerable biographies."
                                    Carlyle

Lewis and Clark
1806

Members of the Lewis and Clark Expedition walked the lower reaches of Hells Canyon in the spring of 1806 during their eastward return from the Pacific Ocean. Snow on the Bitterroots lay higher than their saddle skirts, forcing the men to camp impatiently with the Nez Perce near today's Kamiah, Idaho, for almost a month.

During this time a three-man contingent consisting of John Ordway, Robert Frazier and Peter Wiser (for whom the Idaho town and river of Weiser are named) was taken by Indian guides across the Camas Prairie to gather fish at the Salmon River. The journals of both Captain Lewis and Captain Clark record the party's observations on June 2, when the men returned. Lewis's journal reads, with major variations from Clark shown in parenthesis:

> The Indians inform us that there are a plenty of Moos to the S.E. of them on the East branch (Salmon River) of Lewis's (Snake) river which they call Tommanamah R. (Clark: Tommawamah River.) about Noon Sergt. Ordway Frazier and Wizer returned with 17 salmon and some roots of cows (kouse); the distance was so great from which they had brought the fish that most of them were nearly spoiled. These fish were as fat as any I ever saw; sufficiently so to cook themselves without the addition of grease; those which were sound were extreemely delicious; their flesh is of a fine rose colour with a small admixture of yellow. these men set out on the 27th ult. and instead of finding the fishing shore at the distance of half a days ride as we had been informed, they did not reach the place at which they obtained their fish untill the evening of the 29th having travelled by their estimate

near 70 miles. the rout they had taken however was not a direct one; the Indians conducted them in the first instance to the East branch of Lewis's river about 20 miles (Clark: about ten miles) above its junction with the South branch, at a distance of about 50 Ms. where they informed them they might obtain fish; but on their arrival at that place finding that the salmon had not yet arrived or were not taken, they were conducted down that river to a fishery a few miles below the junction of the forks of Lewis's river about 20 Ms. further, here with some difficulty and remaining one day they purchased the salmon which they brought with them. The first 20 Ms. of their rout was up Commeap Creek and through a plain open country, the hills of the creek continued high and broken with some timber near it's borders. the ballance of their rout was th(r)ough a high broken mountanous country generally well timbered with pine and soil fertile in this quarter they met with an abundance of deer and some bighorned animals. the East fork of Lewis's river they discribe as one continued rapid about 150 yds. wide it's banks are in most places solid and perpendicular rocks, which rise to a great hight; it's hills are mountains high. on the tops of some of those hills over which they passed the snow had not entirely disappeared, and the grass was just springing up at the fishery on Lewis's river below the forks there is a very considerable rapid nearly as great from the information of Sergt. Ordway as the great falls (rapids) of the Columbia the river 200 yds. wide (Clark: about 150 yards wide). their common house at this fishery is built of split timber 150 feet long and 35 feet wide flat at top. The general course from hence to the forks of Lewis's river is a little to the West of south about 45 ms. The men at this season resort their fisheries while the women are employed in collecting roots. both forks of Lewis's river above their junction appear to enter a high Mountainous country.

While it is impossible to ascertain with certainty whether the three-man party actually visited the Salmon-Snake confluence, it seems probable from the evidence, and they were obviously the first white men to explore the lower portions of the middle Snake.

Wilson Price Hunt
1811

Fifteen cottonwood canoes embarked on Henry's Fork of the Snake River, October 19, 1811, as part of an expedition that was to suffer privations severe as any experienced in the westering history of America. They were pilgrims bound for the canyon of hell — and not all of them would return.

The journey originated in the mind of John Jacob Astor, German-born New York merchant of furs and pianos. Astor had the vision, resources and opportunity to establish an empire. The United States had recently purchased the Louisiana Territory; Lewis and Clark had returned from the area with reports of abundant furs, and Canadian traders had taken only token advantage.

Astor conceived a grandiose scheme: build a chain of forts along Lewis and Clark's route to the sea, establish a post at the mouth of the Columbia to collect furs, monopolize trade with the Russians at Sitka, supply the coastal trading post with ships from New York, use the same vessels to haul the furs to China and return to the Atlantic carrying cargoes of Chinese tea, silk, and wares. These ships would meet company vessels from England loaded with inexpensive Birmingham goods for the Indian trade. Cumulative profits would be enormous. J. J. Astor told Washington Irving, the biographer of this enterprise, that he considered his establishment at the mouth of the Columbia "the emporium to an immense commerce, a colony that would form the germ of a wide civilization, that would in fact carry the American population across the Rocky Mountains and spread it along shores of the Pacific — as it already animated the shores of the Atlantic." Aware of the political effects that could result from expanded American activity in the Oregon Country occupied by the British, Astor had consulted with President Jefferson, then covered his bets by offering partnership or cooperation to the Canadian North West Company in his venture. The company turned him down.

John Astor then formed the Pacific Fur Company in 1808, taking several partners. He chose a young, intelligent, conscientious, and amicable St. Louis merchant as his field marshall. Wilson Price Hunt had been born in New Jersey, but moved to St. Louis the year it transferred to American sovereignty, where he opened a store with bright prospects for trade. Hunt was not a mountain man, however. He was a

Drawing of Wilson Price Hunt from the Missouri Historical Society.

"businessman first, last, and always." After conferring with Astor in New York, he went to Montreal and began organizing an expedition with two experienced ex-North West Company Scots, Donald McKenzie and Alexander McKay. French voyageurs were hired as boatmen there, and others, along with supplies, were gathered in St. Louis. The brigade, now bigger than Lewis and Clark's, wintered 450 miles upriver from St. Louis, where plentiful game made it easy to feed the crew, and where an early start could be made in the spring. Astor's ship, the *Tonquin*, sailed from New York for the mouth of the Columbia in September, 1810, to rendezvous with the overland party. The plan was underway.

As Hunt's boatmen pulled and poled their craft against the Missouri's spring flood in 1811, a wholly separate but engaging epic in river history was enacted. Manuel Lisa of the Missouri Fur Company, desiring protection from the Sioux that would be afforded by a larger group, set out from St. Louis to overtake the Hunt party, which had a three week start. Lisa sent a messenger to request that Hunt wait for him, but two of Hunt's partners suspected Lisa would turn the Indians against them, so urged their party to remain in the lead. Thus ensued the most famous keelboat race ever recorded; Lisa pushing his men to lengths never equalled (75 miles in one day *upriver!*), and finally overtaking the Astorians two months and 1100 miles later.

On advice from John Colter, as well as three Kentucky hunters headed downriver, Hunt abandoned Lewis and Clark's route in order to avoid the Blackfeet. The group now numbered 65 people, including an Indian woman, Marie Aioe Dorion, and her two children. Horses were purchased from the Arikara Indians and the party set out across the plains of South Dakota. They traveled the rolling grasslands of Wyoming, through the Big Horns, over the Wind River Mountains and across the difficult divide between the Green and the Snake. In early October they came down the snowy summit of Teton Pass into what is now Idaho. A few days later the men arrived at Henry's Fork, the north fork of the Snake. They set about felling cottonwood trees in order to make log canoes. It was from this point that they pushed off downriver on October 19, and trouble began camping on their trail.

No one had yet traced the route between the Snake and the Columbia. The Astorians were confident of a swift, brief journey, but as they merged with the main river they first encountered tumultuous rapids. Portages interrupted the flow. Nine days later the boatmen entered a lava canyon in southern Idaho near today's Burley, where the river often formed impassible cataracts. When one of the canoes struck a rock, its steersman was flung into the water and swept away. The French-Canadians began referring to the water as "maudite riviere enragee" — the accursed mad river. They pulled their canoes out on the jagged shore while Hunt and three of his man scaled the basalt cliffs to scout downriver. A 35 mile survey was disheartening. The river was choked with rocky rapids and the canyon walls were so sheer Hunt found access to the water in only two places. A group that reconnoitered the river from the opposite rim was more optimistic, but after a six mile carry with four canoes, the boats were flushed away along with their equipment. The men decided they needed fins instead of feet.

John Astor's expedition was in a perilous position: no horses, little food, isolated on the bleak Snake plains with winter about to pitch its tent and no idea how far it might be to the Columbia.

Hunt decided to conquer by division. He split the party into five groups: Ramsay Crooks was to lead one back 300 miles for horses. Two other groups, under Reed and McClellan were to search downriver for Indians with food, and the fourth was to go with Donald Mackenzie north across the arid plain in quest of the Columbia.

Hunt remained in the canyon with the balance of the party to cache supplies, catch fish and beaver. After a few days, Crooks' group returned saying land travel was too difficult.

The Astorians decided to follow Reed and McClellan, and the commander split the men into two bands which pressed forward on foot. Crooks and 19 men traveled along the south rim, while Hunt with 22 others, including the uncomplaining Marie Dorion — 7 months pregnant, carrying a two-year-old on her back and leading a four-year-old by the hand — proceeded along the north edge of the palisades.

Day after weary day, they struggled across the lava shards and sage-splashed emptiness of the Idaho desert, suffering a tantalizing thirst as the inaccessible river glinted below them. Crooks' party was reduced to eating their moccasins. Hunt's group lagged behind, and scrounged an occasional dog or dried fish from impoverished Shoshone Indians. Due south of present Boise, Hunt led his people away from the Snake's canyon, cutting across the barren waste until they struck the Boise River. The laconic sentences of his journal reveal their predicament:

On the 20th, the rain, which had commenced to fall the previous night, gave us a little water. This alleviation was timely, as several Canadians had begun to drink their urine.

10

It continued to rain all night. On the 21st, at sunrise, we saw
before us a river (the Boise) which flowed westerly. Its shores
were fringed with cottonwoods and willows. Some indians
had established their camp there. They had many horses,
and were better clad than those we had seen previously.
They informed us that beaver are common further up in this
small river. Very few of them are in the neighborhood of the
camp. On reaching the huts, I lost my horse. An indian told
me that it had been stolen from him.

The weather was constantly rainy. We could not make
much progress. On the 22nd, we met some Indians. From my
observations and the few words I could understand, the
distance from this place to the Big River (the Columbia) was
very considerable; but the indians told me nothing of the
route I must follow. We followed the river. On the 24th, we
crossed it a little above our Canoe River (the Snake), which
continued to flow toward the north. The mountains in front
of us were everywhere covered with snow. On the 25th, despite the severe weather, our fatigue and our weakness, we
forded another river (the Payette) which came from the east,
the water was waist-deep.

On the 26th, the hills began to appear. They stretched
along the snowy mountains. We crossed another small
stream (the Weiser) which flows from the same direction as
the others. It led us, on the 27th, to a defile (Mann Creek) so
narrow as to leave scarcely space enough to pass through. We
frequently were obliged to remove the baggage from our
horses and to travel in the water. On the previous evening, a
beaver had been caught, which furnished us a scanty breakfast. We had supped off bouillon tablets. I therefore had a
horse killed. My men found the flesh very good. I ate it reluctantly because of my fondness for the poor beast.

Hunt had followed the Weiser to the mouth of Mann Creek, ascended Mann Creek to the headwaters of Monroe Creek and crossed to
the head of Wolf Creek, following it down to its mouth on the Snake,
about 25 miles upriver from the present location of Brownlee Dam. The
Astorians were now entering Hells Canyon:

On the 3rd (December), it rained and snowed all day.
We could advance only 9 miles. Our horses were unloaded to
allow them to go along the river. The baggage was carried by

11

hand. We travelled toward the northeast. On the 4th, it was necessary to leave the banks of the river and to climb the mountains. They stretched all around us, and were covered with snow. Pines and other green trees grew on the sides of some of them. The snow came above our knees. It was excessively cold. We were almost succumbing to its severity when, at sunset, we had the good fortune to reach a cluster of pines. We made a good fire, which comforted us. Although we marched all day, we were, because of the meanderings of the river, only 4 miles from our encampment of the preceding night (south and north ends of the Oxbow).

On the 5th, the abundant snow which was falling did not allow us to see three hundred feet ahead of us. We succeeded, however, in reaching the river's bank by letting ourselves slide. The sound of the running water guided us. A horse with his pack fell some hundreds of feet in depth, but was not hurt. The weather was much less severe in the valley than on the heights. It rained there. The snow was only ankle-deep. I killed another horse.

On the 6th, we had just started out, when — What was my astonishment and distress! — I beheld Mr. Crooks and his party on the other side of the river. I immediately returned to camp, caused a canoe to be made out of the skin of the horse killed on the preceding night, and sent enough food to our famished companions. Mr. Crooks and one of his party came to us. Poor man! — he was well-nigh spent from fatigue and want. He told me that he had gone three days' march further down; that the mountains there are even higher and come closer to the river, which at that spot is compressed into a canal not more than sixty to a hundred feet wide between precipitous rocks; and that it was impossible for men in their condition to proceed, because, for six days, their only animal food had been one of their dogs. Mr. Mackenzie and Mr. Reed with their party had gone on. Mr. Crooks had spoken with them a few days earlier. They told him that Mr. McClellan, on leaving the small river, had crossed the mountains with the hope of falling in with the Flatheads. The river, at the spot where we were, flows almost easterly. Mr. Crooks tells me that it continues in this direction.

I spent the night in considering my situation. I had to provide for the needs of more than twenty starving people and, in addition, give my utmost aid to Mr. Crooks and his party. Notwithstanding all the discouraging reports to me concerning the region below here, I would have continued my journey on the mountains if it had not been, as I already knew from experience, that the depth of the snow would make the undertaking impracticable. It was necessary therefore, to my great regret, to retrace my steps, hoping to encounter in the meantime some indians on one of the three small rivers above the mountains. I counted on buying from them a sufficient quantity of horses to feed us until we should reach the Big River, which I flattered myself to be able to accomplish this winter. I feared nevertheless that Mr. Crooks and some of his men would not be able to follow us. What an outlook! We must expect having nothing to eat for several days; because, on this side of the indian huts which we left November 29th, we have found only cherries; and perhaps there would be no more of them in the same places.

The skin canoe had been lost. A raft was made, so that Mr. Crooks and his companions, with the remainder of the meat, might cross to the other side. The attempt failed. On the 7th, we were reduced to marching slowly, because Mr. Crooks was so feeble that he had great difficulty in keeping up with us. Most of my men had gone on ahead.

On the 8th, another raft was made; but, after repeated trials, Mr. Crooks and his man were unable to cross owing to the violence of the current. Therefore I was obliged to wait for them. Whereupon my men grumbled, saying we all would die of hunger; and importuned me in every way to go on. To add to my troubles, Mr. Crooks was quite ill in the night. Seeing that this mishap would delay for two days my arriving among the indians, I left three men with him; and departed on the 9th with two others to rejoin my party. I had three beaver skins, two of which I left with them. We supped off the third. The weather was extremely cold.

On the 11th, we had another calamity. One of Mr. Crooks's men was drowned while crossing the river in a canoe which capsized with many goods.

The Hunt party had managed to catch five Shoshone horses and fashioned a horsehide boat to ferry the food to Crooks' band starving on the opposite shore.

Washington Irving relates the incident in *Astoria:*

". . . A poor Canadian, however, named Jean Baptise Prevost, whom famine had rendered wild and desparate, ran frantically about the banks, after Jones had returned, crying out to Mr. Hunt to send the canoe for him, and take him from that horrible region of famine, declaring that otherwise he would never march another step, but would lie down there and die.

The canoe was shortly sent over again . . . with further supplies. Prevost immediately pressed forward to embark. Delauney refused to admit him, telling him that there was now a sufficient supply of meat on his side of the river. He replied that it was not cooked, and he would starve before it was ready; he implored, therefore, to be taken where he could get something to appease his hunger immediately. Finding the canoe putting off without him, he forced himself aboard. As he drew near the opposite shore, and beheld meat roasting before the fire, he jumped up, shouted, clapped his hands, and danced in a delirium of joy, until he upset the canoe. The poor wretch was swept away by the current and drowned, and it was with extreme difficulty that Delaunay reached the shore.

Hunt left Crooks, John Day, and three French Canadians to regain their strength with a band of Shoshone. He had the men make a boat from two skins, ferried the party to the west side of the river, and with three Indian guides resumed the overland trek. They discovered a feasible route through the Blue Mountains to Umatilla Valley, which with slight variations would become famous as the Oregon Trail. Marie Dorion paused to give birth to her baby, then caught up with the group the next day.

The Astorians crossed the Columbia and took to canoes near The Dalles. They arrived at the mouth of the Columbia in mid-February, 1812. There they found the sea group had arrived a year earlier and built a fort called Astoria. However, the ship and crew had been destroyed afterward by Indians at Nootka.

Hunt also found the members of the McKenzie, McClellan and Reed parties who had preceded him to the post by a month. They had skirted the eastern slopes of the Seven Devils Mountains and descended to the Little Salmon where friendly Nez Perce gave them food and guided them to the Clearwater. There they obtained canoes and paddled to the Snake and thence to the Columbia.

The epilogue to the whole venture is stranger still. Hunt took another Astor ship, the *Beaver,* to Sitka where he traded its cargo to the Russians for 75,000 seal skins. The furs had to be picked up in the Pribilof Islands which required a six week detour. Short of time, the *Beaver* headed for Canton, dropping Hunt in the Hawaiian Islands where he could get a supply boat back to Astoria. But the War of 1812 disrupted Astor's dreams and supply lines as well. Hunt was forced to charter a ship from Oahu to Oregon, only to find the interference and uncertainty of the war had persuaded the men at the post to abandon the project. Hunt had to go back to Oahu and buy another ship — the *Pedler.* It sailed into Astoria in 1814. This time Hunt learned that word of a British vessel en route to seize Astoria had arrived with North West Company trappers, and in Hunt's absence Duncan McDougal decided to sell the fort and all its provisions to the North West Company at a fraction of their value. Hunt was obviously indignant, but there was nothing he could do.

He sailed with the *Pedler,* gathering what he could from Pacific Coast trade, alternately arrested by the Spaniards and the Russians; took his gains to China to exchange for silk and tea and returned to New York in 1816, two years after his employer had formally dissolved the Pacific Fur Company. Wilson Price Hunt went home to St. Louis in 1817, bought several thousand acres, built a grist mill and settled into the life of a provincial merchant — which was what he had wanted all along.

And Astor? He made large earnings from real estate transactions on Manhattan Island, scrutinized his investments, ruthlessly foreclosed on mortgages, lived unostentatiously, and became the richest man of his time. On his death in 1848, he left $400,000 to New York City for a library and $20,000,000 to his son, who shortly doubled it.

Donald McKenzie
1819

They called him "Perpetual Motion" and no wonder: after a 600 mile trip on snowshoes to Fort Nez Perces (ten miles below the confluence of the Snake and Columbia), he rested scarcely a week before setting off up the Snake River to attempt a reverse passage of Hells Canyon.

Donald McKenzie's indefatigable manner was proportional to his size — he weighed over 300 pounds. He was cousin to Alexander McKenzie, first man to cross North America. Donald was no stranger to rivers or the region. He had traveled with the Wilson Price Hunt expedition in the upstream race against Lisa, and led the party which seven years earlier had bypassed the main chasm in favor of the southern spur of the Seven Devils. During those 21 days, the eleven men struggled northeasterly through Six Lake Basin, or Rapid River, and down to the Salmon by way of the Little Salmon, subsisting on two mountain sheep and five beaver. At Fort Astoria, Alexander Ross, the clerk who recorded their travails, wrote:

> At this time some of them were so reduced that M'Kenzie himself had to carry on his own back two of his men's blankets, being a strong and robust man, and long accustomed to the hardships and hard fare of the north. He alone, of all the party, stood the trial well; and, by still cheering and encouraging his men on, he brought them at length to the main waters of the Columbia. . . .

But McKenzie had participated in the discussions which resulted in the sale of Astoria to the North West Company before he traveled east with the Nor' Westers to Montreal. He reported to Astor in New York, and John Jacob apparently decided the burly Scotsman had actively intrigued against him and refused him re-employment. At that point, McKenzie went back to work for the North West Company and was placed in charge of the Department of the Interior.

He was anxious to determine whether the Snake River would provide an avenue of transport for the furs of the upper Snake country, particularly since Fort Nez Perces was advantageously located if the route proved feasible. McKenzie left in March, 1819, "through snow and ice," according to Ross, with six French-Canadian boatmen on a "barge" headed upstream.

16

Donald McKenzie.

The men had a favorable stage of water and the use of many sand beaches (which have since been eroded by dams) but their voyage was still incredible. They may have resorted to a square sail, as was often rigged for upriver wind on the Missouri; certainly they used poles, paddles, and cordelle.

Two months after their departure, four of the boatmen returned by river to the Fort with a message from McKenzie for Alexander Ross:

Point Successful, Head of the Narrows, April 15, 1819:

The passage by water is now proved to be safe and practicable for loaded boats without one single carrying place or portage, therefore the doubtful question is set at rest forever. Yet from the force of the current and the frequency of the rapids it may still be advisable and perhaps preferable to continue the land transport, while the business is being carried on in a small scale. We had often recourse to the line. There are two places with bold cut rocks on either side of the river, where the great body of water is compressed within a narrow compass, which may render those parts doubtful during the floods owing to rocks and whirlpools but there are only two and neither of them long.

Point Successful has never been satisfactorily identified, but was likely in the vicinity of Buck-Thirtytwo Point Creek. McKenzie must have had some reservations about the route, as it was never used. And Peter Skene Ogden, of the Hudson's Bay Company, ten years later noted that half-loaded boats might proceed from Fort Nez Perces upriver to the mouth of Burnt River (a tributary of the Snake) in three weeks, but he added that "fully loaded pack stock could traverse the same distance overland through the Blue Mountains in only six days."

Hudson's Bay Company subsumed the North West Company in 1821 and many of McKenzie's achievements in opening the Snake River country were lost in the merger. He went east and was chief factor of the Red River District until he left the Company for health reasons in 1833. The indomitable Scot retired to New York and made an attempt at writing his memoirs. But he hated paperwork of any kind and became so upset with his efforts at times that his wife cast his manuscripts in the fireplace rather than see him distressed. Her solicitude caused an inestimable loss to the early history of Snake River.

Captain Bonneville:
1833

When Thomas Paine was in exile in France he became a close friend of the Nicolas Bonneville family. Paine persuaded the family to emigrate to America, and on his death left a portion of his farm in trust for the education of the Bonneville children.

Benjamin Louis Bonneville was one of the French children who benefited from the trust's provision. He graduated from the U.S. Military Academy in 1815 and began a lengthy military career. While at Fort Gibson he formed plans to explore the Rocky Mountains at the head of a fur brigade. He wrote Major General Alexander Macomb requesting leave of absence to "examine the locations, habits, and trading practices of the Indian tribes, visit the American and British establishments, and study the best means of making the country available to American citizens." He asked for nothing from the Government except U.S. and Mexican passports. Macomb granted him leave with orders "to collect any information which may be useful to the Government."

Most of Bonneville's motivations and financing are shrouded in obscurity. He may have been a spy for the government to report on British holdings in the Pacific Northwest. The only person definitely known to have been an investor in the Captain's undertaking was Alfred Seton, who 20 years before was a clerk at Astoria and was now a New York fur dealer. Bonneville left St. Louis in May, 1832, with 110 men and 20 wagons of trade goods. He was to spend three years wandering the west.

In the winter of 1833, while encamped at the Portneuf River (near present-day Pocatello), Bonneville prepared to reconnoiter Hudson's Bay Company territory around Fort Walla Walla (formerly Fort Nez Perces). On Christmas day he departed with three companions, hoping to ride horseback on ice down the Snake River. The plan melted with an unexpected thaw. Oblivious to the Astorian experience, the quartet followed the Snake into the canyon, probably as far as Thirtytwo Point Creek, just as Ramsey Crooks had done. Here the basalt bluffs made horses a hindrance, and the awesome rapids dissuaded them from committing their lives to a horsehide bullboat. Mauled by the weather and short of food, they began to retreat.

Knowledgeable local informants like J. Himelwright and G. Tucker believed Bonneville's group must have retraced their path upriver four miles to the vicinity of Kirby Creek, climbed a small ridge and moved north along the Squaw Creek benches as far as far as the divide between Thirtytwo Point Creek and Steamboat Canyon. After two days of floundering through the white wash of winter they topped out, just south of Post Office Saddle, and descended the opposite side of the ridge into Post Office Saddle itself. The men traveled north along the main divide to a point near the head of Smith Canyon, then down

Captain Benjamin Louis Bonneville.

Summit Creek to its confluence with the Imnaha River. A few miles downstream they were received hospitably by families of Nez Perce and proceeded down to within four miles of the Imnaha-Snake confluence before turning toward the Grande Ronde Valley. From the Grande Ronde, Bonneville moved to the Snake-Clearwater junction, and by Nez Perce Trail to the Hudson's Bay post.

The American contingent was received coolly at Fort Walla Walla and were refused supplies for their return trip. The Captain headed back to the Portneuf, where he arrived two months later than anticipated.

On returning to New York in 1835, the soldier-trapper reported first to John Jacob Astor, then learned to his consternation that he'd been declared absent without leave and dropped from Army rolls. After an interval, he succeeded in being reinstated on the recommendation of the Secretary of War to the Senate.

B. L. Bonneville was with General Winfield Scott during the 1847 invasion of Mexico, after which, in an amusing display of military doublespeak, he was promoted to brevet lieutenant colonel "for gallantry and meritorious conduct in the battles" and found guilty on three counts by a court martial for "misbehavior before the enemy." He was then assigned to command Fort Kearney on the Oregon-California Trail, and later was in command of the military department of New Mexico Territory.

Bonneville retired at age 70, as a brevet brigadier general, and at his deathday was the oldest retired officer in the U.S. Army. In a manner as curious as his career, the general's name is commemorated by a peak in the Wallowas — and by a concrete barrier across the Columbia River.

◆

The Stubadore Company
1862

The story of Levi Allen's trip up the Snake River and the resulting discovery of the Peacock copper lode in the Seven Devils has been repeated with frequency. The original account of the journey is specific enough to persuade a reasonable man of its authenticity. Two subsequent narratives contained sufficient ambiguities to raise a number of questions.

The winter of 1861-1862 was the worst on record. That spring's floodwaters have never been equalled. It also happened to be the spring that a party of prospectors decided to examine the upper reaches of the middle Snake. *The Golden Age,* a newspaper in Lewiston, carried the following account on February 5, 1863:

Since our last issue, we have had an interview with Mr. Allen, one of the party of thirteen who went up Snake river last season. They took with them one of Mr. Sam Smith's large batteaus, and with their provisions and mining tools, the boat drawed 18 inches of water. It was so overloaded that they could not row the boat, consequently they cordelled it all the way up Snake to the mouth of Salmon. They travelled on the bank of Snake on the east side, thus proving conclusively that a trail exists to Salmon, close by Snake river. Mr. Allen states that from Lewiston to Salmon the depth of the water varies from three and a half to twelve feet, and no obstruction exist of any kind to the successful navigation of the river. From the mouth of Salmon they took their boat up 12 miles to Wapshalee or Billy's camp. There navigation of Salmon ceased with them. The party here separated, and part of them took the Indian trail, and crossed over the Snake river, a distance of 14 miles, in their opinion. The road was good all the way. The only mountain was the one that rises immediately after Raving Salmon, and is not so steep as to prevent a good wagon road being built at a small expense. Three of the party, among them Mr. Allen, returned and took a canoe at Wapshalee, returned down Salmon, and proceeded up Snake. The first seven miles they walked along the banks; afterwards for 20 or 25 miles, went through a deep canon, water very deep, no rocks; river twenty-five per cent better for navigable purposes than that of Snake below Lewiston. About 10 miles this side of Wiser river, left the canoe, and took the Indian trail around Wiser a few miles above its mouth, and proceeded across Piette to the Boise mines. The trail is good, the country level, and from Wiser river a good wagon road can easily be built. This side of Wiser the mountains come down to the Snake, but steamers can go between Powder and Wiser and have a fine landing, and packers, miners and others will not be necessitated to cross the dividing ridge, or what is called Salmon River Mountains.

Some additional information can be gleaned from a biographical sketch concerning Edmond Pearcy included in the 1899 *Illustrated History of Idaho:*

> On the 14th of March, 1862, Mr. Pearcy, with a party of fourteen, set sail in a large bateau for a prospecting tour up Snake river. This was a perilous trip, because of the numerous ice jams, but notwithstanding the fact that the river was so full of ice they reached Lewiston safely. They prospected up Salmon river twelve miles and then, with packs upon their backs, went into the country, but found nothing of value. After this they went to Pittsburg Landing on the Snake river, twenty miles above the mouth of the Salmon river, where they hired horses of the Indians and went up Little Salmon to the head of Salmon valley, whence they started for Snake river. They camped at the big canyon and discovered the Peacock country copper and gold mine, which afterward sold for sixty thousand dollars. That was the first discovery of the Seven Devils. The party camped out, killed mountain sheep to supply their table with meat, and enjoyed life there, although they celebrated the Fourth of July with snow, six inches deep, upon the ground. When their provisions gave out they returned to Lewiston . . .

The *Lewiston Morning Tribune* in 1939 carried an account of Allen's trip drawn from an "old letter." Levi Allen wrote:

> The year 1862 found me in the employ of the Oregon Steam Navigation Company (O.S.N.). Orders were given to explore the upper Snake River canyon above Lewiston. A boat was purchased at Fort Walla Walla on the Columbia, a supply of provisions was loaded aboard, and with 14 men the journey was commenced, the company being known as the Stubadore company. The season was early spring, ice was still on the water and along the river banks with great chunks floating down the river. Ten men walked on the shoreline and pulled the boat with a long rope. At length the party reached Lewiston . . . After two days we left and began our trip up the Salmon River to the upper part of the canyon which we explored to its upper end. Our party returned and

made our camp to the west of the Seven Devils mountains. A party left this place for a trip through the mountains but returned in a week as the traveling was very rough. Trading with some passing Indians we secured several ponies and with packs left for the Seven Devils mountains where we found deep snow and were forced to return the horses to our main camp up the Salmon river.

The members of the party then started on foot, packing supplies on our backs. By starting early each morning we were able to walk on the heavy frozen crust for some hours each day until the mountains had been crossed. After five days we reached the Salmon River, up which we traveled until it turned eastward. We then continued south up a smaller branch and passed a large lake (Payette Lake) the water from which flowed south. This we followed until we came to a large bend in the river (Horseshoe Bend on Payette River) where we camped, having covered about 140 miles from our main camp.

After resting several days we decided to return as our supplies were getting low. Two months' time had been consumed in reaching the camp at the river's bend, no white men had been seen since leaving Lewiston. The party returned by nearly the same route. Provisions were nearly exhausted before they reached their main camp.

Lewiston was reached in another 30 days. No paying gold mines were found during the prospecting trip. An account of the turbulent Snake river canyon was brought back by the members.

There are some obvious inconsistancies between the first version and the last. Only the first account asserts that the Stubadore-Allen-Pearcy company took the batteau above Pittsburg Landing. But in light of the testimony, the journey appears rooted in fact. (W. W. Lloyd, an old-timer who came to Oregon's Pine Valley country on the Tim Goodell wagon train by way of Boise and Weiser, reported that Chinese miners brought boats up the river to Connor Creek, 16 miles above Powder River, in 1877.)

Captain Ankeny's Crew
1862

Navigation of the Snake River above Lewiston suddenly became a matter of enormous consequence — at least to the citizens of Lewiston — in the fall of 1862. Reports of the Boise Basin placer mine discoveries in August had left no doubt that the next big gold rush would sweep thousands of miners into the Boise region. Although the geography of the intervening country remained unclear to most Lewiston pioneers, scarcely anyone there could doubt the urgency of turning up a good route from Portland and Walla Walla through Lewiston to the new mines.

Lewiston hoped the Snake River would provide an attractive and feasible means of reaching the Boise country. In event of a choice between a hard stage trip through the Blue Mountains and an easy steamboat excursion up the river at seven miles per hour, the water route would command a decisive advantage. But if steamboat service should fail to materialize, traffic from most of the Pacific Northwest would go over the more direct Oregon Trail. So the immediate future of Lewiston hung on the possibility of finding a suitable Boise route.

Dispatching a scouting expedition to determine once and for all the much discussed "possibility of navigating Snake River with light draught steamers from that point to Fort Boise," the hopeful promoters of Lewiston were overjoyed to obtain a positive answer. (A year or two later, they may have had reason to wonder a little about the competence of their scouts, but the 1862 examination of Snake River canyon took place under the most competent direction available, and the results were credited in Portland as fully as they were in Lewiston.)

This happy, if somewhat optimistic, report attracted widespread attention over the northwest after publication in Lewiston's *Golden Age,* November 22, 1862:

> The party consisted of three reliable men — Charles Clifford, Washington Murray and Joseph Denver — and started from Lewiston under the auspices of Capt. A. P. Ankeny (of the O.S.N.), on the 20th of September. They followed the meanderings of Snake to the mouth of the Grande Ronde, and found the distance to be 27 miles, due South. It is an open river with no obstructions. From Grande

Ronde they proceeded to intersect the old emigrant road, and reached it at or near its crossing of Powder river; a short distance further on diverged towards Snake river, and followed it up to Boise. For several miles the river runs through deep canyons or mountain gorges, and has the appearance of being very deep, and shows by the banks that during certain seasons of the year, it rises to the hight of sixty feet. The party met several Indians, but none were unfriendly. A great similarity exists in the whole country between Fort Boise and Lewiston, as it does between Lewiston and where Snake river empties into the Columbia. Sometimes bold rocky sides, then beautiful rolling table lands, interspersed with trees and prairie lands. The party passed through some of the most beautiful farming land in the world; deep, rich, dark loam, well watered and well timbered, with gold in all the ravines and gulches for the miner, and soil to provide him with the necessaries of life.

After their arrival at Fort Boise, they proceeded to construct a boat, or more properly a raft, to navigate the river with. In a few days they were rested and prepared, having taken the precaution to lash their provisions on to the raft, bade adieu to Fort Boise, and came dashing, foaming down the wild, tortuous Snake.

The first canyon of note was twelve miles in length, and here the banks gave indication of the water rising 60 or 70 feet. After this came an open space of eight miles, in which you could observe, for a long distance, the glorious open country. The weather was delightful and the scenery inviting. The next canyon, or gorge, was fourteen miles in length, and penetrated the two ridges of the Blue Mountains. The course seemed to be north, showing that Snake river runs north and south. After passing this canyon there came an open place, alternately changing, but of no perceptible difference. About sixty miles brought them to the mouth of the Salmon, making a distance, as they reckon, of about one hundred miles from Fort Boise to Salmon. From Salmon to Lewiston the distance is inside of forty miles, so the entire distance from Lewiston to Fort Boise is only one hundred and thirty-five miles!

They found nothing in the river to impede navigation whatever, and pronounced it feasible at any season of the year unless it be by ice. The examination of the river, has resulted in establishing the fact that Snake is navigable for steamers, and will be much safer to travel than the river is from Lewiston to the mouth of the Snake.

This is equally gratifying to the projector of the scheme as it is to the citizens of Lewiston, and the country at large. A new route will now be opened for steam, the results of which cannot now be foretold. We shall penetrate Nevada and Utah Territories by steam, as it is well known that it is only 90 miles from Fort Boise to Salmon Falls on Snake river. Salmon Falls is within 250 miles of Salt Lake City. A new avenue of trade will then be opened and those who have risked their fortune and periled their lives are justly entitled to the gratitude of the people, and a rich reward will be their portion. But a few more suns will rise and set before the shrill whistle of the steamer will reverberate along the banks of this noble river, and its echo will be heard for ages yet to come through the ravines, gorges, canons, and on the mountain tops of our golden land, as a symbol of ambition, perserverance, and goaheadativeness.

John H. Scranton, the editor of the *Golden Age* (who forecast such a happy future for Lewiston once the Boise and Salt Lake trade were diverted up Snake River), had just left an eight year career operating steamers out of San Francisco and on Puget Sound. Two years went by in which neither he nor anyone else seized the opportunity to reap a fortune in the Snake River steamboat business. Traffic to Boise was still going up the Columbia as far as Umatilla, and then over the Blue Mountains. Very likely someone found out in those years that Snake River navigation above Lewiston was more obstructed than the somewhat unobservant scouts had made out. In fact, those scouts underestimated the distance from Fort Boise to Salmon River by a hundred miles, and gave such a general description of the canyon that one could conclude they neglected to inspect the main portion.

The Colonel Wright: Tom Stump
1865

The gold rush to Fort Colville and the subsequent Indian wars had stimulated up-river trade, inducing numerous individuals to invest in steamboats to serve that traffic. The navigation of the Columbia above its junction with the Willamette was obstructed at the Cascades and The Dalles. Railroad portages were established around these two rapids, with separate boats operating between and above the whitewater impediments.

John Ainsworth, William Ladd, and Jacob Kamm formed a corporation with the owners of the Cascade and Dalles portages to secure a monopoly on the Columbia River passenger and freight traffic. The corporation was known as the Oregon Steam and Navigation Company and ruled the river from 1860 to 1880.

Fares and freights were high. The company charged freight, not by weight, but by the "ship's ton", figuring 40 cubic feet as equivalent to a ton. To obtain the measurement of an article, "the full length, height, and thickness were taken and carried out full size, the largest way of the piece." To measure an empty wagon, the tongue was extended for length, then raised to give its height. The story has been told that in order to "make the measurement come out right" for a small cannon which the government was shipping, a pair of mules had to be hitched to the cannon so that the proper extension of length and height could be secured.

Competition for control of the Boise and Owyhee passenger and freight traffic finally forced the O.S.N. to experiment with steamboating in the Boise region. North Idaho had no opportunity to escape from the clutches of the O.S.N. South Idaho, however, enjoyed the advantage of having more than one group of competitors seeking its trade. Freight and stage lines overland from Salt Lake reached southern Idaho on a route comparable in length with the O.S.N. connections to Portland. Direct service from San Francisco and Sacramento also became available to Boise and Owyhee after 1864. The California Steam Navigation Company (C.S.N.), which transported Idaho goods by sea from San Francisco to Portland, also served the Sacramento River. When the California company began to divert Idaho traffic via the Sacramento and over the Red Bluff and Chico routes directly to Boise, the O.S.N.

attempted drastic action to regain the southern Idaho trade. Extension of O.S.N. steamboat service to Snake River in the Boise country, together with operation of an ocean steamer between San Francisco and Portland, was the O.S.N. reply to the C.S.N. challenge.

Getting a steamboat into service on Snake River in the Boise-Owyhee area posed a major problem. The boat either had to be sailed up through the deep canyon, or hauled piecemeal across the Blue Mountains and assembled in the area it was to serve. Neither alternative seemed satisfactory. Should steamboat navigation from Lewiston to Owyhee Ferry — or even from Olds Ferry to Owyhee Ferry — prove feasible, the O.S.N. would be able to recapture the southern Idaho trade. (A steamboat line up the Snake from Lewiston to Owyhee Ferry — along a stretch of the land route then in use — was expected to give the Portland-Umatilla O.S.N. route a much better chance to compete with the direct California service.) In either event, the first step was to dispatch an O.S.N. steamboat from Lewiston up the Snake to the abandoned Hudson's Bay outpost, Fort Boise.

The ship chosen was the *Colonel Wright*. It was built at the Deschutes above Celilo in 1859 by Lawrence W. Coe and Robert Thompson. They named it after the commandant of the military post at The Dalles who had sent soldiers to protect the settlers on the steamer *Mary* when she was under attack by Indians.

The *Wright* was the first steamer to run the rapids of the upper Columbia and the first to arrive at Lewiston. She was 110 feet in length and carried a mast rigged with a supplemental square sail. This steamboat had also ventured above Lewiston once, almost to the forks of the Clearwater, during the gold rush to Pierce, Idaho.

The pilot selected for the historic mission was Captain Thomas J. Stump. He was brought up from the Sacramento River to replace Captain White, who had resigned when Ainsworth cut his salary from $500 to $300 a month.

Stump, a native of Nashville, Tennessee, had come across the plains to California, and was running a small sternwheeler between Sacramento and Marysville for the C.S.N. when Ainsworth hired him away. Later, he would be in charge of all the O.S.N. upper Columbia and Snake River fleet for nearly 20 years, and would die in the pilot house of the *Spokane* on its downriver run from Lewiston in 1881.

CAPT. THOMAS STUMP

But all that was in the future, as Captain John Stump headed up Snake River in mid-June of 1865, with a young assistant pilot, William Polk Gray, who recorded the adventure as a member of the crew:

We went up the river to about twenty-five miles above Salmon river. In attempting to make a dangerous eddy at this point, the boat was caught in a bad eddy, thrown into the current from Idaho shore. It carried away eight feet of her bow, keel and sides to the deck. Things looked desperate for a moment. Captain (Thomas J.) Stump gave an order from the pilot house to get out a line on shore. You never saw such a universal willingness to get on shore with that line. Every deckhand, the mate, the chief engineer, the fireman and our two passengers, who were standing forward watching the boat, seized the line by both ends, the middle and wherever they could get ahold of it and jumped ashore. The only people left on the boat were Captain Stump and myself in the pilot house, and second engineer, who was below, and old Titus, the cook. Before they could make the line fast the boat was caught by the current and went down the river half a mile. Here Captain Stump succeeded in beaching her. We were joined here by the ambitious line-carriers who walked down the shore to where we were beached.

Captain Stump set the mate and crew to work to repair the forward bulkhead which had been strained and showed signs of leaking . . . . When the bulkhead was finished, we ran back to Lewiston, covering the distance it had taken us four and a half days to come up, in three and a half hours.

Perhaps Captain Stump was fortunate to get turned at the point he did. He had reached the head of practical steamboat navigation for anyone going upstream, and even if he had been lucky enough to get through the eddy that stopped him, worse hazards would have halted his passage.

In any case, by the summer of 1865, the O.S.N. had good reason to doubt the adequacy of the 1862 report of Snake River navigability. The *Colonel Wright* had been so severely strained that only her engines could be salvaged for another O.S.N. steamer.

◆

The Shoshone: "Bas" and "Buc" 1870

Establishment of a shipyard at Old Fort Boise, (at the confluence of the Boise River with the Snake), now seemed to be the only practical way to get a steamboat built for the Boise-Owyhee trade. A San Francisco plan to put a steamer on the middle Snake had already been announced as a rival project. John Ainsworth had mining interests and a mill in the Owyhee District which couldn't operate without a solution to the freight problem. And news that the C.S.N. had reduced its rates on Idaho freight over the Red Bluff route made the O.S.N. even more determined to compete, by putting a steamboat in service.

The C.S.N. had an overwhelming advantage in gaining passenger traffic: the distance from San Francisco to Portland exceeded the distance direct from San Francisco to Boise and the $123 O.S.N. fare was more than twice as much as that of C.S.N.'s route.

On his way from California to Lewiston in order to captain the *Wright,* Thomas Stump had examined the Snake River in the Olds Ferry-Owyhee Ferry vicinity and reported it navigable for a boat of light draft.

O.S.N. vice-president and manager, Simon Reed, wrote upon Stump's return from the Snake:

> ... the building of a boat seems not to be a matter of choice but a necessity as we must divert all the trade and travel of that country over our route on the Columbia River, hence we have decided to build a boat to be commenced this fall and winter, and completed for the early spring trade. We will use the machinery originally purchased for the *Owyhee* (an O.S.N. steamer on the Snake).

Agents for the O.S.N. reached Boise shortly after DuRell's Umatilla, Boise & Idaho Express and Fast Freight Line got underway with inexpensive, six-day service over the O.S.N. route from Boise to Umatilla. The agents contracted with A. H. Robie for delivery of the necessary lumber to Old Fort Boise by December 1, and wagons began hauling planks October 20. Workers began to assemble at the shipyard, and by Christmas everything was ready for the arrival of the building superintendent, "Mr. Gates, the greatest steamboat builder on the Columbia River." Shortly after the boatbuilding crew celebrated New Year's, Captain Gates turned up and construction of the *Shoshone* got underway.

The mouth of the Boise River was scarcely an ordinary site for a shipyard. The Snake War of 1866-1868 got off to a good start during the time that the *Shoshone* was being assembled — and the old fort definitely was in the zone of hostilities. Assembling building materials there turned out to be no easy task. Four brief reports of construction progress indicate some of the difficulties faced by the builders:

> Mr. Scranton came up from the boat at the mouth of the Boise yesterday (February 2, 1866), where he has for several weeks been at work. Capt. Gates has twenty men employed, and the work is progressing well but it is likely to be hindered for want of lumber. The roads are thawing out and getting almost bottomless for a heavily loaded team.

Next, in mid-February:

> Captain Gates, who has been in town (Boise) for a few days, tells us that the boat at the mouth of the river is going ahead finely. The frame is up and ready for planking. The cabins will be commenced next week, and in three weeks more the hull will be nearly finished. The boilers and engines, and all the heavier parts of the machinery, are on the ground, and the engineers will soon begin to put it in place.

Captain Gates will start in a day or two for Umatilla, with Creighton's teams, to bring up what necessary machinery and furniture was left behind. It is the intention to have her ready to run by the middle of April, and certainly by the first of May. This is good news to those who feel an interest in the progress of our Territory. Those who pay most attention to the subject (in this case, James S. Reynolds, editor of the *Idaho Tri-weekly Statesman*) are firm in the belief that this little boat will form a link in stream communication between the Columbia river and Salt Lake, at no distant day, and perhaps as soon as the Pacific railroad shall be built to Salt Lake. May the day soon come.

Then, a little more than a month later:

We learn (March 24) that the boat for Snake river is nearly completed — except putting the machinery in place. We are also glad to learn that an old California friend (of J. S. Reynolds) and engineer, Mr. G. B. Underwood, has been sent out by the Chief Engineer of the O.S.N. Company to put up the engines and set the boat running. Mr. Underwood knows how to "fix the irons" and is the right man for the job. The boat will be afloat with steam up in a few weeks.

Finally, the president of the O.S.N. reported that:

De Orsey (who made the original lumber contracts with A. H. Robie) has returned (to Portland) from the New Boat on Snake River, has had a hard time, came near losing his life by the Indians, had his horse shot from under him at one time, and his hair brushed with bullets at other times, this was no fun, and he has no desire to go back. He has paid out about $19,000 for lumber and hauling, and about 400 cords of wood, these are frightful figures but there is no backout now. The last of the machinery shipped the second time by Lew Day, is now lieing at the foot of the Blue Mountains on the other side, the man having it in charge refusing to move till the roads dry up, unless paid some $700 extra. I (J. C. Ainsworth, president of the O.S.N.) am more and more disgusted with the doings of Lew Day, the boat cannot be launched till these wagons get through.

In spite of their difficulties, though, the shipyard workers were keeping the construction of the *Shoshone* on schedule.

33

Public opinion in southern Idaho divided over the issue of whether the O.S.N.'s new boat would be an asset to the transportation system of the region. Jim Reynolds and his Boise *Statesman* endorsed the O.S.N. plan as providing an ideal freight and passenger service. Reynolds' only complaint was that the O.S.N. had not built more steamboats sooner. In Ruby City, though, the *Owyhee Avalanche* firmly approved of the C.S.N. and the Red Bluff-Chico route, and scoffed at the attempt to combat the C.S.N. by extending steamer service into southern Idaho:

> This navigation vampire (the O.S.N.) . . . covets our trade and sends agents to deprive us — if in the power of man and money — of a vital necessity . As the Pacific Railroad extends eastward (from Sacramento toward Winnemucca, so that the Boise and Owyhee traffic would go direct to California), the O.S.N. Co.'s pap will diminish, their tears increase, and their extortionate and feverish grasp slacken. Were it not for bitter experiences, their howls would incite pity. Like snakes, their boats run and bite everything in their way during the Summer and hole up in Winter.

By the time the *Shoshone* was launched the C.S.N. and Central Pacific retaliated with rate competition even the O.S.N. could hardly meet — the first 150 tons of Boise freight would be delivered to the Central Pacific terminus free of charge.

Invitations to leading citizens of Boise and Ruby City to attend the formal opening of service by the *Shoshone* provoked considerable disparagement. The *Avalanche* declined the invitation quite disrespectfully:

As for the "Blow out," that'll come off sure, but it would have been better to have built two steamers — you see there would have been a bigger "blow out." . . . Steamboats are good things for navigators — shouldn't ever be without a few. Are glad the O.S.N. Co. are building some up in Snake Valley. They'll be handy for emigrants in case of a storm, and fully demonstrate that steamboats can be constructed up this way. Recent examinations show that the steamer can run up Sinker Creek to the N.Y. and O.F. Mill (high up in the Owyhee mountains) as easily as to its mouth. A country don't amount to much without steamboats, and the more the better. Waitah, pass along a few steamboats.

A number of prominent leaders did attend the *Shoshone's* celebration, but aside from J. S. Reynolds (who was even more convinced of the value of the steamboat enterprise than were the O.S.N. officials) and B. M. DuRell, none of them stayed to complete the opening voyage.

James S. Reynolds was convinced he was witnessing an epoch in the history of Idaho when he recorded the story of the *Shoshone:*

The first link in the chain of steam communication, to be made continuous at no distant day between Salt Lake and Columbia river, was welded to-day (May 16, 1866). The new steamer *Shoshone* of the O.S.N. Company, put on steam yesterday and ran from this place (Old Fort Boise) up to the Owyhee ferry, distance, forty-five miles. It being late in the afternoon when she started. Captain Myrick laid over at dark last night and ran up to the ferry this morning, arriving at ten o'clock, in nine and a half hour's running time with fifty pounds steam. This was the first time her lines were let go, and she behaved in a manner to reflect credit upon builders and officers. The boat has been built under disadvantages, particularly in getting her machinery in order, every piece of which had to brought from shops on the Columbia. She draws light — about twenty inches water and is of capacity to carry one hundred and seventy-five tons.

Anticipating the arrival of the boat at Owyhee Ferry a small party of gentlemen from Ruby City and another from Boise City, came over on the stages this morning just in time to hear the music of the steam whistle reverberate for the first time along the sage brush solitudes of the Snake. It was pleasant music to the ears of us who have for two years heard no other than the whoa-haw, driver's whip, or the Jehu's horn. First taking a good dinner at the hospitable invitation of Captain Myrick, we started down the river at half past one o'clock, running down to the Boise Ferry in five hours, including time to wood and other delays. The wind several times blew a gale as it generally does on the Snake and Columbia. The boat being entirely light it was difficult to keep her head in the wind. Two or three times it turned her completely round in spite of helm and steam.

The banks of the Snake are nearly level full, and the current strong, but there are no rapids of any consequence in this part of the river, and but few dangerous rocks to be observed at the present stage of water. There is no better water to navigate in western rivers than this portion of the Snake; how it is above and below remains to be tried. Tomorrow we start down the river for Old's Ferry.

Except for a vigorous thunderstorm, the trip from Old Fort Boise down to Olds's Ferry was uneventful:

Nothing has happened to stop the boat a moment or prevent a single turn of her engines since the lines were first cast off, which is saying much in favor of the skill of her engineer, Mr. Geo. B. Underwood, considering the many difficulties under which her machinery was put together.

The running time, down from Boise Ferry (Old Fort Boise) was four hours and forty minutes. When regular trips shall be established they will afford passengers up or down a pleasant relief from the dust and jolt of the stage over ninety miles of land travel between this place and Boise or Owyhee . . . .

This boat is made considerably out of the ordinary course of steamboat building. Usually the first boat built on a newly navigated river is an inferior, slow concern and built in the rudest style, but in this instance the O.S.N. Company have at once taken the risk of building a first class boat, believing that if any boat is needed at all a good one will pay better than a poor one. The *Shoshone* has already shown that her running time is as good as the average of the boats belonging to the company.

Exploration of the Snake above Owyhee Ferry revealed that steamboat navigation was practical at least as far as six miles above the mouth of the Bruneau River. At that point, Captain Myrick tested the head of a rapid with full steam for a half hour but was unable to go over the top. He turned back, feeling that with a good line he could have made it to Salmon Falls — that this stretch of the Snake was no worse than the falls of the Willamette and Columbia, which were crossed regularly by O.S.N. boats. Thus extension of O.S.N. service to intercept the Overland road from Salt Lake in the Hagerman valley was thwarted.

As the *Shoshone* commenced her regular run, DuRell's fast freight and passenger line dropped its rate by two-thirds, as it had agreed to do in advance with the O.S.N. President J. C. Ainsworth rejoiced June 6 that the steamboat was succeeding in drawing off the C.S.N. Red Bluff-Chico traffic:

> The *Shoshone* will not make any money for us this season if she ever does, but I think she will enable us to compete successfully with the Chico Route for supplying the 'Owhyee' District. If she does this she is a success.

But he had to admit that:

> Our Snake River boat will not assist us much in the Salt Lake trade, we find she cannot run successfully much higher up than the Owyhee Crossing. She reached a point some sixty miles above, within twenty miles it is thought of the Ferry below Salmon Falls. Much of this river is through canons and over Rapids, that at a low stage would be difficult and unsafe to navigate. The distance she will run tri-weekly will be about the same as from Celilo to Wallula, and the Route about as direct.

On June 21, he still had confidence in the *Shoshone:*

> Our Snake River boat is now making tri-weekly trips from Olds Ferry to the Owyhee Landing, has not and cannot pay expenses this season, but will warrant our running her by the facility she will offer in securing to us the Owyhee trade, as against Chico, we are in my judgement, to get the trade and next year I think the *Shoshone* will pay a direct profit.

Aside from the rate competition, the perils of the Snake War had helped block the C.S.N. route from California to Idaho and the Indians may deserve considerable credit for the resurgence in the Portland O.S.N. trade to Boise-Owyhee.

Unfortunately for the O.S.N., the triumph of the *Shoshone* was brief. In August, Ainsworth reported a ruinous difficulty confronting continued operation of the vessel in that region:

> Our Snake River boat is laid up for want of wood. We do not think of starting her again before next spring at which time, if we succeed in getting wood, and making the proper connections she will do a fair business and indirectly be of great service to our company.

*This is the only surviving photograph of the **Shoshone**. She was 136 feet in length with a 27-foot beam.*

The Central Pacific was completed in Nevada to Winnemucca, and California passenger traffic for Idaho ceased to go to Portland. As a result, the purpose of running the *Shoshone*, at a loss if necessary, vanished before the wood supply problem was solved.

The steamer lay alongside the bank at Owyhee Ferry for three years. Finally, John Ainsworth dispatched Captain Silas Smith to bring the ship down to the Columbia or wreck her in the attempt. Nothing is impossible for the man who doesn't have to do it himself.

Shortly before mid-June of 1869, Smith left Owyhee Ferry with the *Shoshone* for Lewiston and the Columbia. He proceeded cautiously, and waited for hawsers to lower her down some rapids below Brownlee's Ferry.

CAPT. SEBASTIAN MILLER

Apparently shortage of rope and fuel forced the *Shoshone* to spend the winter in the canyon near the stream still known as Steamboat Creek. Low water that summer may have also been a factor in Smith's decision to abandon the project.

Early the next spring, the O.S.N. sent the highly experienced Sebastian "Bas" Miller back to the canyon to rescue the steamboat. Miller was born in Ohio in 1827 and learned the engineer's trade on the Ohio River. He went to Oregon in 1852 and worked on the *Canemah* and the *Willamette* for seven years, until he got his master's papers and went to the other end of the boat, where he had a varied career. He commanded over 40 different steamboats on the Willamette, Columbia and Snake during a period of 30 years.

CAPT. DANIEL E. BUCHANAN

Captain Miller brought an equally impressive engineer with him, Daniel E. Buchanan. Also from Ohio, but eleven years younger, Dan had been orphaned in childhood, and served a six year apprenticeship as a blacksmith and machinist in mills and on locomotives. He journeyed to the Pacific Coast in 1859, worked in mills, mines, and then on ferries. Buchanan began steamboating as a master and engineer of small steamers that towed rafts and scows. He would eventually be the Government's chief engineer in charge of all Columbia River channel improvement and maintenance from the mouth to the head of navigation and would supervise the building of all dredges, tugs, and snag boats engaged in that endeavor.

Miller and Buchanan left Portland March 21, and after reaching Umatilla Landing were compelled to travel on buckboards, sleds, wagons, horseback and afoot to arrive at Lime Point three weeks later. Two more days downriver brought them to the *Shoshone.*

The steamer was banked in the care of Livingston and Smith. The former shipped as mate, the latter as fireman. W. F. Hedges was employed as a general utility man. These five men constituted the crew, and before undertaking the journey the boat was thoroughly overhauled. The machinery was disconnected and put in good operating order.

The steamer had been constructed of mountain pine, which is quite brittle and soft when seasoned. Without materials with which to rebuild, and with no time to caulk the seams, they started the deck pump and wet down the hull until the planking swelled and closed the gaps. As the work progressed, the river rose and when it reached the proper stage they decided to attempt the run over Copper Ledge Falls. (this was a stretch of rough water, more pour than falls, which was located at the site of present-day Hells Canyon Dam).

Captain Smith had reported that the falls could not be run in safety. The start was made April 20th. Due precaution against accidents had been made by placing lighted candles in the hold so that a leak could be detected immediately and stopped. The plan of navigation adopted was to drift with the engines backing, steering the boat by the pressure of water against the rudders.

In approaching the rapid, Captain Miller miscalculated the force of a large eddy where the river was divided by a small island of boulders, and the steamer was spun around three times before she cleared the whirlpool and finally faced the plunge, out of position to avoid the rocks in the middle and lower part of the rapid. When she reached the declivity, the stern hung over until the wheel was entirely out of the water and the engines began racing. When the stern wheel took hold again, the weathered portion was destroyed and the paddles were useless in checking her speed. She collided with the rocks at the foot of the falls, carrying away about eight feet of the bow. The shock threw the weight off the safety valve, allowing the steam to escape.

A landing was made as soon as possible, and the crew was employed all day repairing the wheel. The breech in the bow was above the waterline, and the forward bulkhead kept most of the water out.

At nine o'clock the next morning, they again steamed down the uncharted river, passing through several bad rapids. At eleven o'clock they landed near a small clump of trees, which were soon converted into fuel, and got underway again at two-thirty, passing before nightfall some of the worst rapids yet encountered. A landing was made at five p.m. to make further repairs to the wheel. It was patched with stage planking and other available lumber on the boat.

This work occupied the men until the morning of the 23rd, at which time they again cast off, but were compelled to moor at 11 a.m. because of wind, which prevented the captain from keeping the boat properly headed.

On the 24th another start was made, the nature of the river traversed being about the same as the day before, necessitating frequent stops in order to scout the water ahead.

After making 10 miles, the steamer secured at the base of a mountain where fuel was plentiful. Captain Miller was nearly killed at this spot, when a large tree rolled on him, inflicting injuries that kept him from working the next day.

On the evening of the 27th the *Shoshone* steamed up to the Lewiston dock. While rounding to, Captain Miller shouted with elation through the speaking tube to the engineer, "I say Buc, I expect if this company wanted a couple of men to take a steamboat through hell, they would send for you and me." After landing, he turned the boat over the O.S.N. agent, stating that while "she might look a little rough, she did not leak a drop."

While going over Copper Ledge Falls, the jackstaff was carried away and was picked up at Umatilla so long before the boat was heard from that she had been given up for lost.

The *Shoshone* was taken on to Celilo by Captain Holmes and in June was run down the middle Columbia. She was hauled out for extensive repairs at The Dalles, then used as a cattle steamer until the spring of 1873, when Captain Ainsworth piloted her over the Cascades. He took the vessel to Portland, where she was sold to the Willamette River Transportation Company.

The *Shoshone* was used on the Willamette, running there until the fall of 1874, when en route to the Yamhill River she struck a rock opposite Salem and sank. All efforts to raise her were frustrated, so in November the machinery was removed and the hull left to its fate.

In January the hull floated down to Lincoln, where a thrifty granger salvaged it and the remains of the pilot house were used as a chicken shed.

The Norma: Captain Wm. Gray
1895

The magnet of mining activity once again drew a steamboat to Snake River in the 1890's. Substantial copper deposits had been discovered in the Seven Devils on the Idaho side of Snake River. Albert Kleinschmidt, from Prussia by way of Montana, had become wealthy in the freight and mining business of the "Treasure State." He was impressed with the returns on ore shipped from the Blue Jacket mine in the Seven Devils to the smelter at Anaconda. Wisely deciding cheap transportation was the key that would unlock the lode, he engineered a road from the Devils down to the river.

Kleinschmidt apparently reached an agreement with Jacob Kamm and Jaspar Miller of Portland, inducing them to construct a steamboat which would haul the copper ore from the foot of his road up to the Union Pacific railhead in Huntington, Oregon. (This railroad was also known as the Oregon Short Line.)

Kamm had made a snug fortune from the now defunct O.S.N., and aware of the *Shoshone's* saga, had business acumen that would have required impressive reasons for constructing a second steamer in the area. Nonetheless, the 165-foot vessel was built near Huntington, and named *Norma* after Kleinschmidt's oldest daughter. The ship's capacity was 300 tons.

Captain Miller was sent to Huntington in March of 1891 for the trial run. (This pilot was probably not "Bas" Miller, since that captain would have retired about ten years earlier.) Miller had to wait six weeks for an auspicious water level.

On April 21 the *Norma* steamed up and down past the Devil's Gate, Bay Horse Rapids, and Blacksmith Point without difficulty.

Kleinschmidt's road was finished three months later, but the *Norma* only made two trips. Some accounts say Albert then refused to pay for the steamer, but there appear to have been other factors at work. Kleinschmidt had sold his shares in the Devils' mines for stock in the newly organized American Mining Company. His control was jeopardized and years of litigation ensued. The price of copper dropped, and the panic of 1893 discouraged development.

During the interim, the *Norma* was unable to travel up river from Huntington because the Oregon Short Line's bridge across the river had no draw allowing steamer passage.

C. W. Williams, the ship's owner in 1892, petitioned Secretary of War Stephen Elkins:

> ... to cause the Union Pacific Railroad Company to put draws in three bridges which the company has across the Snake .... It is alleged that it is the desire of the owners of the *Norma* to ply to a point on the Snake above all these bridges in the Silver City section, to carry ores from the Seven Devils mining district, and also to engage in a general freight and passenger business.

Williams had already lost a case in federal court to have the bridges abated, and his efforts with the War Department proved equally futile. Two more years of inactivity led to the decision that the time had come for another spectacular steamboat voyage down Snake River to Lewiston. The *Oregonian* reported:

> Jacob Kamm yesterday (May 11, 1895) sent W. P. Gray and a crew up to Huntington to bring the steamer *Norma* down to Pasco. This is a great undertaking and will be watched with interest by all steamboat men in the Northwest. Compared with it, the bringing of a steamboat down over the Cascades is an easy task. The *Norma,* which is a large sternwheeler, was built at Huntington in 1891 by Mr. Kamm, and was intended for the trade between Huntington and the Seven Devils country. She made only two trips and was then laid up. Mr. Kamm finds that he can put her to good service on the lower Snake, whereas the boat is useless at Huntington. At any rate, it is worth while making the trial ....
>
> The *Norma* will be overhauled and strengthened in preparation for her perilous voyage. The boat already has fore-and-aft bulkheads and several thwartship bulkheads will be put in. This trip has been made only once before, and will probably never be made again, as no one is likely to build another steamer on the upper Snake. Many years ago, the steamer *Shoshone* was brought down to Lewiston from the upper waters and it is believed the trip was made without accident. It is expected that everything will be ready for the *Norma* to leave Huntington the latter part of the week....

*The **Norma** on the Snake River, 11 miles below Almota.*

If "courage is the virtue necessary for the practice of other virtues", then Kamm had an admirable man in William Polk Gray. Born in Oregon in 1845, the son of an incredibly resourceful father, W. P. Gray had accumulated river experience the way a backeddy gathers driftwood. This was the same Gray, who as a 20-year-old assistant pilot, had recorded the attempt of the *Colonel Wright* to steam up Hells Canyon. Two excerpts from Gray's reminiscences convey a fascinating glimpse of his career.

While working as a cub pilot on the steamer *Yakima* between Celilo and Lewiston, Gray met a Mr. Atwood who had a sawmill near Asotin, ten miles up the Snake from Lewiston. Atwood was despondent because his repeated attempts to raft lumber down to Umatilla Landing, where it would fetch four times the Asotin price, had all ended in disaster at the rapids. Gray said he could get a raft down. Atwood persuaded the captain of the *Yakima* to release the young pilot for a trip.

The story in Gray's words:

Atwood and I went to his mill at Asotin, where he built a raft containing 50,000 feet of lumber. . . . When he came to the big eddy above Lewiston (where Atwood had always had trouble, and had missed landing at that place with several rafts and as a consequence lost the lumber as there was no market farther down the river), I threw the raft into the

45

center of the eddy. Atwood protested, believing that we certainly would miss the Lewiston landing, but as the raft returned up the eddy and shot out towards the Lewiston shore, his face was wreathed with smiles.

We took on 10,000 additional feet of lumber here. Next morning at 2 o'clock I cast loose and started down the river. Whenever we came to a rapid I sent the raft into the center of the rapid. The rapid would give the raft such impetus that it would carry us through the slack water. Atwood said, 'The very thing we have been trying to avoid — getting the raft in the rapids, seems to be the reason for your success.' We were averaging nine miles an hour. I told him we would get along all right until we came to the Palouse rapids and we were going to have a serious time of it there. The water pours through a narrow chute and empties into the eddy, which boils back toward the current from the south shore.

When we got to the Palouse rapids I sent the raft into the center of the rapids. The current was so swift it shot us into the eddy. The forward part of the raft went under water and the current from the chute caught the back end of the raft and sent the raft under water. We stayed on the raft until the water was up to our knees. The skiff which he had on the raft started to float off, but I caught the painter and we got aboard the skiff. We brought the skiff over where the raft had been and felt down with the oars but we could not touch the raft.

We floated down with the current. All I attempted to do was to keep the skiff in its course. Atwood said, 'I knew you couldn't do it. With such rapids as the Palouse it was foolish to expect we could.' I felt pretty serious for I was afraid the eddy had broken the fastenings on the raft and we would soon run into the wreckage of floating boards. About half a mile below the rapids our skiff was suddenly lifted out of the water by the reappearance of the raft. Our skiff and the raft had both gone with the current and, oddly enough, it had appeared directly under us, lifting the skiff out of the water. This may sound 'fishy', but it is a fact.

You never saw a man more surprised or delighted than Atwood, for the raft was uninjured. As a matter of fact, before leaving, I had taken special pains to see that it was strongly fastened, for I knew what kind of treatment it would get in the rapids.

We went through the Pine Tree rapids without accident, but a little ways below there we struck a wind strongly upstream, so we had to tie up. Next morning at 3 o'clock, just before daybreak, we started again, arriving at Wallula at 10 o'clock in the forenoon.

The steamer *Yakima* was just pulling in from below. From Wallula to Umatilla was plain sailing, so I left Atwood to go the rest of the way alone and rejoined the *Yakima*.

In the past they had tried to manage the raft by side sweeps, while all I had used had been a steering oar at the rear. Atwood paid me $20 for carrying the raft successfully through the rapids. He told me that he would have been just as glad to pay me $500 if I had asked that much. This was the first lumber raft ever taken down the Snake river, but it was the forerunner of scores of other rafts.

For this lumber, which was worth only $900 at Lewiston, he got $3,300 at Umatilla, or in other words, he made a profit of $2,400 on the $20 investment in my services.

On another occasion, William Gray made a reconnaisance of the Columbia from the mouth of the Snake River to Rock Island rapids. He sent a report to the president of the Oregon Railroad & Navigation Co., saying he thought it was possible to run a boat through Rock Island rapids. On the strength of that report, a couple of years later some friends with mining interests in the Okanagan district had a steamer built in Pasco, Washington, with the expectation that it would haul their supplies over Rock Island rapids to their Okanagan claims.

Unable to find anyone who would attempt the trip, and out the expense of the boat because they credited Captain Gray's report, they were able to prevail upon him to drop his own interests long enough to prove it could be done.

Again, the narrative as he wrote it:

The only point at which Rock Island Rapids is really difficult or dangerous is at Hawksbill Point. It juts into the river at an acute angle from the island, on the left hand side of the island as you go up the river. It required delicate calculation to overcome this difficulty. I put out three lines at the same time. One to line her up and the others to keep her from swinging either way. It took us two hours to pass Hawksbill Point. We had another cluster of reefs near the head of the island to pass. Here the current turns in strongly toward the bluff, 40-feet high, which projects from the mainland on the right hand side at an acute angle. We had no rope long enough to fasten to the right point to take us around this bluff. The boat's power was insufficient to hold it in place, let alone making headway across the current. The current drew the boat in at the head. We bucked the current for over an hour without success. I finally decided a desperate remedy must be taken. I threw her head across the current toward the island and swung almost against the island. It was necessary that I should let the stern wheel of the steamer go within four feet of the rocks and directly above them, to get out of the main strength of the current. If the current here was too strong the boat would go on the rocks, break her wheel, and leave us disabled in the current. For a moment the boat hung where she was. It was a mighty anxious moment for me, for, with all steam on, she seemed only able to hold her own. She was neither going forward nor back, but slowly, inch by inch, she pulled away from the rapids and out into the open river. That was the first time a steamboat had ever been through Rock Island Rapids.

The president of the company owning the boat was on board. His enthusiasm had ranged from fever heat to zero on most of the rapids. When I swung the boat over in the last effort, he wrung his hands and sobbed, 'You'll wreck her, you'll wreck her sure!' But when we began to gain headway and he was sure we were over Rock Island Rapids, he threw his arms around my neck and yelled, 'You've saved us — I knew you would!' Then I thought, what a narrow line divides failures and success. Failure is 'I told you so'; and success is, 'I knew it!'

Captain William Polk Gray.

Captain William Gray and his assistants arrived in Huntington during May, 1895. They worked over the steamer, preparatory to their trip, and awaited the river's spring rise. Gray furnished details concerning the trip, a quarter century later, at the request of the director of the

U.S. Geological Survey. If he seems to exaggerate at times, he was a seventy-five-year old boatman, whose exploits entitled him to stretch the blanket a bit:

Pasco Washington
December 2, 1920.

Director,
U. S. Geological Survey,
Washington, D. C.
Dear Sir:

Your request for a description of the voyage of the Steamer *Norma* through the Snake River Canyon is received. I kept a complete log of the trip but after several days hunt among sixty years relics, cannot find anything but the 'time book' of the crew, and must depend upon my memory for an account of the incidents of the trip.

The steamer was a light draft stern wheeler.

Hull length – 165 feet
Hull breadth – 35 feet
Hull depth – 6 feet, 6 inches
Length from stem to fantail – 185 feet
Width over guards – 40 feet, 4 inches
Deck house – 120′ x 35′ x 10′
Cabin – 80′ x 35′ x 9′
Pilot house – 12′ x 8′ x 8′

Crew for the trip:

W. P. Gray, master and pilot
A. W. Gray, first mate
Ed Lyons, second mate
C. H. Jennings, engineer
E. D. Kellogg, second engineer
A. B. Gardner, fireman
Jas. Duffey, watchman
Walter Young, deck hand
Mike Quigley, deck hand
Martin Condry, deck hand
Pat Westwood, deck hand
Geo. Binnard, cook and steward
Thos. Wright, carpenter
F. D. Farwell, signed on as clerk but was a reporter for papers.

We left the O.R. & N. Bridge across Snake River near Huntington, Oregon, at 2:00 P.M. May 17th, 1895. At Bay Horse rapids, three miles down, while drifting in a channel improved by Government engineers (a copy of their report was in the pilot house) we touched on what afterward proved to be a piece of two inch steel drill which had been broken off and left when the engineers were working there some years before. The drill ripped several holes through the bottom and the boat swung around and damaged the stern wheel badly. Working the boat clear with spars and lines we went down to J. A. Gray's Landing and repaired the wheel and patched the holes in the bottom.

Left Gray's Landing on the 19th — no wind. I was steering, my brother, the Mate, watching the Government chart. I saw indications of reefs or shoals and remarked: "It don't look good, what does the chart say". He replied: "All clear — there is a black rock marked on the shore." But I was not satisfied and rung the bell to stop. Almost instantly she struck the starboard knuckle making a hole forty feet long and four feet wide. I grabbed the chart and flung it out of the window and we touched no reefs or rocks afterward except at Copper Creek Falls. We had struck the edge of a reef about a foot under the muddy water which the Snake carries while in flood.

We were drifting while the mate inspected the damages. I knew they were bad but the crew had been a little discouraged at the "Bay Horse" trouble and I was afraid they would jump the jb if we landed above Sturgill Rapids, three miles below us. From where we were the boat could easily steam back to the Bridge. I heard that Sturgill Rapids were very swift and it would be almost impossible to bring the boat back over with our damaged side so I kept on down slowly. The men gathered on the forward deck and one man asked if I was going to land. I made no reply and soon we were below the rapids where we landed. There was some talk and I told them we would repair damages as much as possible. We had plenty of lumber and forty cords of wood in the hull. The boat had bulkheads all through her. We built a bulkhead as close as we could to the hole in her side and pumped out the six bulkheads that had been flooded. The men had under-

don't get excited and jump overboard. Snake River never gives up her dead. Now get ready to go."

When we dropped over the fall we seemed to be facing certain destruction on the cliff below, but I knew my engineer was "all there' and would answer promptly. Back slowly and within ten feet of rock to starboard her bow passed the mouth of Copper Creek, where an eddy emptying, gave her a slight swing out and I backed strong with helm hard to starboard — the bow must take its chances now, the stern must not. Almost before one could speak the bow touched the point of the cliff just hard enough to break three guard timbers without touching the hull, and we bounded into the still water below. The carpenter who had stationed himself on the hurricane deck outside of the pilot house with two life preservers around him stepped out in front of the pilot house and shouted: "Hurrah, Cap! You start her for hell and I'll go with you from this on."

A little below Copper Creek Falls we entered the canyon and although a bright sun was shining outside, in the canyon it was twilight. I was too busy watching the surface of the river but the men on deck said they saw the stars through the gloom. Shortly after coming out of the canyon we passed down a straight cataract that had cut its way through a plateau of Blue Clay and granite boulders. The canal was not over sixty feet wide and a mile or two long with a drop estimated at one hundred feet to the mile. We tied up on account of wind for the rest of the day and all night at Johnson Creek, which is now the head of navigation, and reached Lewiston May 24th. The dates given are taken from the crews' time book in which I kept the account of supplies bought at different places.

The signature to your request is unintelligible to me so I don't know whether I am writing to a stranger or friend, but as you must have heard of me it seems a good opportunity to 'toot my own horn' and a man seventy five years of age can't have many more chances to toot.

Will say that I should not be expected to remember the details of one short trip when it is know that I have been captain and pilot on steam vessels from outside the Columbia River Bar (when there was a bar there) on all its reaches up and into the Okanogan River, the Willamette from mouth to Harrisburg, the Snake from mouth to the Imnaha, the Fraser from mouth to Fort Yale, the Stickine from Fort Wrangel to Telegraph Creek, and took a stern-wheel steamer from Seattle through the inland passage to Icy Strait and across the North Pacific Ocean, up Bering Sea to St. Michael's to White Horse Rapids. I am the only man that ever took a steamboat carrying freight and passengers both up and down over Priest Rapids and Rock Island Rapids on the Columbia River where all others that have tried have failed.

On all these voyages I had no chart or pilot but found my way by reading the character of swift water which has been my vocation since as a boy thirteen years old I handled canoes and batteau on the Fraser River in British Columbia. I was called by telegram from Pasco to Chicago by parties I had never heard of to give evidence on the navigability of the Des Plain River in Illinois. After examining the river one afternoon my evidence decided a lawsuit involving millions of dollars by saying "When water crafts cannot compete with wagons along the banks of a stream it is not navigable."

Yours very truly,

/s/ W. P. Gray

The *Norma* was leased to the Oregon Railway and Navigation Company at different times and used on the Snake from Lewiston to Riparia until 1906, when the North Bank Railroad leased her for construction work. During the building of the Deschutes railroad, the ship served as a ferry across the Columbia, and on completion of the bridge above Celilo Falls, the *Norma* was taken to Portland where she was dismantled in 1915.

*The **Norma** on the Lewiston waterfront.*

*The **Norma** at Portland.*

When river passengers comprehend the feat of Captains Miller and Gray, their incredulity lessens with the assumption that those pilots had far more water than the dams now pass.

Water records since 1896 indicate two spring floods, measured at the mouth of the Weiser, exceeded 120,000 cubic feet per second. The same records for a 30 year pre-dam period show April-May flows (months used by the steamboats) averaged 48,000 c.f.s. — with highs of 50-60,000 c.f.s. not uncommon. (Even with many reservoirs above the gauge and irrigation depletions for two and a half million acres, the river has twice run over 84,000 c.f.s. since 1952.) There was more water in earlier days — and there were channel obstructions, since cleared by the Army Corps of Engineers. But given the length of the steamboats, the additional flow can scarcely diminish the audacious accomplishments of Captains William Gray and Sebastian Miller.

Imnaha and the *Mountain Gem* 1903 - 1904

The tropism that seems to exist between mines and steamboats drew two more ships upriver after the turn of the century.

The sternwheeler *Imnaha* was financed by corporate mining interests at a cost of $35,000. She was completed at Lewiston in 1903 as the transportation workhorse for the Eureka Bar/Fargo Group copper claims up Snake River at the mouth of the Imnaha River. Captain Harry G. Baughman took the vessel for her first run to Eureka on June 30, 1903. This cruise revealed the need for installation of rings on shore in order to line through Mountain Sheep Rapids, an obstacle which caused a two-day delay in the initial trip. Similar hazards existed at Wild Goose Rapid and at the mouth of the Salmon River, so lining rings were also implanted in the rocks at these places. A month later the *Lewiston Tribune* reported that the *Imnaha* had departed for Mountain Sheep Rapids with a party of government engineers who would blast away the large rock in that "menace to navigation." The following day, according to the newspaper, the steamer made the round trip to Eureka without the use of lining rings.

For about five months the vessel successfully navigated the river, carrying passengers, machinery, and supplies up the 53 miles to the mines. Downriver passage required about three hours. On her fourteenth voyage, November 9, 1903, while transporting equipment essential to the new concentrating mill under construction at Eureka Bar, disaster struck.

*The steamer **Imnaha** at Lewiston.*

To understand the problem it is necessary to realize the method used to surmount rapids like Wild Goose. The cable attached to the ring had a barrel floating on the downstream end. The steamboat would retrieve the barrel, wrap the free end of the cable around the capstan and winch over the broken water.

The *Imnaha* had cleared Mountain Sheep Rapid and the cable was cast off by command, but the cable buoy of the lining system became entangled in the eccentric rods, broke them and disabled the paddlewheel. Helpless, the craft drifted back into the rapid. As the 125-foot steamer swung crosswise between the narrow walls of the canyon, passengers and crew scrambled for the safety of the Oregon shore like ants off a burning log. Mounting water pressure crushed the hull, the deck splayed open and mill machinery sank like stone.

There have been rumors ever since that the ship was deliberately sunk — a conspiracy by mining promoters who knew they could not deliver the copper ore expected by their stockholders. The speculation seems no more credible than the accident. Race you to Moot Point.

Lewiston businessmen took up a subscription to replace the *Imnaha* with the *Mountain Gem*. The *Gem* was fashioned with a stouter hull and made a successful trial run in August, 1904. However, in October of 1905, it was leased for service between Celilo and Pasco with W. P. Gray as pilot, which signaled the demise of steamboats on the middle Snake, and of mining operations at Eureka Bar.

*The **Mountain Gem**, built to replace the **Imnaha**.*

Ed MacFarlane
1910

Stockmen and miners trading at the Asotin, Washington, "Glover and MacFarlane" hardware store in 1909, brought news of the railroad coming north downriver from Huntington. They carried word of new homesteaders upstream, fending families and fresh mineral strikes. Edwin Glover MacFarlane must have listened close as a deer while he sold barbed wire, traps, and nails to ranchers that called. For E. G. had spent five years with boats in British Columbia and Alaska — on Puget Sound and the Kootenai Lakes, and rivers like the Yukon, Skeena, and Stikine, before being drydocked as a partner in the hardware business at Asotin. Snake River flowed past his front door, and like a raft on its painter, the live-water life tugged at his memory.

Aware of the isolated homesteaders, and longing to be back on the river, MacFarlane decided to combine business and boating by offering the first regular transportation service on the Snake. The evolution of this decision on the part of the "father of Snake River navigation" is best told in his own words:

There was a miner by the name of Holly Solan came into the shop at the store one day and asked for a price on four-inch galvanized pipe and a Sibley stove. He wanted this to draw powder smoke out of a tunnel he was driving on his hard rock property up the Snake River.

The way he talked I thought he might have a good prospect, and after meeting him a few times through the winter I decided to go up the following spring and look his property over.

So along in the summer Mr. Glover (Richard Glover, McFarlane's uncle and senior partner in their hardware store) and I made an agreement with him and his partner for one half interest, providing we install an air drilling outfit on the property, and Solan and his partner to drive the tunnel and cut the ledge.

The drilling outfit consisted of St. Clair air drill, Fairbank engine, compressor and air tank, water tank, pipe, hose and tools and to deliver this equipment at the mouth of the Grande Ronde River.

One day Mr. Glover asked me how we were going to make delivery of this shipment. I told him 'we can build a boat and take it up.' So we decided to do just that.

Late in the fall we started to build a little steel hull 36-feet long and 6-foot beam behind the shop. We worked on it at odd times. Finally we launched it about the first of February, 1910.

The gas engine was a two-cycle, three-cylinder Fario (25 hp). Well I remember the time I spent getting acquainted with it. Hugh (Onstot) and I would take turns cranking it. Then we would talk about its stubborn qualities, pat it on the back and call it a few questionable names, then do it all over again.

After performing like this, snorting and sputtering at intervals for about two days, it decided to go. What a relief!

As we got on better terms with the engine we began to think it wasn't such a bad animal after all, but when it took a notion to stop, stop it would, just like a balky horse. I had a long 14-foot oar and oar lock on the stern, and when necessary I would skull the old boat to shore or eddy.

*The **Flyer** under construction in Asotin in 1909.*

Different times I took it down stream for miles by skulling it along with this big oar.

The first trip with the *Flyer* was on Feb. 7, 1910. Hugh Onstot and I had loaded on about 1,500 pounds of this machinery the evening before. We saw the steamer *Lewiston* coming so we let her go by and dock at the grain warehouse. Then we started. The steamer *Lewiston* crew gave us the once over as we slipped past.

We weren't blessed with a lot of power but we kept plugging along, and finally made our destination about 1:30 at the Grande Ronde, and that's 30 miles, and unloaded it and beat it back to Asotin and tied up at Asotin about 4 pm.

As we walked back to the store everyone wanted to know how far we got. We didn't give them much satisfaction as it had been noised around by some that we would never get there. After we had made two or three trips everyone seemed to think we were getting through all right.

It wasn't long until this one and that one wanted some freight hauled. Then we put on a scheduled once-a-week trip, and soon we were making quite a few trips during lambing, and hauling a few sheep shearers.

Ed MacFarlane looking down at the Snake River.

Mac gradually extended his operation from the mouth of the Grande Ronde to the confluence with the Salmon, to Eureka Bar, and finally Pittsburg Landing. In December of 1911 he ascended to Defiance Eddy, four miles above Pittsburg. (This was the boat noted by the railroad survey crew in the next section.) The partners ordered a 60 horsepower Sterling engine to meet the growing demands placed on their craft.

The *Flyer's* success proved the river's navigability, and gave evidence that enough business existed to turn a profit. So Glover and MacFarlane launched their second venture, the *Prospector,* in the spring of 1912. This vessel was 65-feet in length, with twin 100 horsepower Scripps engines and twice the carrying capacity of its predecessor. While the *Flyer* was making three trips a day from Lewiston to Asotin, charging a 50-cent fare each way, the *Prospector* began advertising picnic excursions to Wild Goose Rapid for $1.50.

In May of 1914, according to the *Lewiston Tribune,* Mac took the *Prospector* with 19 passengers upriver to see how far he could go. His friend, Stewart Winslow, a steamboat captain on the lower Snake, accompanied him with his fast little launch, the *Tillicum.* They left the *Tillicum* at Johnson Bar, and powered to Rush Creek where the passengers helped rope the *Prospector* up from the Idaho side.

They motored on to Granite Creek, where all the people were put ashore except Winslow, and then Mac humped the *Prospector* up the rapid like a homesick salmon. He nosed the craft to the crest of the tongue, but when water began breaking over the bow he had to back her down.

The **Prospector.**

Low water in the fall of 1914 allowed MacFarlane and the Army engineers to improve the river channel with the aid of explosives. The engineers had appropriated $25,000 for this purpose at the urging of the Lewiston Commercial Club.

That year John Platt recalls an amusing incident, with some fellow cowhands on a roundup, who hitched a ride downriver one evening with Captain Mac to Asotin. They agreed to meet Mac at five o'clock the next morning so he could have them back in their camp by seven.

But the boys got so drunk they couldn't hit the ground with their hats in three throws, and consequently turned up two and a half hours late at the landing. Mac was irritated. In Platt's words:

> Up the river we went. The early river boats were largely
> experimental, and their power was so limited that much time

was consumed in navigating the rapids. Wild Goose Rapids alone took 20 minutes to traverse. Just above these rapids McFarlane shot a big mallard duck. The bird fell, and McFarlane couldn't maneuver the boat around fast enough to get hold of him before the rapids caught the bird. The duck had a broken wing, so he killed him and threw him on the deck.

Four of our crew lay in the blankets McFarlane carried for just such emergencies. I slipped the duck down between two of the sleepers, and just as we cleared the rapids the second time, one of the sleepers was awakened by the wet bedfellow. He grabbed the duck and heaved him out of the boat and down through the rapids he went. McFarlane swore he'd have that duck, and we followed him through the rapids again!

We had now wasted most of an hour's time. The early boats had the engine in the open on the deck. The fellow who had thrown the duck was now fully awakened. He stood up, with the blanket wrapped around him Indian fashion. The fashion was all right, but he backed too close to the engine's flywheel, the blanket tangled with it, and killed the motor. We drifted for a mile below the rapids before McFarlane got the blanket out and the motor started again. We reached camp at 12:00 o'clock!

PROSPECTOR

E. G. MacFarlane also ran a boat called the *Wild Goose* from Lewiston, Idaho, to Asotin, Washington, prior to national prohibition. The *Goose* had a tendency to roll and was ballasted with a thousand pounds of scrap iron. Her purpose was to haul passengers from Lewiston, which was dry as a covered bridge, to Asotin, which was wet under local option. There the folks could drink their cheerwater and then be chauffeured safely home.

Just after World War I, MacFarlane went partners with A. M. Peterson and constructed the *Clipper*. She was on the river in 1920, a lithe and handsome vessel, with leather and mirrors in the passenger cabin; but a "roller" too. They operated the concern as the Snake River Boat Company.

*The **Clipper** hauling Dobbin and Huffman sheep across the river.*

Over a period of twelve years, Captain Mac hired Press Brewrink as a deckhand and twice formed partnerships with him which ended in dissolution. Their arrangement when it functioned was called Snake River Transportation Company.

Ed McFarlane had acquired a contract to deliver mail as far as Pittsburg Landing in 1926. Service was dependent upon water levels — he could always get to Pittsburg until late June, but sometimes Temperance Creek Rapid would block the run to Johnson Bar. If summer water was too low, service might be renewed in the fall. Many people still got their mail at Imnaha or Lucile. He shared the contract with Press Brewrink in the 1930's.

65

Mac and Press built the *Chief Joseph* in 1935. This craft was about 65-feet in length, shallow draft with a sled, prow and capable of carrying almost 30 tons. Mac had always designed his own boats from magazine plans, but Press insisted on using a marine architect for this boat. Ironically, she was a failure — a fuel hog, too slow and clumsy for river use. After a few trips she was docked, and sat sunning herself for four years until the Russell Towboat and Moorage Company of Portland bought her as a ferry on the Willamette for the Kaiser shipyard workers.

MacFarlane sold his interest to Brewrink in the mid-Thirties and swallowed the anchor. He lived with his wife, Maude Powell, in a lovely house in southern Lewiston. At his retirement he took the steering wheel and ship bell from one of his river craft and placed them in the hallway of his home. When river friends left his place they were always bid farewell with a strike of the bell and a spin of the wheel.

Captain E. G. MacFarlane, born in Ontario, Canada in 1872, and 35 years a boatman, crossed the last bar October 15, 1949.

Captain E. G. MacFarlane at Lewiston in 1940.

An unusual discovery along the Snake River in 1936 led to a lovely, perpetual remembrance for Captain Ed MacFarlane, river pilot. In the spring of that year, he pointed out a flower he admired to some botanists from Washington. It was a variety new to science — MacFarlane's four o'clock. The Latin name is *Mirabilis macfarlanei*. Mirabilis means "wonderful." The plant, which grows only on the middle Snake, is a stout perennial with rose-purple funnelform flowers that open on late afternoons each May — MacFarlane's memorial. *(See drawing page 335.)*

The Union Pacific Railroad Survey 1911

In the fall of 1911 the Northwestern Railroad Company, a subsidiary of the Union Pacific, was still serious enough about plans for a railroad through Hells Canyon to launch a six boat survey crew on the Snake at Homestead.

The Adams family of Massachusetts must have been even more confident of the results. They owned enough U. P. stock to be represented on the board of directors, and using their inside information, invested heavily in land where the city of Clarkston now stands. The Adamses platted the townsite, set aside ground for the railroad yard, and developed an extensive irrigation system behind the future city. A toll bridge was constructed across the Snake from Lewiston to the Adams' location to replace the aging ferries. One more instance of unwarranted anticipation.

The survey party rowed out of Homestead on October 3rd. The diary notes of assistant engineer S. C. Martin are available from the U.S. Geological Survey. Some excerpts transmit a sense of the difficulties:

> Oct. 3, 1911. Left Homestead in six row boats loaded with camp equipage and supplies and sixteen men, Olie Taleen, boatman, at 10 A.M. Passed a number of rapids successfully but at 3 P.M. arrived at Lynch Creek rapids, some fifteen miles below Homestead, where there is very rough water. One of the boats in attempting to shoot the rapids was swamped and all of the personal effects of the

men in the party were lost; that is, their suitcases and valises, none of them ever being recovered. One transit was saved by one of the three men who were in the boat when it upset. He swam to shore with the instrument in hand. The stationery chest drifted ashore in an eddy one and a half miles below the rapids. The boat drifted across a large boulder in the stream and was broken in two by the force of the current, a complete loss.

Oct. 4, 1911. Made portage of stores and tents by Lynch Creek rapids, set boats adrift and caught them below the swift water.

Oct. 5, 1911. One mile farther down stream to Squaw Creek rapids. Lined four boats, partly loaded, through the rapids. Camped for the night.

Oct. 6, 1911. Reached Buck Creek rapids at noon. Lined four boats over the rapids. Two of them upset, to one of which the camp range had been lashed in with hay wire; it was swept out of the boat and lost.

Oct. 7, 1911. Shot Pine Creek rapids and landed just below them. One boat had a hole knocked in it by running onto a boulder. Repaired it.

Oct. 8, 1911. Arrived at Steamboat rapids at 3 P.M. Overtook one boat that got away from us at Buck Creek rapids. A boy had salvaged it at Fisher's ranch, where we bought fruit and bear meat.

Oct. 11, 1911. Down river to Battle Creek bar. Lined boats around rapids ¾ of a mile above Battle Creek. One boat stranded before starting and the same boat swamped on a rock at Battle Creek bar. Mr. Winchester and family reside on Battle Creek bar in a small cabin. Alfalfa patches and a few apple trees. It is a placer mining claim and some free gold.

On Oct. 12,1911. Left Battle Creek at 8:15 A.M., arrived at Two Creeks by noon. Very rough water and rapids. Had to take boats over a portion of the rough places by hand. Camped half mile below Granite Creek which flows from the Idaho side into the river. Made three miles today.

Oct. 13, 1911. Lined boats over rapids. Arrived at Three Creeks rapids at 1 P.M. Carried bedding around and shot boats through the rapids. Made Squaw Creek rapids, one mile below Saddle Creek at 4 P.M. where camped for the night. Ranch at Three Creeks and Squaw Creek on the Idaho side and ranch at Saddle Creek on the Oregon side.

Oct. 14, 1911. Attempted to line boat over rapids below Squaw Creek; swamped it and lost boatman's bed roll and two sacks of flour. Also a few other articles. Made portage of cargoes in other boats and shot the rapids with empty boats. Lined boats through next rapids and camped for the night. Three miles today.

Oct. 24, 1911. George Heydrick, rodman, one of the men who was in the boat that upset in the Lynch Creek rapids Oct. 3, is sick in camp; a severe cold and high fever. Beverige, draftsman, is rodding in his place.

Oct. 27, 1911. Took George Heydrick, who is very ill, in a boat down the river to a ranch, two miles above Pittsburg Landing, where he was taken in a buggy to White Bird, Idaho, for medical attention. Nurses were employed to wait upon him. He had incipient tuberculosis before the party left Homestead, but I did not know about it until after he became ill in camp.

Nov. 12, 1911. Party on line. Beverige reported that George Heydrick had died at 9:30 P.M. Friday, Nov. 10, 1911, of typhoid pneumonia. His body was sent by express to his mother at Norristown, Pa. All expenses were defrayed by the O. S. L. Co.

Nov. 21, 1911. Moved camp from Summers Creek to Rowland's Bar — 6 miles down the river, just below Dodson's ranch. Shore travel is very difficult: Detours far back from the river necessary for safety. The line had to be pushed along the cliffs by the aid of the boats.

Nov. 25, 1911. Party on field work.

Sent list of claims for loss of personal effects that were lost from the boat that capsized at Lynch Creek rapids, Oct. 3, to Mr. Stacey, accounting by Mr. Stradley and paid from the appropriation for the survey. Rain at 3 P.M.

Dec. 4, 1911. Party on field work. The *Flyer* passed on way down the river in A.M. It had gone to a point four miles above Pittsburg Landing where the navigation became impracticable.

Dec. 15, 1911. Moved camp in motor boat "Flyer" from Dug Creek to Cache Creek. Passed through a box canyon gorge below the mouth of the Imnaha River for a distance of some four or five miles. Some rapid and rough water. A wild ride in a motor boat.

Dec. 25, 1911. Christmas — In camp — Cook gave us a chicken dinner.

More snow today.

Jan. 13, 1912. Broke camp and went down the river in six row boats to Lewiston. The river was a flowing stream of cake ice. Stopped at noon for lunch. Arrived at Lewiston at 2:30 P.M. having made 39 miles on the water. Passing through some rough rapids; the boats drifting with the current, it being impossible to steer them with the oars. Often the ice floes covered the river from shore to shore, so there was nothing to do but to go with the flow of the stream.

Met Mr. Stacey at Lewiston where we cached our boats and shipped outfit to Salt Lake City.

The men had completed a strenuous task through terrain so rough a bloodhound couldn't track it, but their labors were as useless as salt in the ocean. Cost analysis showed construction would run about $200,000 a mile. The Panama Canal opened in 1914, diverting much traffic from the railroads. Then the Union Pacific and Northern Pacific agreed to share the Inland Empire trade and jointly constructed the Camas Prairie line to feed the terminals at Lewiston. The arch of the Homestead railroad rainbow never alighted on the Adams's plan.

◆

Press Brewrink:
1912

William Pressly "Press" Brewrink was sometimes Ed MacFarlane's partner and sometimes his most able competition on the river. Brewrink went to Washington State College where he studied mining engineering. He was attracted to the Snake River by his interest in the AA1 mine at Wild Goose Bar.

Brewrink's first boat was the *Swastika,* and he was operating it in 1912. It was slower than a horse with hobbles, so he bought a boat called the *Billie Bryan* from its builder, Jim Chapman. Chapman had used the vessel in 1915 to carry his shearing crews up and down the river. Jim had dubbed it the *Bryan* after the three-time Democratic presidential nominee, William Jennings Bryan, because he said it was "always running but never got there."

The Brewrinks: left to right, Jimmy, Edna, and Press.

The first river route mail contract, according to U.S. postal records, was awarded to Brewrink in 1919. It called for weekly deliveries and he held the right until 1922. The contract was let for $1,950 at that time; by 1970 it was worth more than $10,000.

As previously mentioned, Brewrink worked for and with MacFarlane at times. He owned boats like the *Let's Go* and the *Clipper* which MacFarlane had operated earlier. Johnny Ames and Archie Rowland subcontracted the mail run to Press from 1924 to 1926.

*The **Bryan** on the lower Snake River.*

*The **Let's Go** with Jay Rhodes, bank land inspector, on deck.*

Brewrink and MacFarlane built the *Idaho* in 1922, a twin-engine, gas powered 58-foot ship with an eight-foot beam. She was a dependable craft, could carry eight tons, and with a diesel transplant remained in irregular service until 1953.

Press and Ed hauled household goods, grocery orders, salt blocks, wool, mail — whatever their customers needed. The upriver trip to the head of navigation took a day and a half (without mishaps) and half a day for the return. Captain, deckhand and passengers carried bedrolls and food for the trip. In winter a small coal-burning stove at the rear of the canvas-curtained cabin lent some warmth to the journey.

Captain Brewrink lost the mail contract to Kyle McGrady in 1938. He left the river when competition for freight reduced his business.

Brewrink had a wife, Edna, and a son, Jim. They lived by the dock on Snake River Avenue in Lewiston. Captain Brewrink was a good businessman and well-liked. He died after surgery, in 1942, far short of old age.

There were five other pilots on the river during the MacFarlane-Brewrink era whose names should be mentioned here. Johnny Ames and Archie Rowland were the most active. They held the mail contract from 1922 to 1926. Joe Hart was on the river as early as 1913, running passengers and freight from Asotin to Rogersburg. Lawrence Sitkus and Roy McCoy also boated with some frequency.

The **Idaho** headed up the Snake.

Amos Burg
1925

A young man beached his canoe at Homestead during the fall of 1925, looking for someone willing to accompany him through Hells Canyon. The voyageur had embarked on his journey the 9th of July at the source of the Snake, almost 9000-feet above sea level in the southern part of Yellowstone National Park. He had survived the loss of his first canoe, many difficult portages (once six in an afternoon), and intimidating rapids. He was no novice — the 24-year-old boatman had already spent years at sea, canoed Alaska's Inland Passage to the mouth of the Fraser, twice floated the Columbia from its Canadian source to the Pacific, and canoed the Yellowstone, Missouri, and Mississippi from Livingston to New Orleans. In addition, he was a journalism student at Oregon State College. His name: Amos Burg — one of the intrepid pioneer boaters on western whitewater.

Amos Burg (left) and John Mullins (right) at Granite Creek in 1925. The wooden "Old Town" canoe is covered with canvas and the men are wearing cork life jackets. Mullins had shot a man a few months earlier who killed his dog.

Burg found his companion in veteran riverman and prospector John Mullins. Mullins claimed to know the canyon and every rock in the river. They departed Homestead in the canoe *Song o' the Winds* on the morning of October 20. John sat in the stern with the steering paddle; Burg had a rowing arrangement midship. They fought the breakers in Kern Rapid, had a close call at Squaw Creek, capsized the canoe at Buck Creek when a tow line broke, shattered the stern at Thirtytwo Point (Sawpit Rapid), washed out of the craft at Steamboat, and nearly dumped at Copper Ledge Falls. John kept saying he "knew every rock in the river," and Burg allowed "that he ought to since he'd hit them all."

The difficult stretch of the trip behind them, John Mullins lassooed an old range horse above Johnson Bar. He said it belonged to Ralph Barton and he'd give him three dollars for it if they ever cut trails. Mullins rode back to Homestead, proud of having wielded a paddle on the first canoe through the canyon. Burg continued downriver to the Columbia confluence and paddled on to Portland.

Amos Burg made the Hells Canyon run three more times. He returned with a canoe in 1929, and ran the river again in 1946, with a 16-foot rubber raft called *Charlie*. That trip had a party of four: Doc Russ Frazier from Utah, Charles Wheeler, vice president of McCormack Steamship Company in San Francisco, and Alexander Paterson of Seattle. There were two other rubber boats along — six-foot *Junior* and 12-foot *Patches*. Junior flipped in the rapids at the foot of Eagle Island. Deciding they could use additional support, the men bought a 12-foot wooden boat for $15 from a ferryman they met below Homestead.

The group lined Squaw and Buck Rapids, then damaged the wooden craft while lining Thirtytwo Point. An impromptu bandage from socks and towels was fashioned for the leaking hull. They stopped to fish at Steamboat Creek and found it thick with trout. The smaller boats were lined through Wild Sheep and Granite Rapids. Nine days had been allowed for the trip, but their decision to take more time caused an Army search plane to come looking for them. Wheeler and Paterson flew out at Pittsburg Landing; Burg and Frazier floated down to Lewiston.

Burg party portaging Buck Creek in 1946: Wheeler at the stern, Doc Frazier midship, and Paterson on the bow. This was the craft purchased from the ferryman.

Burg's adventures had just begun in 1925. He canoed from Skagway, Alaska, to Portland the next year, ran the Yukon River for the National Geographic, and descended the Athabaska, Slave, and McKenzie Rivers. The latter trip was completed alone, by packing a six-foot rubber raft five days across the Peel Portage, with the help of Indians and dogs, in order to float down the Bell and Porcupine Rivers to Old Crow.

Amos rafted 72 days down the Green and Colorado Rivers with Haldane "Buzz" Holmstrom in 1938 — Burg's rubber raft was the first to be used in the Grand Canyon. The following summer he ran Idaho's Middle Fork with Doc Frazier. Later he sailed a 26-foot sloop around the southern tip of South America via the Strait of Magellan, and visited China, Europe, South America and Alaska, completing 25 educational films for the *Encyclopedia Britannica* and 12 articles for the *National Geographic*.

Amos settled in Juneau, Alaska, in 1952, where he served 20 years as education and information officer for the Alaska Department of Fish and Game. He retired in 1974.

In the summer of 1978, Burg returned to run Hells Canyon with his wife Carolyn, whom he married in 1958. The Burgs had their own 12-foot Avon raft, and were accompanied by friends in four additional boats. Amos discovered with dismay, in his words, "that dams had destroyed one of nature's most magnificent masterpieces."

Amos Burg.

Kyle McGrady
1938

An Irish garage mechanic from Lewiston, born the year MacFarlane began running the Snake, was the dominant powerboat personality on the river through the Forties. He was Kyle McGrady, and unlike MacFarlane and Brewrink, he could not say he'd never lost a boat.

While fixing a stock truck, McGrady overheard one rancher telling another that he couldn't continue operating without reliable riverboat service. On impulse, Kyle withdrew his savings and bought an old boat, the *Dawn*. After half a dozen trips, he chose the wrong channel through Zigzag Rapid and slammed into the rocks. From shore he watched his fuel ignite and the boat sink.

Kyle and Florence McGrady.

McGrady had to top out over the canyon rim on the Idaho side where he met a sheepherder that put him on the trail to Lewiston. He arrived home, appearing to his wife and children like the survivor of a shipwreck — which he was. Undaunted, he decided to try again. Joe McClaren, a rancher at Lightning Creek, took up a collection. McGrady mortgaged his house. With these loans he purchased the old *Idaho* and used his mechanical abilities to convert her to a twin-engine diesel with three rudders. The ship averaged seven miles an hour upstream.

McGrady's River Transportation Service left Lewiston every Wednesday and Saturday morning. The service had the mail contract to Johnson Bar. There were about 350 people on the 99 mile river route. The boat carried passengers and cargo under the supervision of the I.C.C. Round trip tourist fare from Lewiston in 1942 was $5.00. Five years later it had jumped to $17.50. The dudes were expected to bring their own food and bedroll.

Kyle had two unsung helpers for his transport business: his wife Florence, and Mrs. Ruth Sapp. Ruth ran a grocery store in Lewiston and was trusted by every rancher, herder and miner on the upper stretch of the river. McGrady would bring their golddust and want lists to her market. She would shop for those items she didn't have — size 12 socks or the latest *True West* magazine, a house cat or a birthday card. For 39 years she fulfilled such requests with exactitude. Meanwhile, the river pilot would bank their money, pick up pension checks, pay bills, and drive his truck by to load their groceries. On the trip back upriver, the Irishman was so busy delivering mail, selling stamps and money orders, and notorizing papers that he had to have a deckhand to handle cargo. In this manner, McGrady's River Transport obviated the need for any residents of this remote canyon to make their way to civilization — most were immensely grateful for the favor.

Having hauled all the materials, including cement and bricks, for three houses on the river, Kyle decided in 1946 it was time to build his own lodge — for tourists. Under special-use permit from the U.S. Forest Service, he constructed a capacious building on the flat at Sand Creek, across from Willow Creek. Dick Rivers helped him boat the supplies. The finished lodge could accommodate 50 guests.

McGrady operated a twin-screw 46-foot boat called the *Florence* — after his wife. The ship was built in Clarkston, Washington, in 1939. It had dual 100 horsepower engines and a ten ton capacity. In low water, he could haul 12 passengers in the *Flyer*, a 28-foot Chriscraft. Since radio contact was impossible in the canyon, Kyle even tried an experiment with carrier pigeons as shipboard messengers.

While traveling the river, Captain McGrady baited trot lines with eels and caught impressive amounts of sturgeon. The meat and caviar provided him with an extra $75 a week.

Kyle McGrady (with cap).

But the river took as well as it gave: Kyle's boat was frozen in the ice at Buffalo Eddy for 33 days in 1948. Then his 18-year-old son, Ken, drowned in May of that year, while trying to swim from an island near Cave Creek. McGrady lost most of his enthusiasm for the river business after that personal tragedy, and sold a half interest to the Tidewater Barge Lines in 1950. Tidewater lost its bid for the mail contract, and McGrady left the river. He farmed for 20 years in Whitman County, Washington, until his death in 1970.

Buzz Holmstrom
1939

"I'd have to say he was the best."
"If he'd been shootin' folks instead of rapids
  his light would shine with the cowboys."
"Always calm and cool, knowing what to do and
  having the skill and power to do it."
"Best boatman of his time."

That's what those who knew him say about Haldane Buzz Holmstrom — extraordinary river runner during the brief, adventurous years that preceded the commercial whitewater business. For Buzz, river running was not an acquired taste — he took to it naturally. His handprint is in the boatman's annals and his fingerprint in Hells Canyon of the Snake.

This blonde, blue-eyed Swedish farm boy was born in Gardiner, Oregon, in 1909. Plowing, milking, and haying developed his powerful body: a cask of a chest, large hands, and arms of a blacksmith. All agreed he was strong as a jail.

From the time he was old enough to look over a hay bale, Holmstrom had seen loggers and boaters on the Umpqua and Coquille Rivers. Moving water captivated Haldane, hooked him with the magic of its challenge. In 1935 he ran the Rogue, then the "River of No Return" from Salmon to Lewiston in 1936. Between times he worked in a Coquille gas station. He read Kolb's *Down the Colorado;* it was the genesis of a dream that finally resolved itself in action. The Colorado would be his next dare.

Buzz went to the woods and selected a Port Orford cedar that he felled for its light, durable wood. Days laboring in the service station were followed by nights spent shaping a boat from the fragrant cedar. In his basement he fashioned a fifteen by five-foot hull with a center cockpit and water-tight compartments fore and aft. Preferring to enter rapids stern foremost (this reduced speed and increased control), he designed a stout, square stern. Handles were affixed to the bow in order to drag the 450-pound vessel around risky rapids. Then coats of lobster red paint brought the long task to completion.

Holmstrom loaded his craft on a rickety trailer, hitched it to his five-dollar Dodge, waved goodbye to his mother, and drove off to Green River, Utah. His friend Clarence Bean was expected to accompany him, but got sidetracked by an ocean voyage. So Haldane Holmstrom went alone. It was 1937, and he had a rendezvous with river history.

Over the next 52 days Buzz Holmstrom became the first person to make a solo transit of Grand Canyon of the Colorado. He portaged five rapids, realizing an accident could have fatal consequences. A year later he returned, and accompanied by Willis Johnson and Amos Burg, who ran a rubber raft, piloted his boat through all the rapids without mishap. It was a longer journey, begun near the Continental Divide and ending at Boulder Dam. A conversation on that trip gives insight into Holmstrom's values: Burg recalled that Buzz said he would "rather live on beans and bacon than kill a canyon deer." The gun they carried was never used.

Buzz Holmstrom at the end of his Grand Canyon run. Photograph taken by Bill Belknap.

An excerpt from a note to his mother, which he wrote on the shore of Lake Mead reveals more: "The last bad rapid is behind me. I had thought that once past that my reward would begin, but now everything ahead seems kind of empty, and I find I have already had my reward in the doing of the thing."

The publicity generated by the Coquille boatman's exploits spawned his next venture. He was contacted by Edith B. Clegg, a wealthy 53-year-old widowed mother of four, and grandmother of nine. At a hundred pounds she was scarcely big enough to keep, but she possessed

Amos Burg (left) and Haldane Holmstrom (right) in Grand Canyon.

an admirable resiliance in temperament and character. Her husband had been an English diplomat, but the couple had lived in Vancouver for years.

Mrs. Clegg presented Holmstrom with a startling proposition. She wanted to make a transcontinental water voyage to New York, where she would take in the World's Fair, before going on to visit her daughter in England. Buzz agreed.

He designed two 14-foot flat-bottomed spruce boats that were built by Art Ellingson, of Coquille: the *Mongoose* and the *St. George.* They had water-tight cargo holds fore and midship, with passenger wells fore and aft. Spare oars were lashed to the deck and a ten-horse Johnson outboard provided power. Crew consisted of Holmstrom, Earl C. Hamilton (a pre-med student) and Clarence Bean, all of Coquille, and Willis Johnson, Utah friend and boatman.

The party began their 4,000 mile expedition from Portland on April 14, 1939 — 120 years to the day since McKenzie and his voyageurs completed the first upstream passage of Hells Canyon.

Mrs. Clegg disdained publicity. Cornered by reporters, she always said the trip "was just a private venture, just for the interest" and she seems to have enjoyed each day. In a letter, Buzz wrote: "One good thing is that she doesn't want publicity . . . won't talk to a reporter . . . doesn't write."

Saint George and the *Mongoose* scudded up the Columbia and the Snake — sometimes fast as a dog could trot, 35 miles a day, other times slow as a long afternoon. They had no schedule. Gasoline was cached by the mail boat upriver to Johnson Bar. At that point they entered the fortress cliffs of the main canyon. They left behind skeptics on the shore who scoffed at their "mosquito fleet." "Somebody's going to get a dunking that will get his name in the obituary column", one of them sneered. Another remarked, "The state border is the only thing that runs through that gorge without getting drowned."

Yet with only three portages (Granite, Squaw and Buck), the group arrived at Kinney Creek May 30, taking 18 days from Lewiston. The skeptics could eat their words with knife and fork.

Willis Johnson left the trip at Weiser to run the Middle Fork with Frank Swain and Doc Frazier. Clarence Bean headed back to Coquille. It was at Weiser that Holmstrom made a surprising statement. He said he had found the uphill run through Hells Canyon four times more difficult than his 1938 trip down the Colorado. He had been fighting a 15,000 c.f.s. flow, had fallen out of the boat once, and the rapids must have tired him.

The Holmstrom-Clegg voyage at the mouth of the Weiser River in 1939. Left to right: Earl Hamilton, Buzz Holmstrom, Willis Johnson, Clarence Bean, Edith Clegg.

Holmstrom and Clegg at the Weiser on the Snake in the **Mongoose.**

The expedition pressed on to the headwaters of the Snake, trailered across the divide to the Yellowstone River and re-embarked a couple of miles below Gardiner, Montana, June 21. Earl Hamilton left with the *St. George* at the Yellowstone, as support was no longer considered necessary. Three motors had been exhausted at that point. The couple followed the Yellowstone to the Missouri. Buzz and Edith reached Kansas City in early August. They floated down the Mississippi to Cairo, turned northeast up the Ohio, then into the Alleghany, across the Great Lakes to the barge canal and down the Hudson, arriving in New York the second week of September. The fair was an anticlimax.

Holmstrom at Lake Mead in November, 1938. Photo by Belknap.

World War II interrupted Holmstrom's river running. He joined the Navy and spent duty time in New Guinea as a carpenter's mate. "Boos" was such a favorite with some of the islanders in the South Pacific that they offered him a wife and land if only he would remain. But after three and a half years in the service, he returned to Coquille. He took a job with the Bureau of Reclamation on a core-drilling project at potential damsites on western rivers.

Then in May of 1946, Buzz was back on the river — happy as a lost soul with hell in flood. He had been hired to boat supplies on the Grande Ronde for a U.S. Coast and Geodetic Survey party, piloting an 18- by 6-foot craft. On that river his inexplicable death occurred. Surveyors said that he came into camp and borrowed a .22 rifle, saying he was "going to kill some chickens" (sage hens). His body was found with a fatal head wound. The crew said he was depressed about not being able to handle such a large boat on the Ronde. But 1946 was a high-water year. (The river is now run by commercial outfitters, sometimes with wooden boats.) Holmstrom's death was listed as suicide, and there is evidence of some problems which could have induced it. On the other hand, his many friends and the people of Coquille were never satisfied with that explanation. No autopsy or inquest was held.

Haldane "Buzz" Holstrom's river accomplishments covered less than a decade, and like the streak of a falling star, have slipped from sight. He is buried in Coquille, beneath a granite gravestone that bears this epitaph: "Home is the Sailor, Home from the Sea."

Floating Through the Forties

Five parties have left accounts of their downriver trips through Hells Canyon in the early Forties. To round out the record, some of their experiences are included here.

Robert J. Wood, postmaster of Weiser, Idaho, decided to see the canyon with five friends in the summer of 1939. They launched their 18-foot wooden boat near Homestead. At Granite Creek, even after scouting, their craft bought the river. Boatman Oren "Mac" McMullen, who was big enough to hunt bears with a switch, pulled so hard on the oars one lock broke and the other grasp got away:

Seconds seemed like hours . . . The prow of the boat rose
as she stood on end as the water hit the rock. Mac grabbed
the tow rope as it dropped past him. Pledger fell off into the

water. Parker grabbed a hand rope and hung on — put his foot out and the next second Pledger grabbed it and before you could say it, he had his arms around Parker's neck. (The boat) stood on end — how long I do not know. I do know that two still cameras (on the shore) set and ready to push the button were forgotten entirely . . . and . . . the crucial moment remained unrecorded. Finally, a backwash brought the boat to an even keel and it slowly backed up into the stream and on down the river. We all drew a sigh of relief.

It was several miles more before a swimmer could drag the boat to shore. After the upper gorge, Wood's party found the remainder of the river calm as a horse trough.

Clarence Moore and Paul Jones, reporters from the *Lewiston Tribune,* accompanied a July, 1940, Hell's trip that embarked from the Red Ledge mine road. John Olney ran a boat called the *Snake Charmer.* Kyle McGrady manned the other skiff and it was christened *Hell's Belle.* John's brother, Lawrence, was along, as was Paul Laudien of Oregon.

The men portaged the worst rapids on the top end. Even so, as McGrady was filming *Snake Charmer* in another rapid, his own boat flipped and cost him his camera. Moore wrote:

Seaworthy as our boat was it could not stand being pushed upward on one side and sucked down on the other. It flipped over so quickly that I was still in a sitting position when I tumbled out, head first and bottom up. An undercurrent caught the three of us . . . and swept us under the river. It must have been more than fifteen feet (deep) because my ears ached from the pressure for about six hours. I recall the changing current turning me about in the water in slow motion as some 'amazing stories' report that men do in mythical space ships, and all the time I was wondering if I was apt to hit any rocks.

The Olneys pulled out at Dug Bar where they lived; McGrady went on to Rogersburg. (John Olney had a wife and five children, and lived for a while on a boat tied by the river. He piloted McGrady's motor launches at times.)

Oregon boatmen Dayton Thompson, John Miliron, and John West carried four Army engineers in three wooden McKenzie driftboats through the canyon in the fall of 1941. With expensive equipment and a government contract, the boatmen lined and portaged nine rapids. The group reported seeing deer, bear and lions. The Army engineers were reticent about discussing the purpose of their float, but were undoubtedly surveying power site locations along the river. Their trip required nine days.

In August, 1946, Norman Nevills brought a party of 14 people in four wooden "sadiron" boats through Hells Canyon. Nevills was the first outfitter to run dude trips through Grand Canyon. He operated Mexican Hat Expeditions on the Green and Colorado Rivers until 1949. Norm came to see Hells Canyon because he had heard it was a deeper gorge than Grand. One of the boatmen on the 1946 trip was Otis "Dock" Marston, foremost historian of the Colorado River. Marston was accompanied by his wife, Margaret, and their twin daughters, Maradel and Loel. A fourth lady, Feris Dodge, of San Francisco, was along. As far as can be determined, they were the first women to float through Hells Canyon.

The other boatmen on the trip were Preston Walker, and Kent Frost. Walker was thrown from his boat in Buck Creek Rapid and fished out by Nevills.

The group shot 10,000 feet of movie film on their voyage. In Lewiston, The Idaho Scenic Land Association gave them all "One-Way Club" certificates.

A 39-year-old California steel construction worker, Emil Anderson, made a solo trip from Robinette to Lewiston in August of 1948. He used a 12-foot rubber raft.

The second day out, just below Kinney Creek Rapid, he flipped his boat and lost all his equipment except a tarp, two blankets, a container of water-soaked food and one oar. But Anderson continued.

"I always wanted to make a trip like that," he recalled. "I just looked and looked at them pinnacles until my eyes and neck were tired. Then the first thing I would know, I'd be craning my neck to see some more."

As soon as Emil reached Lewiston he headed for a shoe store. His footwear was lost in the turnover and he had paddled the canyon barefoot.

The Amos Burg party in 1946 (discussed earlier) used three rubber boats on their excursion. These rafts, like Anderson's, were a token of things to come. Durable, inexpensive inflatable craft, made surplus by the close of World War II, rapidly expanded river running into a desireable profession and pastime.

Blaine Stubblefield
1950

Blaine Stubblefield is generally credited with being the first boat-man to run motorized passenger trips through Hells Canyon. He had succeeded at several careers before he turned to the river.

Blaine Stubblefield motoring the twin-pontoon **Chief White Hawk** *near Lewiston.*

"Stub" graduated in journalism from the University of Idaho, where he was student body president, then did graduate work at the University of Washington. In the mid-Twenties he was a publicist for the Spokane Chamber of Commerce and the American Automobile Association. He was commissioned lieutenant in the Air Corps during World War I, and served as an instructor in Texas.

Following the war, he was public relations manager for Varney Airlines (now United) in San Francisco, and then was editor of McGraw-Hill Publication's *Aviation* magazine for several years in Washington, D.C. He attended Roosevelt's weekly press conferences as

Stubblefield in 1956, running Buck Creek Rapid.

*Blaine running Buck Creek with the **Chief Joseph.***

a newswriter. Blaine spent his leisure time during this period recording folk songs from remote areas of the Appalachians for the Library of Congress. Being a singer and guitar player himself, folk music was an abiding interest.

In 1949, he decided to leave the complicated existence of the nation's capital and returned to the tranquility of Snake River country where he had been born — in Enterprise among the Wallowas in 1897.

He chose Weiser, Idaho, as his headquarters and served as secretary to the Chamber of Commerce there, doing stories on the Hells Canyon region for national publications. He also originated the Weiser National Fiddle Festival.

A long-held dream of running the Snake River caused Stubblefield to design and build the 31-foot *Chief Joseph* in Portland. It was powered by twin props turned by two jeep engines. Blaine and Stewart Winslow took passengers on the *Joseph* through the canyon to Lewiston in June of 1950. The boat didn't handle well and was too wide and heavy for haulback purposes; it was scuttled in favor of some 33-foot war-surplus bridge pontoons propelled by 25-horsepower Evinrude outboards. Stub called them "alley cats." He used hard-hulled wooden boats designed by Glen Woolridge of Grants Pass, Oregon, for day-trips on the upper end.

Blaine ran Hells Canyon excursions during the summer and Dan Cole, who operated the service station and grocery in Homestead, worked with him three years as a guide. Cole said steering the big rafts through the obstreperous rapids of the upper canyon was "like running an angle worm." Dan quit in 1955 to work as a crew foreman on the Brownlee Dam and Ray Holt took his place. Ralph Page also ran a Woolridge boat as a licensed guide, starting shortly after Cole, and continuing for 11 years. He was a hunting and fishing guide as well.

When Brownlee diversion began, Stubblefield had to move his boating operation downstream to Homestead. He ran shorter trips from there to Kinney Creek Rapid and back. Many people were saddened by Blaine's death from cancer in 1960.

Cole and Page ran power boats at a site downriver for a couple of years where crews were doing feasibility studies on the Pleasant Valley damsite. Then ground was broken for Hells Canyon Dam, more rapids were sentenced to a slackwater death, and boatmen began to look like an endangered species.

◆ • ● • ◆

Oliver McNabb
1950

When Inland Navigation successfully underbid Tidewater Barge Lines for the U.S. river-route mail contract in 1950, the company hired Oliver McNabb, of Umatilla, Oregon, to run its boat.

McNabb operated the *Wenaha*, a 52-foot, twin-engine diesel. She

*The **Wenaha**.*

could carry 16,000 pounds or 49 passengers from Lewiston to Johnson Bar in twelve hours. Oliver handled the mail run until 1958. At the time of this writing, he lives in Clarkston and is employed as a river pilot by Tidewater Barge Lines on the lower Snake.

The *Wenaha* was taken to The Dalles, Oregon in 1961 and then to Kotzebue, Alaska.

Georgie White
1954

A woman who had first floated Grand Canyon in a life jacket In 1945, then several trips later started her own river outfitting business, arrived on the Snake in September, 1954. Georgie White Clark, "the grand lady of whitewater," idol of thousands of her "Royal River Rats," came north from Grand Canyon to test the rapids of the Middle Fork and Main Salmon that fall. She brought her triple-rigs; surplus ten-man rafts lashed side by side and powered by a six-horse outboard. Georgie ran Hells Canyon as an extension of her three week Middle-Main Salmon floats. She went through once a summer for four years. Unfortunately, the Idaho guide's board hassled her about a license, and though she detested the idea of such strictures, she finally sent in the fee.

White pulled her Salmon expeditions out at Riggins Hot Springs and trucked equipment to Homestead in order to do the Snake, taking out at Lewiston. Licensing requirements and dam construction eventually caused her to phase out the Idaho operation, as had Ralph Page. Georgie was always disappointed in the Salmon River rapids, but of the upper Hells Canyon she said, "Wild whitewater has a very low political priority, but I think it would have been worth the trouble to have made a greater effort to save the only really good rapids in the Pacific Northwest."

Georgie White (center, white helmet) running Kinney Creek Rapid with her triple-rig.

Georgie White in Buck Creek.

Don Harris in 1953, on one of his five Hells Canyon trips. The motors were only used in quiet water. In 40,000 miles of river-running Harris capsized three times, and two of those turnovers were in Hells Canyon: at Sawpit as a boatman, and in Buck Creek when Brennan was rowing.

Jack Brennan running Kinney Creek Rapid in 1952 with a 16-foot Cataract boat.

Richard Rivers
1958

With a surname like Rivers, what more suitable employment than captain of the largest vessel on the middle Snake?

Dick Rivers was born on the river, at Asotin, in 1919. He took to the outdoor life like a trout to a fly. Father of five sons, Captain Rivers first came up Hells Canyon in 1938 with Kyle McGrady. He ran McGrady's boat to Sand Creek in the Forties. Then he worked as a logger for 15 years, in the Blue Mountains of Oregon and at Aberdeen, Washington. Most of the time since he has spent on the river.

For two years in the mid-Fifties, Dick ran a diesel tug, the 32-foot *Anatha,* on the Snake. He was running a logging show on the head-waters of Corral Creek and trucked the logs down to the Idaho shore. Because the Snake is considered a navigable waterway, the logs had to be towed in rafts to Lewiston. Any that escaped the binders had to be retrieved. By boating the logs the men could work through the winter, despite snow at higher elevations.

The **Anatha,** *diesel tug.*

Rivers ran a tug for the Missouri Valley Dredge Company for a year while they were putting a natural gas line across the Snake at the mouth of Tucannon River. He also ran a drilling barge part-time for the Army Engineers on four Snake River dams below Lewiston.

In 1958, Rivers bought the mail contract that Oliver McNabb had handled for Inland Navigation. He called his business "Rivers Navigation Company" and operated the 30-foot *Idaho Queen I*. It covered the same distance as the *Wenaha,* but in half the time. Eventually he switched to a slightly larger and more powerful *Idaho Queen II*. Besides

Idaho Queen II hauling a damaged plane out of Temperance Creek (1961).

Idaho Queen IV loading wool at Temperance Creek.

hauling ranch supplies and supplemental feed for cattle and sheep, Rivers' company began taking an increasing number of tourists who wanted to ride the mail boat to Hells Canyon. In the summer he was busy transporting 300-pound sacks of wool downriver to Lewiston. But as ranches consolidated and the number of families in the canyon dwindled, it became obvious that the future of the river business lay with the tourist trade.

Captain Dick Rivers at the wheel.

Dick obtained a use-permit from the Forest Service to build an outfitter's camp at Copper Creek. Over a period of years he hauled and assembled the materials that now occupy Copper Bar. The pleasant camp can accommodate two dozen people.

At the time of this writing, *Queen I* has been sold down the river for use as a fishing boat at the mouth of the Columbia. *Queen II* is used for the same purpose in Kotzebue, Alaska. Their replacements, *Idaho Queen III* and *IV* now serve the middle Snake. The *Queen IV* was built in 1973, and her 49-foot length is propelled by twin diesel V-8 engines with 14-inch Jacuzzi jet pumps. (Jetboats are propelled by water drawn through a hull intake and then expelled from a pump with great thrust at the stern. Jets are less susceptible to damage and cavitation than are propellers.) The two boats run the gauntlet of the Snake twice weekly during the summer as Captain Dick Rivers continues to provide reliable service on a unique mail route that forms the pathway to his popular cabins at Copper Creek.

◆

Don and Ted Hatch
1962

The well-known river runners Don and Ted Hatch ran a Hells Canyon trip in 1962, after coming off the Main Salmon. Don ran a

27-foot pontoon, while Ted rowed a 10-man raft. Smus Allen, Dave Rassmussen, and Bruce Lium were along, with some members of the Appalachian Mountain Club as passengers. Les Jones accompanied them in his decked Grumman aluminum canoe with oars on outrigged locks. Jones wore a football helmet with an eight-mm. movie camera mounted on it, and a rubber band attached to a pencil that could be held in his mouth to trigger the camera. The only problem on the trip was a tip-over with the 10-man in the curlers below Buck Creek Rapid.

* ● *

Smith and Filer
1962

In 1962, a 24-foot aluminum boat with twin 50 horsepower outboard motors powered through all the rapids of Hells Canyon and returned downriver from Oxbow the same day. Donald McKenzie would have been surprised as a pup with his first porcupine. As far as is known, it was a one-time feat.

Bob Smith and Paul Filer, Salmon River boatmen, were aboard. They had been guiding fishermen on the Snake when they decided to attempt the upstream run to the dam under construction at Oxbow. They headed upriver with Dr. Howard Smith and Grace Julius as passengers. Bob remarked, "If the engines quit you might as well throw your hat in and go after it."

They did have motor problems on the way back — both engines swamped in Kinney Creek Rapid but were revived. Then one failed in Copper Ledge Falls. It was dusk when they greeted Bob's father, Don, who was anxiously awaiting their return at Granite Creek. The men brought a case of eggs from Dan Cole's store in Homestead to prove their success. They left the eggs with Bud Wilson at Sheep Creek.

Construction began on the coffer-dam above Copper Ledge Falls — the start of Hells Canyon Dam. Beneath twice a hundred feet of water went cliffs and rapids that had snaffled explorers and boatmen for a century and a half.

The impounded waters are now contoured by a road, and some who drive it can't help regretting the vigorous river lost to a flat-faced reservoir. They might remember a philosopher's comment on mutability: he said, "The only enduring effect of man's work is that the earth may cast a slightly different shadow on the face of the moon."

The Snake Subdued:
Cambridge to Hells Canyon Dam

"Our heritage is composed of all the voices that can answer our questions."
— Malraux

Cambridge is situated at the confluence of highways 95 and 71 — the town of departure for parties visiting or boating through Hells Canyon from Idaho or eastern regions. (Halfway, Oregon, serves as a similar point for visitors approaching from the west.)

The community is the stepchild of an earlier town — Salubria, which was located across the Weiser River about two miles east of Cambridge. Settlers began taking homestead ranches in Salubria Valley, also known as upper Weiser Valley, in the early 1880's. Irishman John Cuddy installed a grist and saw mill in 1879 on Rush Creek. Pat Hickey established a store at the corner of William Allison's homestead in 1884. Salubria sprouted at the crossroads like a mushroom after rain.

The two roads which meet at the intersection were flanked with buildings of commercial enterprise. The L-shaped Salubria Hotel with 17 rooms upstairs, occupied one corner and Mart Hannan's saloon was on the opposite corner. Along the street there was a bank, blacksmith shops, two feed stores, a couple of general merchandise stores, Haas hardware, and Smith's sawmill. Cuddy's flour mill also moved to the new location.

In the 1890's, Salubria was a thriving town: a telephone line arrived from Weiser, the *Salubria Citizen* began publication, three doctors and a dentist became residents, a two-story schoolhouse and an Odd Fellows hall were constructed, and board sidewalks aided pedestrians. The stage arrived from Weiser at the Salubria Hotel each day, bringing passengers and mail.

Margaret Hannan Petersen, who lived in Salubria as a young girl, and in Cambridge since then, remembered the community as:

"... a beautiful little city, hemmed in by mountains and hills. Many tall poplars and shade trees, as well as shrubs and lawns made the homes attractive. It seems to me that hollyhocks, white iris, yellow roses and lilacs grew in every yard."

100

Salubria Valley in the 1880's.

Salubria in the late 1880's. The Odd Fellow Hall is on the left.

John Keats wrote: "Circumstances are like clouds continually gathering and bursting — while we are laughing the seed of some trouble is put into the wide arable land of events . . ." A rather insignificant disagreement during the town's development proved fatal to its growth. The Pacific and Idaho Northern railway thrust north from Weiser through Middle Valley. It was intended to serve the Seven Devil's mines and the planned route included a depot at Salubria. But Mrs. Miller, who owned the land in town required by the P & I N, refused to sell a right-of-way at the railroad's price. Mose Hopper had property on the west side of the Weiser River and offered the Idaho Northern every

Salubria Hotel in 1896 owned by Mr. Day.

Weiser stage at the Salubria Hotel. George Ingman (right) and Mart Hannan (left) in front seat. In good weather the trip could be made by noon, when the road was bad it took all day.

other lot in exchange for relocating the route to his side of the stream. The railroad accepted Hopper's inducement, and its arrival on the far side of the river in December, 1900, meant the future of the little town with the pretty name was anything but salubrious. As Cambridge prospered, Salubria faded like an autumn leaf, then vanished. The new

Salubria school in 1896 with Ernest Hunt (teacher) and his wife.

Harry Smith's grain threshing crew on the Smith Ranch in Salubria Valley.

Methodist church never even got a coat of paint before its lumber was salvaged. Only the schoolhouse and the top of the *Salubria Citizen* printing press, embedded at the crossroads to protect Hannan's saloon from corner-cutting freight wagons, remain as testimony to the location.

Cambridge, Idaho 1912. Although the Village of Cambridge was founded in 1900, 12 years later it appears to be quite a town. The only recognizable buildings pictured that still stand are the Fred M. Jewell store on corner at left, and the Williamson building near the end of the street on the right. A two-story frame building is shown where Bucky's Cafe now stands.

The Hagadone Hotel, just off Main Street in Cambridge.

Cambridge today is largely an agricultural community, dependent on cattle, dairy and hay production, along with some timber harvest. It is the location of the Washington County fairgrounds and serves as eastern gateway to Hells Canyon.

Cambridge, Idaho, 1911. Picture taken from Cambridge Elevator, loaned by Margaret Peterson. At left is depot and old feed mill along tracks. At right center is Pitzer Livery Stable. The two-story house was the home of Emma Brown; behind it is the Co-op Creamery (now Cambridge Metal Works). At right center is the Lorton Drug Store where Hunter's Inn is now located. On the right is the back of the building which is now the Medical Clinic.

This photograph of Cambridge is thought to have been taken about 1920. In the right foreground is the building that later became the Cambridge Telephone office. Across the street is the News-Reporter building which was built in 1919. Left of the N-R office is a hardware store. The building on the corner was at one time a bank, pool hall and rooming house. Across Central Blvd. is the back of the old post office. Up the Blvd. is the first Masonic hall and across the Blvd. is the old Hagadone Hotel. On 1st street where the Jerry Hughes-Carole Finley house now stands is an old saloon. Along the right side of the Blvd. are the Clare Lorton, Millard Beigh and Gertrude Rhodes homes. The old Methodist church (Grange Hall) is on the corner. Across the street is a frame school house which burned in 1921.

105

Highway 71 heads northwest along Pine Creek from Cambridge. Just before the road begins to drop down Brownlee grade, about 20 miles from town, one can see a fine view of the Cornucopia and Wallowa Mountains to the west, if the weather is clear.

The highway winds downhill along Brownlee Creek. Hugh Beggs recalled that the wagon road which existed before the present highway crossed the creek with great frequency. In spring the water was often too high to cross safely with a horse. The Civilian Conservation Corps in the 1930's blasted some of the worst rocks out of the road, but its present improved condition is a legacy of the dam construction era.

Mr. Little's shearing crew working on Pine Creek in the early 1900's, along the road to Brownlee.

Judge Frank Harris, in his *History of Washington County*, published in 1941, relates that Tim Goodell, mountain man, guided a train of 60 wagons along the east side of the Snake to the mouth of the Weiser River, then up the Weiser through Midvale (Middle Valley) and Salubria Valley in 1862. The group was headed for Oregon and camped temporarily near present-day Cambridge.

Some of the men rode down to Brownlee's ferry and Mr. Brownlee offered to take their wagons and stock across the Snake without charge if they would clear a road from Salubria Valley to his boat landing. The men agreed.

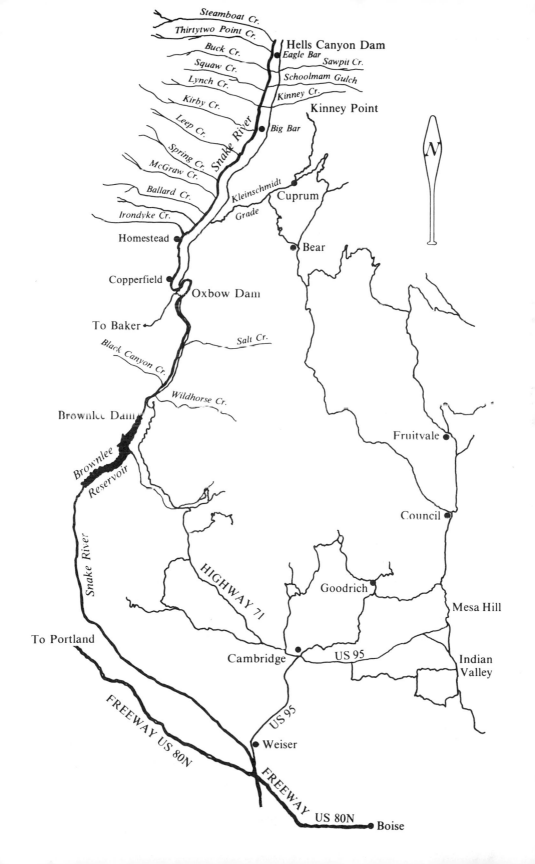

Once the wagon train was on the Oregon side of the river, Brownlee offered each man with a team and plow $2.50 a day in gold to build a similar road up Brownlee Canyon to the top of Zig Zag hill. In this manner, a trace was cleared to Pine Valley. The train then rejoined the Oregon Trail by way of Eagle Valley and the Powder River.

Brownlee operated his ferry on the Snake for many years. After his death, others took his place. The Ada County records in October, 1875, carry the following notation:

William A. West, G. W. Hunt, O. Gaylord and James M. Stevenson. Granted a 8 year franchise to run a ferry across Snake River at a point known as Brown Lees ferry — exclusive right 1 mile up & 1 mile down-river. Have 6 months to construct a suitable ferry boat. License per year — $25. $1000 bond.

Toll Rates: Horse & Rider — .50

Footman — .25

Horse & carriage — 1.50

Wagon & 2 horses, mules or oxen — 1.25

Each additional span — .50

Pack animals — .25

Loose animals — .12½

Sheep or hogs — .05

In January, 1876, the Idaho *Tri-Weekly Statesman* carried this brief note:

William A. West and Gaylord have a ferry running at old Brown Lee ferry. Has been in operation for two months. They are building a graded road six miles east to Weiser mines from ferry, to be done by next May. Also plan to build road from Weiser Mines to Salubria, a distance of 18 miles. This road to be financed and built by subscriptions of the Weiser Valley residents. To be finished sometime in June. This road will give people a through route from Salubria to Baker City, a distance of 75 miles.

A ferry operated at the site until replaced by the bridge built for construction of Brownlee Dam.

Brownlee Dam — at 395 feet, among the world's highest rock-fill dams — confines the river below the mouth of Brownlee Creek. The dam was built by Idaho Power Company. Idaho Power is a corporation (that marvelous legal invention that allows individual profit without individual responsibility) chartered under the laws of Maine in May,

1915. The company grew out of the bankruptcy of Idaho-Oregon Light and Power Company. I-O L & P had been organized to exploit the power potential at the Oxbow site downriver. Expenses exceeded estimates on that project and the company failed to meet its first mortgage bond. Electric Investment Company, an organization of I-O P & L bondholders, was successful bidder at the foreclosure. This company worked out a merger whereby five hydroelectric companies were consolidated as one, integrating potential markets and resources. The property and systems of the five were transferred to Idaho Power Company for operation and development as a combined system.

The Federal Holding Company Act, passed in 1935, required that parent utility corporations confine their interests to systems physically interconnected or located in contiguous territory. Electric Power and Light Company owned Idaho Power's common stock and was simply a holding company for Electric Bond and Share of New York. In the summer of 1943, Electric Bond had to dispose of 450,000 shares of that stock, so it was offered to the investing public. Idaho Power became an independently owned utility at that time. However, even at present (1979) less than 10 percent of the company's common stock is owned by people in the seven western states, so it remains an "Idaho company" in name only.

By 1941, Idaho Power had joined a power pool which included electric service companies in Oregon, Washington, Montana and Utah. The systems in five states were linked so that power could be exchanged at peak demand periods which vary with time and weather among the states. After World War II, the company quadrupled its generating capacity in six years. With eight dams on the Snake between Twin Falls and Mountain Home, Idaho Power fastened eager eyes on the energy possibilities in Hells Canyon.

The late 1940's were a time of fierce debate over the plan which would best utilize the river's hydroelectric potential. The Army Corps of Engineers issued a report with a preliminary plan for a 600-foot dam in Hells Canyon at Hells Canyon Creek. The Interior Department's Bureau of Reclamation favored the idea and hoped to build the dam. Idaho Power still had 10 years left on its federal site-withdrawal certificate which had been issued to one of its predecessors in 1906 for a dam at the Oxbow, downriver from Brownlee ferry. In the summer of 1947, the company filed for a preliminary permit with the Federal Power Commission to develop the Oxbow site, thereby giving the Corps of Engineers notice of a prior claim to the area. The horse race was on.

The same year, Lewiston was the scene of hearings by the Corps of Engineers on its preliminary proposals. Support for a federal dam began to gather momentum as the Army Engineers and Bureau of Reclamation reached an agreement in 1949, giving the Bureau jurisdiction over projects above the mouth of the Salmon River and the Corps control over dams below the Salmon. Within a few months, Idaho Power counter-attacked by filing with the FPC for a final construction permit at Oxbow and suggesting at the time four other projects it was prepared to build in the canyon which would use the same head as the high federal dam. Arguments like "cheap federal power" versus "tax giveaway" flew thick as seagulls over garbage.

The Truman administration backed the federal dam proposal and legislation was actually introduced in both houses of Congress authorizing construction of the single high dam. But Dwight Eisenhower's election in 1952 initiated a policy favoring power development by private utilities. The FPC held hearings and Idaho Power filed two more construction applications: one for a low dam at Hells Canyon Creek, the other for a dam at Brownlee ferry. The FPC hearings on the tri-dam proposal lasted for a year. The Examiner recommended a license be issued to Idaho Power solely for construction of a dam at Brownlee. Two months later the full board of the FPC overruled his recommendation and decided in favor of the three-dam complex. On August 4, 1955, the FPC issued a construction license to Idaho Power for all three dams and within weeks company equipment was raising more hell along the river than a turtle when the tank goes dry.

Brownlee is a rock-fill dam with a clay core. The rock to build it came from the excavation for the spillway and powerhouse. The clay, which is impervious to water, was taken from a hill on the Idaho side of the river above the dam site. A base was excavated 120 feet below the riverbed and the clay core (135 feet wide at the base) was sandwiched between layers of sand and gravel. Hydraulic nozzles watered the fill continuously in order to increase its density.

At the height of the Brownlee-Oxbow scheme, 3400 workers were employed in shifts seven days a week. The dam was completed in 1959. It has a usable storage of a million acre-feet and a reservoir length of 57 miles.

The FPC required that the dam be designed with space for two additional generators. In 1975, construction began on a fifth generating unit at Brownlee and it was finished in 1979. The newest hydro turbine runner is the second largest in the country and its output more than

Rock-fill being dumped and compacted at Brownlee.

equals the peaking capacity of the entire power plant at Oxbow Dam. There is sufficient water to operate the turbine only in late spring, and energy produced at that time is traded to systems in other states in return for electricity they produce during the summer when Idaho Power experiences deficiencies due to high agricultural demand.

The FPC license to Idaho Power to develop three dams required a program to conserve the salmon and steelhead runs on the Snake River. The goal of the FPC was passage of the fish around the dams to their

Brownlee Dam under construction.

Intake gates for Brownlee Dam.

Brownlee spillway under construction, looking north downriver. Construction camp is on the Idaho side of the Snake.

spawning grounds. One might as well hunt a horse thief in heaven as build a high dam compatible with anadromous fish runs. The dam was too high for fish ladders. Upstream, fish were to be trapped and trucked around the dam. To handle downstream migrants, the company adopted a plan which involved stringing a net of plastic mesh across the reservoir a mile upriver from the dam. Barges with siphon pumps were anchored along the net to capture the fingerlings. The net was plagued with problems: young fish went through it like ants through chicken wire. The director for the Oregon Fish Commission found that only a quarter of the million fingerlings that should have passed downstream made it through the turbines or over the spillway. In 1962 the net was scrapped and fish runs above Brownlee, up the Weiser, Payette and Boise Rivers became a wonder of the past.

The storage waters of Brownlee disrupted another life cycle — that of **Robinette:** an Oregon community on the riverbank about nine miles upstream from the dam.

Jim "Ed" Robinette was born in Maryland in 1852, and left his parents' home in Missouri when he was 17, for Eureka, Nevada, where he mined for nine years. In Elko, he married Eva Lincoln, a second cousin to President Lincoln. They moved to the Cornucopia mines in

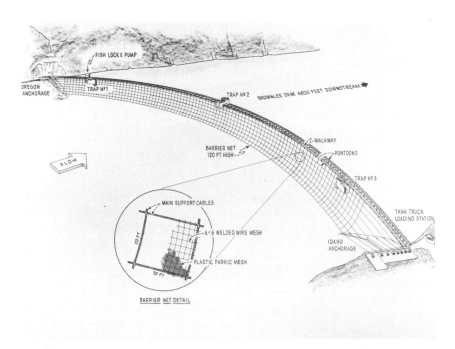

A drawing of the downstream-migrant fish net build by Idaho Power. The plan was a failure and the net was scrapped in 1961.

New Brownlee runner for the turbine being trucked down White Bird grade in 1978.

Oregon in 1885, then down to the Snake River a couple of years later.

Ed and Eva built a frame house on the homestead that would bear their name. Ed farmed hay across the river from Sturgill Bar, placer mined for gold, and helped raise a family of four children.

Anticipating the railroad's arrival from Huntington in 1910, lots for a townsite were surveyed on the Robinette property. A stage terminal existed in the growing community where people from Cornucopia, Richland, and Pine Valley could pick up mail rather than go to Baker.

Eventually there was a general store with a post office, a two-story hotel, tavern, train depot with living quarters for the station keeper, a coal forwarding company, petroleum storage for Standard Oil tank cars (that left fuel to be distributed by truck), and an Idaho Power substation. In addition, a cable ferry operated across the river.

James Robinette (far left) with surveyors platting the town of Robinette.

Gold ore from the Cornucopia mines, and Pine Valley timber and cattle were shipped from Robinette. About 100 people were living around the community in its heyday.

The hotel burned in the 1920's and ore shipments ceased a few years later. The railroad track was removed in 1936. But Robinette's economy received a boost in 1951 when the Stillwell Lumber Company constructed a drying kiln and planer shed in town. Then Idaho Power's

View of Robinette.

Gas station/store at Robinette.

plans for the river surfaced and the small town's days were measured.

The powerhouse and school were moved to Homestead, Oregon. Barney Edison's store was transported to Richland and converted to a residence. Other structures were dismantled or burned.

The town died February 27, 1958. Fortunately, Ed and Eva didn't live to see its demise. They are buried near Richland.

Wildhorse River or Creek flows from Idaho into the backwaters of Oxbow reservoir, about half a mile below the Brownlee bridge. This stream is formed by Bear, Crooked, Lick, No Business and Starveout Creeks. Frank Harris wrote that horses belonging to John McCullough fattened on bunchgrass in this drainage summer and winter. The animals became wild as deer, but were gradually killed off by prospectors who didn't want the stud horses mixing with their stock.

Black Canyon Creek comes into the reservoir from the west side of the road less than half a mile below Wildhorse Creek. Finley Gordon, a native of Scotland, settled at the mouth of this canyon in 1911. He ran cattle on a section. One of his three children, Mabel Ray, was still living on the homestead in 1979.

Salt Creek comes through the draw on the Idaho side of the water, about seven and a half miles south of Black Canyon. The building with the metal roof belonged to Albert Campbell and his 24,000-acre OX Ranch which extended along the Idaho shoreline in this area.

Albert was the eldest son of Charlie Campbell, who founded the Circle C Ranch in New Meadows, Idaho in 1879. (At the time that ranch was sold in 1973 it had holdings of 29,000 acres of deeded land and 130,000 acres of leased grazing land.) Albert started his own cattle ranch with acreage bought on Wildhorse Creek in 1910.

The OX Ranch is headquartered on Lick Creek, about 30 miles from Council, Idaho. OX cattle swam the river twice a year so that they could be wintered near Halfway in Pine Valley, Oregon. In later years, Albert used the Brownlee ferry to get his cattle across the river. The water was higher than a scared cat's back in April, 1952, when the ferry sank with Campbell and Lovell Gover aboard. The men were carried two miles down the river before they were rescued.

Albert Campbell was 91 years old and living in the Council hospital at the time this was written.

Copperfield
"No Place For a Presbyterian"

Oxbow Village on the Oregon side of Snake River, just below the bridge across Pine Creek, occupies a site which carries a compelling history.

The first white settler known to have built a cabin near this location was Andy Culver. He was there in the 1870's, raising horses and trading them to Indians and white men for necessities. Culver had a second cabin a dozen miles downriver. He was said to have arrived by way of the Willamette Valley.

Dick Makinson and Ike Lloyd came down along the river hunting in 1883, and discovered Culver badly crippled in his cabin. They went for help and returned with two men and a stretcher in order to carry Andy to Pine Valley. He died there in 1885 and was the first man buried in Pine Haven Cemetery.

There were several prospectors working placer deposits along the river in the 1880's — men such as Bob Jordan, Thad Leep, William McKinnell, Alexander Hopkins, and the four Holbrook brothers.

Mr. Snow also constructed a cabin near the mouth of Pine Creek as early as 1888, and ran horses as Culver had, selling some each fall to Pine Valley ranchers in Oregon.

Jake and Bert Vaughn, brothers who discovered the Irondyke mine behind Homestead, Oregon, in 1897, sold their claim six months later, and Jake invested his share of the money in the 160-acre Copperfield Ranch at the Oxbow. He, and his wife Gertie, had seven children.

The Vaughns sold their land in 1906 to John Schmidt and William Pollman of the Baker Loan and Trust Company.

The Baker businessmen had learned of construction plans for the Oxbow area: a railroad line as far as Homestead to haul ore from the Irondyke mine, and a power plant to be installed at the Oxbow.

The Baker investors selected the benchland of Copperfield Ranch as the logical townsite, laid out lots, and in two years sold most of them to new arrivals, making a substantial profit.

A subsidiary of the Union Pacific, the Northwestern Railway Company, built a track from Grange, Wyoming, to Blake's Junction just east of Huntington, which was completed in 1864. This stretch was known as the Oregon Shortline, since it represented the shortest route east to

Oregon. An initial survey intent on extending this line north through the Snake River Canyon to Lewiston was discouraged by the terrain encountered.

A second survey was undertaken in 1905, and a decision made to lay the line from Blake's Junction through Robinette and Copperfield to Homestead. It was expected that gondolas of copper ore would repay the expense. Construction began in 1907 under the supervision of Utah Construction Company's foreman, George Thompson.

At the same time, Idaho-Oregon Light and Power Company was working on acquisition of the Oxbow site for a power house. In late 1906 the company established water rights to 8000 cubic feet per second, and a month later obtained a federal power-site withdrawal authorization. Within another year implementation of development plans was well underway.

The power scheme involved exploitation of the Oxbow feature which occurs on the river upstream from Copperfield. The water swings in a single hairpin meander two miles around a point just above the village. In that distance the river drops over 20 feet. The plan was to drive a thousand foot tunnel through the rocky point, and by drawing river water into the upstream opening of the diversion tunnel, power a turbine located at the exit on the downstream side.

Construction workers of every nationality began arriving in groups on foot from Baker. They were housed in tent camps at the mouth of Pine Creek. Since both railroad and dam projects involved extensive tunneling, there were ample powder monkeys, drillers, muckers, blacksmiths, and mechanics. They worked hard and recreated harder — tough men in a tough country.

Power for the two projects, as well as for a sawmill a couple of miles up Pine Creek, was provided by giant coal-fired steam engines brought in from Baker.

Pine Valley served as a major source of food for the new community. Beef, mutton, pork, eggs, fruit and vegetables were hauled by wagon 20 miles to the boom town.

Bill Makinson recalled making such trips with his father, W. C. Makinson. Their method of refrigeration for meat was unusual. Green sweet clover was gathered along the road and layered in the front of the wagon. A clean sheet was spread over the clover, the meat distributed on the sheet, another clean cloth on top, and a second mat of clover over all. As they entered town they had to weave their wagon around the drunks lying in the street.

119

If it was necessary to remain in Copperfield overnight, father and son always slept in the livery barn for fear of being robbed. After making deliveries to hotels, W. C. would enter one of the saloons for a beer, secretly cash his large checks, while his son Bill would come in the back door for a drink of water. Discreetly, the bartender would pass the money to the boy, who would then slip out unobserved and unsuspected.

Numerous wooden buildings fronted Copperfield's main and side streets. There were 11 saloons, most with whorehouses behind them, gambling halls, a post office / meat market in 1907, two boarding

Copperfield as it looked in 1909.

houses, a livery barn, barber shop, several stores, a couple of hotels, and eventually a railroad depot. The four-cell jail had an outside stairway to a second floor meeting room.

John Schmidt donated land on the hillside for a school. Some of the Vaughns had been buried on the site, so their remains were moved to Halfway.

Hector A. Stewart, a carpenter, furnished the materials and labor for the building. By 1909 there were 14 students. One teacher, A. W. Parker, commuted to his job from Homestead each day on a railroad speeder car.

Church services were held on Sundays for those who wanted to attend. Worship took place in a covered pavilion which had benches and a wooden floor.

There was a tent hospital and drug store in the community, served by Dr. Spencer of Huntington, who had the medical contract for both railroad and power company. There were several registered nurses available as well.

Copperfield had a model water system with a cement reservoir which drew water from Hunsaker Creek. There was also an adequate sewage system.

Idaho-Oregon Light and Power Company constructed a spectacular suspension bridge across the river in 1911. The Oregon end was slightly upstream from the intake of the diversion tunnel. This bridge

Copperfield about 1910.

stood until flood waters in the early Twenties carried away the supporting abutments.

As early as 1909, Copperfield had a city council, consisting of Sid De Weese, Tom Griffith, Sam T. Grim (a carpenter), Sam Aklin (store owner), and Hector Stewart (saloon proprietor). With Baker, Oregon, the closest sizeable town within a hundred miles, these men represented local government.

There were about 700 men employed at the height of the boom. Perhaps another 400 residents lived in the vicinity. Many of these were family people living respectable lives with permanent employment; undoubtedly infrequent participants in Copperfield's night life. That life was wild as a waterspout and rough as a rasp. Liquor flowed freely; large-scale brawls were common as sawdust at a sawmill. Gambling and prostitution represented a release from hours of heavy labor. Money changed hands faster then dice in a crap game. The jail served as a drunk tank.

Railroad tracks reached Copperfield in the fall of 1909. The whole town turned out for a celebration. Three times a week the train arrived with mail, supplies, and an occasional passenger.

The power company's diversion tunnel was completed, but the electricity it produced was a pathetic return for the effort expended. In the face of bankruptcy, the grandiose 24,000 KW operation had been scaled down to a meager 600.

Construction workers at the Oxbow tunnel.

Energy was leaking out of the boom, though the first contraction was scarcely perceptible. A slightly diminished population resulted from the departure of men whose work was finished. Competition stiffened between local businesses, then gradually became a cutthroat struggle for survival. A 1913 census numbered the town's inhabitants at approximately 400.

Oxbow diversion dam in 1909.

Oxbow tunnel at the downriver exit, taken about 1909.

Establishment owners and gamblers began to feud. One night Martin Knezevich's saloon burned. He complained to the Baker County prosecutor. Sheriff Ed Rand came to Copperfield, but could not unravel the cross-complaints, let alone fix blame for the possible arson. Martin rebuilt.

Then William Weigand's bar caught fire, but with the help of friends it was saved. The Weigand faction hastily decided to incorporate the town. An election made Hector Stewart the mayor; his partner Tony Warner, William Weigand, and his bartender, Charles Kuntz, became councilmen.

The first act of the new council was the issuance of liquor licenses to all saloon proprietors except Knezevich. Martin again complained to county officials, without avail.

This time however, the complaint, along with a petition signed by the school teacher and 50 other residents about the town's gambling, fighting, drinking, and prostitution reached the eyes of the Oregon governor. He issued an order to the county sheriff to clean up the community by Christmas or face state action. Sheriff Rand replied that Copperfield had no problems it couldn't cope with.

Governor Oswald West was a man dedicated to temperance. When he learned of a wild Christmas celebration in Copperfield subsequent to his notice, he decided to act.

West was perceptive enough to send an intermediary. As his representative, he dispatched his secretary, diminutive Fern Hobbs. Ms. Hobbs was a young woman of 25; at 5'3" and 104 pounds hardly bigger than tiny. More important, she was obviously self-sufficient, having earned her own way since high school. Born of New England parents on a Nebraska ranch, she had come to Oregon in 1904. She had learned stenography while acting as governess to the family of a Portland banker. She had studied law while working as secretary to the president of a title guarantee company.

In 1913 she was admitted to the Oregon bar. Governor West hired her as chief stenographer, then promptly made her his private secretary.

And now she was on her way to cleanse what an Oregon minister had recently called "the poisonous toadstool of the badlands." Fern Hobbs boarded the train on New Year's Day, 1914. She carried with her resignations prepared for the signature of the Copperfield councilmen. She also had a formal proclamation of martial law. In addition, there were seven men, inconspicuous in civilian clothes, aboard the train: Lieutenant-Colonel B. K. Lawson and five soldiers of the Oregon National Guard, and Frank Snodgrass, chief of the penitentiary guards. All seven were veterans of the Philippine Insurrection.

Fern Hobbs as a young woman. After her
trip to Copperfield she received marriage
proposals and poems. Temperance
groups compared her to Catherine of
Russia and Oregon suffragettes pushed
her for governor. She was even offered a
role in a stage play. Ms. Hobbs never
allowed the incident to affect her person
or career. She worked for the Red Cross
for two years and then practiced law
until her death.

Ms. Hobbs wired the Copperfield mayor, saying she wished to meet with city officers and citizens at the city hall as soon as she arrived.

After the delegation had entrained, Governor West called a press conference and revealed what he had done. It was a western scenario whose drama was not lost on the newspaper corps. National and even international attention was focused on the confrontation.

The news penetrated to Copperfield, where Mayor Stewart replied, "We are decorating the city with ribbons and we will try to have some flowers for Miss Hobbs."

When Os West learned the response, he observed that flowers were appropriate for funerals.

In the middle of a rain storm on January 2nd, Ms. Hobbs arrived in Copperfield, wearing blue suit, a muff and neckpiece of black lynx, black hat with two green feathers, and gold-rimmed glasses. She proceeded directly to the meeting hall above the jail. The room was packed.

She took the platform while the Colonel stood nearby. Two guards remained at the single doorway. Fern removed some papers from her briefcase and announced that they were official resignations for all of the city officers. The councilmen perused the documents and then stated their refusal to sign.

The governor's representative stood quietly for a moment, then withdrew another sheet from her briefcase and handed it to Colonel Lawson. Lawson read the proclamation of martial law to the audience.

The Colonel then arrested the mayor and councilmen. He quickly informed them that if they did not get their whiskey, bar fixtures and card tables out of town by the next afternoon, he would stack the tools of sin in the streets and burn them. The crowd was asked to check their firearms at the door and disperse quietly. As the assembly left, witnesses say about a dozen guns were left in the custody of the militiamen.

Outside the hall, the townspeople discovered "closed" signs nailed on every saloon, whorehouse, and gambling den.

In less than an hour, Fern Hobbs had returned to the waiting train and waved goodbye to a silent crowd. The six guardsmen remained behind to enforce the governor's proclamation.

According to press releases, Fern Hobbs said:

> I wouldn't have done this for any other man in the world
> except Governor West and I wouldn't do it again for him. I
> didn't want to come. No girl likes to be conspicuous this way,
> but the Governor had to send someone to represent him

because he couldn't go himself. I had been on trips for him before and knew what he expected done. Moreover, everybody will admit that there was something spectacular about sending a woman on a trip of this kind. Some people think the Governor did this to be spectacular. He didn't. He sent me because he knew everyone would be watching me and wouldn't think about six militiamen coming along. The plan has worked perfectly . . .

The city officers promptly hired Baker attorneys to file suit on their behalf. Lawson ignored them, and when additional soldiers arrived, gathered faro tables, roulette wheels, birdcage games, and all the barrels of beer and whiskey they could locate and placed them on the train for shipment to a Baker warehouse where all could be kept under state seal.

Wiegand and Warner tried to leave town on a speeder car at night, but were caught by a guardsman and confined to the depot. An injunction against the militiamen obtained from Baker was also ignored by Lawson until his work was completed. He installed a provisional city council before he left.

William Wiegand pursued his cause to the Oregon Supreme Court, where the judges found against the plaintiff. But Stewart and Warner, who filed similar actions, triumphed and their judgments included damages and restoration of property at state expense.

Martin Knezevich had fled the county when a Baker grand jury indicted him in March for selling liquor to minors and running a gambling hall. He was apprehended in Caldwell, Idaho, but Governor West was unable to appropriate extradition funds, so Knezevich was released and went east. Twenty-four other indictments were returned; some defendants pleaded guilty and paid their fines.

When H. V. Stewart and Tony Warner's cases were decided favorably, martial law was terminated. But the governor had accomplished his objective. Copperfield was a busted flush — the population had plummeted to 50 inhabitants. Only 32 voters were registered in 1914. Hector Stewart was re-elected mayor.

However, Copperfield still had more problems than a rat-tailed horse tied short in fly time. In May, Sam Grim's new house was destroyed by fire. Cattle belonging to homesteaders were stolen and butchered. Mayor Stewart's orchards were deliberately damaged when gates were left open for stock. Sixty-five of his hogs were poisoned. Then while repairing a fence which had been cut, he was shot twice in the back. The train took him to Baker and he survived, living 11 years more.

Bodies were found on river bars, the victims of foul play. George Holbrook had been murdered down at the Herman Creek ranch less than a year before. Cap Wilson's body was found at the base of a bluff at Fisher Bar, a bullet wound the cause of death.

Another mysterious fire struck in August of 1915. The vacant Lincoln Saloon burned, spreading fire over two blocks in the business district. Property valued then at $30,000 was destroyed.

The same year, A. B. Combs came to Copperfield from Baker in order to open a second-hand store, but, robbed of his money, abandoned the project and departed.

In 1918 the train ignited the railroad tunnel timbers. Returning from Homestead before the flames became too severe, the locomotive was able to continue operations from the upper end of the tunnel. The fire created a draft and couldn't be suppressed until the wood was consumed. During the weeks of rebuilding, ore from the Irondyke was trucked over Oxbow hill and transferred to the train.

Sobriety and virtue had settled on Copperfield at last. The farming and ranching families that remained endured to prosper from the grazing lands, hay fields and orchards. It was a pleasant, if calmer place to live.

John and Garnett Denney, who had acquired the store and stock of William Weigand in 1916, relocated the store to Homestead in the spring of 1920.

June of 1927 saw the demise of the town's post-office. The railroad station closed. First used as a flag stop, it was soon not even that.

Flames lit the sky once again in September, 1935. This time the Sam Aklin house, barn, and granary flared together, though the house was saved. An arson suspect arrested by state police was later acquitted by the grand jury.

The old schoolhouse was sold for a dollar in 1945, when the district was annexed to Homestead. The lumber was salvaged by the buyer.

Now stood only the houses of I-O Light & Power. Copperfield had discovered the skull that lies beneath life's skin; cheat grass grew in the streets. A couple of houses, some faded photographs, and memories ever receding, the way train tracks converge in the distance — all that remain of a town once decried as "Gomorrah on the Snake."

Einstein remarked, "We are not stuff that abides, but patterns that perpetuate themselves." Within a not-so-distant decade, this once busy shore would again witness the cycle of congested construction followed by familiar stasis.

Fern Hobbs when she revisited the site of Copperfield after the town had disappeared.

When construction of Brownlee Dam was well underway, concurrent work began at the Oxbow site. At the time the company received authorization for Oxbow, the old Idaho-Oregon Light and Power generator was still boosting the voltage in the line from Huntington to Homestead with its 600 kilowatts per hour.

Idaho Power used the old tunnel, which fed that generator's turbine, to divert the river while constructing a new 205-foot rock-fill dam. **Oxbow Dam** is similar in design to Brownlee, but has half its generating capacity. Twin tunnels, 36 feet in diameter, were driven 900 feet through the rock point around which the river curves in its three mile meander. When the gates of the dam closed in 1961, river water pooled until it spilled through the tunnels into a pair of surge tanks where it dropped 124 feet to power four turbines on the downstream end of the

Oxbow. The powerhouse is open to the public for an hour each afternoon and the unusual features of this installation are worth viewing.

Fish losses experienced at Brownlee were reinacted at Oxbow, with a variation. The Snake River is the second largest producer of Chinook salmon and steelhead in the world. About 25 percent of the fish entering the Snake passed the Oxbow en route to spawning redds — some going as far as Swan Falls. The runs in the late 1950's ranged from 40-55,000 adult salmon annually. A cement fish trap for the salmonids going upriver had been placed at the mouth of the Oxbow diversion tunnel in 1958. Outwash turbulence caused the structure to fail. River flow was reduced at Brownlee, to 500 c.f.s. at one point, while emergency repairs were attempted. The fall run of Chinook had just started up the Columbia. Despite efforts by Idaho Power and fishery personnel, repairs were not effected before the fish arrived. When a cofferdam, erected to dry the diversion tunnel while repairs were made, was breached, thousands of salmon were stranded in the splash pool below it and exhausted the

The Oxbow dam on the left, turbines located on the right hand top end of the point. The twin tunnels run almost a thousand feet from the reservoir through the neck of the point to the surge tanks 125 feet above the river at the end of the oxbow. Indian Creek enters the river at the bottom center portion of the photograph.

Oxbow fish trap at the mouth of the diversion tunnel.

oxygen in the stagnant water. Some fish were captured and transported above Brownlee, but before oxygen was pumped into the pool with a drilling compressor, at least 4000 salmon died. The loss of this portion of the spawning run was a catastrophe. The fish count made at Oxbow showed a run of better than 20,000 fall Chinook — five years later, when the migration loss was evident, the count tallied 945 fish.

In fulfillment of compulsory mitigation for salmon and steelhead losses caused by its dams, Idaho Power has established a salmon hatchery on Rapid River, an adult steelhead trap and egg-taking station on the Pahsimeroi River, and a steelhead hatchery at Niagara Springs — the sites are in Idaho and run by Idaho Fish and Game personnel. Part of the spring Chinook salmon run has been successfully transferred to Rapid River, a tributary of the Salmon. Unfortunately, tributary habitat is not suitable for *fall* Chinook. Historically, these salmon have only been found in the main Snake.

It is fair to say that the eight Army Corps of Engineer dams on the Columbia and lower Snake are equally responsible for Hells Canyon fish losses — though all of the federal dams are equipped with ladders. It is also fair to observe that Idaho Power is as concerned about fishery conservation as a utility can be, when its primary purpose is to make

View of Homestead, Oregon, taken from the east side of the river. Iron Dyke mine in upper center.

money from a national resource. When the company issues self-congratulatory statements regarding its hatchery expenditures, it should be kept in mind that the money spent is required by FPC license, that it is derived from company customers, and that it is reparation owed the citizens of Idaho, Oregon and the nation.

The highway crosses a bridge into Idaho just below the site of Copperfield and downriver from Oxbow Dam. After a three-mile drive, it is possible to look across the reservoir at **Homestead**, Oregon.

Jake and Bert Vaughn were running cattle along the Snake River in 1896 when they discovered and named the Iron Dyke mine. Jake recalled:

> My brother Albert had gone for water about 50 feet from where we were digging and the nails on his boots scratched a rock ledge the water was flowing over, revealing copper ore underneath. We got pretty excited and dropped what we were doing and proceeded to follow this ledge out. We tunneled in for about 50 feet and down for about 20 feet leading to the discovery of our "Glory Hole," a ledge rich in copper about 40 feet long.

This copper lode is located on the south wall of Irondyke Creek about a third of a mile from the river at Homestead. The Vaughn brothers did some development work on the ore body before selling out for a reported $40,000.

Homestead in 1924. Rough lumber was brought from Halfway, then planed at Homestead. The houses were quarters for married couples.

Frank Pearce took a homestead in the area and J. H. Pearson, as first postmaster for the community that materialized around the mine, suggested the name Homestead in 1898.

In 1900, according to the *Idaho Mining Journal*, the Iron Dyke was held by the Northwest Copper Company, but then was sold by sheriff to C. M. Reed, a wealthy Pennsylvanian. Frank Pearce worked as general manager of the mine at that time.

A smelter that had failed to operate properly for the Blue Jacket mine across the river on Indian Creek was purchased for use at the Iron Dyke. Relocated, it functioned successfully.

Theron and Halsted Lindsay, from Colorado, bought the mine about 1914. They owned a mining concern in Canada called Ventures, Ltd. The Lindsays installed a flotation plant which, along with the smelter, gave Homestead the largest copper concentrator in the state in 1917. Copper was piped in a slurry down to the filter plant on a bench by the river, where it was dry-pressed. The concentrate was then shipped on the railroad, which had been extended from Huntington for that purpose.

Halsted Lindsay brought master mechanic Rudy Lanning and his wife Mona, to Homestead to work for the company. Mona still lives at Homestead at the time of this writing and furnished information and photographs of the town.

The Iron Dyke mine in operation. Photo from Mona Lanning's collection.

Railroad steam shovel clearing a slide caused by a waterspout near Homestead.

The first small school at Homestead was located up Irondyke Creek canyon, but the white schoolhouse which can be seen from the Idaho road was built in 1918. There were two teachers and 30-40 students at that time. The Lindsays erected the buildings on the sloping bench as quarters for the supervisors and miners. Approximately 150 men lived on the bar at the height of production. Homestead had two stores, a post office, meat market and gas station.

Ballard's ferry as it looked before being replaced by the bridge.

Production records for the Iron Dyke for the period of 1910-1934 show 34,000 ounces of gold, 256,000 ounces of silver and 14 million pounds of copper realized from the operation. There is no record of production after 1934 and the mine closed at the start of World War II. A request that 26 men be allowed to work at the mine was denied — output was considered unessential for the war effort. The Lindsays sold their interests to the Butler Ore Company of St. Paul, Minnesota and that company was the owner in 1979 — though Texas Gulf is reported to have the claims under option. A report by Wallace Butler in 1944 states that estimated reserves above the 650-foot level in the mine total 148,000 tons containing 1.16 percent copper.

With the removal of the railroad tracks and the start of dam construction at Oxbow, activity in Homestead slowed to a saunter. Children had to attend school in Oxbow and finally even the post office was transferred there. Most of the buildings that remain stand empty, as if for rent, and Homestead drowses peacefully among the yellow pines.

Azurite Gulch is marked by a small sign next to the road a half-mile north of Kleinschmidt grade. It is named for a vein of pyrites, galena and chalcopyrite located up the drainage. Short adits which were driven show malachite-stained quartz-tourmaline. Not much work has

135

been done on the prospect, though some ore may have been hauled to Homestead.

Ballard Creek enters the reservoir on the Oregon shore across from the foot of Kleinschmidt grade. Eli F. Ballard operated a ferry just above the mouth of this creek around 1893. The crossing was known as Ballard's Landing and Eli served as postmaster there from 1900-1904. Ferry service ended with the completion of an interstate bridge in 1926 at the same location. The 40-year career of the Ballard bridge terminated when Idaho Power dismantled it after finishing the bridge below Oxbow.

The Ballard Bridge in 1927, taken from the Oregon side of the river.

The foot of **Kleinschmidt grade** touches the Idaho highway about three miles north of Homestead, just above the mouth of Ballard Creek. The grade was built to serve as a capillary from the river to the mining interests of the Seven Devils.

The Seven Devils district contains a belt of copper deposits whose ore occurs in irregular, discontinuous bodies within a garnet-rock which rims blocks of metamorphosed limestone enclosed in quartz diorite.

Levi Allen of the Stubadore Company discovered the Seven Devils' Peacock lode in 1862, as mentioned earlier. But mining in the area didn't get into the ground until Albert Kleinschmidt, from Montana, purchased an interest in the Allen-Lewis claims in 1885. Kleinschmidt bought some separate claims on Indian Creek: the Blue Jacket, the Queen, and the Alaska, which had been located a few years earlier. Since the Blue Jacket was closest to a road, Albert had men sort and sack ore all summer, then packed it by horse over the mountain to Bear Creek where it was shipped to a smelter at Anaconda, Montana. The resulting profit pleased him.

Albert Kleinschmidt engaged in the mercantile business in Missouri, New Mexico, Kansas, and Montana. He built irrigation canals in Montana and the Yakima Valley of Washington, planted extensive vineyards and citrus orchards in southern California, and was known as a large-scale building contractor. In his later years, Kleinschmidt founded and managed the wholesale and retail Helena Hardware Company in Montana. Albert and his wife, Ellen, raised a family of three daughters and six sons, all born in Helena. Kleinschmidt died at Berkeley, California in 1920.

Kleinschmidt was now serious about the prospects for the Seven Devils area. He had made a sizeable fortune in the Montana copper strike and sensed history might repeat itself. He turned his talents and $20,000 of his money to solving the ore-transportation problem.

Albert's solution was grandiose: build a road 22 miles down to the Snake River from the Peacock mine, haul ore wagons to the water where a steamboat could carry their loads to a railhead at Olds Ferry or Huntington. In 1889 he put crews to work with picks, shovels, dynamite, and horse-drawn scrappers. Some of the men made a dollar a day. They completed the road in July, 1891. It was "top-hole" job. When Livingston and Laney, mining geologists, examined the grade in 1920 they wrote:

> This road was well located, and of all the mountain wagon roads built before the days of highway construction, this is by far the best graded road that the writers have seen in the state. It rises from about 1,500 feet in elevation at the Snake River to about 7,200 feet on the divide above Helena and there are only one or two really steep pitches in the whole of this distance, and with a little repairing, trucks could be operated over it without particular difficulty. (A passenger car used it in 1909.)

The story of the difficulties encountered by the *Norma* has been related earlier. Kleinschmidt realized some other answer would have to be found.

The settlement of **Helena**, named for the first girl born in the camp, was located below the Peacock mine. By 1890 it had been honored with a post office. Helena was located on the forks of Copper Creek, a tributary of Deep Creek which flows into the Snake River just below Hells Canyon Dam.

The railroad established in Weiser seemed to promise a reasonable alternative for getting the copper to market. Kleinschmidt had formed the American Mining Company with Carl Kleinschmidt and James Millich. A. M. Holter bought the balance of Levi Allen's shares in the claims and in a reorganization of American Mining, Holter became a shareholder and Albert Kleinschmidt lost some of his control over the corporation. Members of the mining company agreed to ship all ore from the Peacock, Helena and White Monument mines over the railroad, which planned to reach the district by 1897. Like an answer to prayer, the railroad was slow in coming.

The town of **Cuprum** (Latin for copper) had been established on Indian Creek, midway between Helena and the foot of Kleinschmidt grade. It was endowed with a post office, two general stores, a pair of livery stables, the Imperial hotel, three saloons, a blacksmith shop, newspaper shop and assay office. A road connected Cuprum with Bear Creek and Council, a distance of about 30 miles.

The Metropolitan Trust Company of New York City had become interested in the Blue Jacket mine and leased the property. It financed construction of a smelter at Cuprum. The water-jacket type smelter proved inefficient, and after two trials was sold to the managers of the Iron Dyke mine across the river.

Cuprum in the Seven Devils about 1910.

The Pacific and Idaho Northern railroad, under the direction of Lewis Hall, had begun building a line from Weiser in 1899, which was intended to terminate in Helena. Men in Helena began working the grade toward Council. By January 1900, the P & I N had reached Cambridge. The year before, Albert Kleinschmidt sold 9/15 of his interests in the Devils to the Boston and Seven Devils Copper Company which was also headed by Lewis Hall. The Boston Company's best claim was the Arkansas — about five miles up Indian Creek from Cuprum.

Thomas G. Jones, former manager of the famous Dakota Homestake mine, filed on a claim adjacent to the Arkansas, had it surveyed and platted into lots, giving rise to the community of **Landore** (Land of Ore). There were nearly 500 people living in the area within a short time. This town was about five miles upstream from Cuprum on Indian Creek.

Landore, Idaho, 1907.

Blue Jacket mine in 1899. Photograph shows mine entrance, blacksmith shop, and shipping dock.

At almost the same time, another settlement clustered around the mines on Garnet Creek, a tributary of Indian Creek, just below Landore. It was known as **Decorah** and a postmaster was appointed in 1901. Its hotel, saloons, and stores mirrored those of Landore and they competed for the trade. A new road that connected Landore with Bear Creek and Council allowed Landore to eclipse Cuprum as the supply center for the mines.

A 1901 view of the Decorah mine.

By now, the P & I N had reached Council, but had shifted its sights from Helena to Landore. The mines were operating 10-hour shifts, plans were aloft for an aerial tramway at the Peacock, and ore was being stored in log bins in anticipation of the railroad's arrival. Freighters were hauling wagon loads of supplies and Pete Kramer's stage was making daily trips from Council to Landore. The Ladd Metal Company of Portland, Oregon, leased some claims from American Mining and constructed a smelter at Landore in 1904. The smelter was woodfired but was not properly designed for obtaining the required temperatures from that fuel. It was remodeled to accommodate coke, which had to be freighted from Council. By fall, 1905, the Ladd Company decided to cut its losses and closed the operation.

The Kleinschmidt interests were entangled in litigation. Lewis Hall had invested $2 million of his father's money in the Pacific and Idaho Northern and had by now grown wholly uninterested in American Mining and the Seven Devils Copper Company. It was 1911 before the railroad reached New Meadows, Idaho.

The boom lasted little longer than a wolf's yawn. Some claims were worked sporadically, and there was occasional production of copper and tungsten. Most of the mines were high-graded and total production is estimated to have reached a million dollars.

Kleinschmidt grade is a vestige of that brief and fevered period. During the summer it is passable to automobile traffic and it is possible to see an active copper mine, the Silver Queen, still functioning on the outskirts of Cuprum.

The **River Queen** mine is located half a mile below Ballard Creek on the Idaho side about 100 yards east of the highway. It was owned by the Haas brothers of Weiser, Idaho, in 1920. Ferdinand Alers obtained a lease and worked it intermittently for a number of years, shipping over 200 tons of ore that averaged 17 percent copper and were worth $20,000. Records show production as early as 1912 and some as late as 1940.

The Seven Devils Mountains.

Spring Creek threads its way down the Oregon side into Hells Canyon reservoir about a mile below McGraw Creek. Charlie Spain farmed here in 1926. His son Kirk went to school at Homestead, and now lives with his wife in Pollock, Idaho. Kirk recalled an amusing incident that occurred on the evening before Thanksgiving Day when the Spains were living at Homestead. Tom Lindsey, who lived a considerable distance up on a bench across the river, raised turkeys. At sunset a big tom came flying down the slope, crossed the water and crashed in the Spain's front yard. Since the bird's legs were broken, the family felt justified in cooking him for the next day's dinner. (They said grace, no doubt.)

Charlie Spain's farm at Spring Creek with orchard, garden, barley and alfalfa fields.

Leep Creek comes down the Oregon slopes to the reservoir 1½ miles below Spring Creek.

One summer day in 1931, a woman so thin she had to stand twice to make a shadow, came walking down the trail on the Oregon side of the river below Pine Creek. She had a pair of rag-wrapped bundles too heavy to be carried simultaneously, so she would tug one a distance, drop it, and return for the other. Leapfrogging her baggage in this manner, she progressed along the trail. It was "slow going" in the afternoon heat.

She stopped at Mrs. Baker's place for a drink of water. Mrs. Baker sized up the situation and offered the lady a wheelbarrow. The aid was accepted, and off she went, trundling her bundles down the canyon. Reports of the "wheelbarrow woman's" progress filtered back: she was seen at Copper Creek, she had crossed McGraw Creek, she reached Fisher Bar at Steamboat. There the rope ladder halted her advance. She retreated to Leep Creek, where an elderly miner, Mr. Van Cleeve, lay sick in his cabin. The lady stayed to help him in his distress.

When Van Cleeve later died, she inherited his cabin, claim and orchard. Though the lady never unpacked her past, she did reveal her name was C. D. "Roxy" Dunbar. She remained in the canyon, sheltered from the Depression. Roxy had a garden and a cow and wheelbarrowed her winter hay to the barn. Van Cleeve's relatives assisted her in return for her kindness to the old man. She used a boat to reach the Idaho side of the river where the Red Ledge road made it easier to reach supplies in Homestead.

The wheelbarrow woman left for Baker one day, with no more explanation than was given for her arrival. She was never seen again in the canyon.

Kirby Creek snakes down from the Oregon hills across the reservoir from **Big Bar** — the terraced bench below the road on the Idaho side.

Two brothers, Bill and Dick Kirby, were early miners on the stream and wintered with their horses in the canyon.

Big Bar was the subject of archaeological investigation in 1963 by the Idaho State University museum in agreement with the Smithsonian Institute, River Basin Surveys. Evidence unearthed indicated the bar was a village site. Several hundred classifiable artifacts were uncovered. The survey concluded that the bar had been intensely occupied for hunting use from A.D. 1600 to historic contact.

White men settled the bar, most of which is now covered by water, in the 1890's and farmed it for fruit and vegetables which were sold in mining camps such as Cuprum and Landore in the Seven Devils.

Two marble gravestones, each protected by a log fence, are located on the bar west of the road. Early pioneers Arthur Ritchie and John Eckels are buried there. Amos Camp and Jess Smith said Mr. Kinney was also interred on Big Bar, in a grave now beneath the water. The land is owned by Idaho Power but the Forest Service maintains the site. The grave markers were provided and packed by A. Huntley, a rancher.

Idaho Power used Big Bar as a trailer camp for employees working on Hells Canyon Dam in the 1960's. The terraces are a vestige of that period. The river edge of the bar served as the gravel source for the aggregate used in the dam's concrete.

The mouths of **Lynch** and **Kinney Creek** nearly kissed each other at the river before the last dam was built. Kinney Creek Rapid was fierce in appearance, but was considered a rather straight-forward shot down the tongue by experienced river-runners.

Dave Vermillion lived a life against the bone in a rock dugout near the mouth of Lynch Creek. It is uncertain how early he was in the canyon because he never advertised his presence, but perhaps by 1870.

Jess Smith, who knew him, said Dave was an old man with long white whiskers, and the wind would blow his beard over his shoulders while he worked his placer claim by the river. "He who never had a cushion doesn't miss it," and Dave's wants were minimal. He told Jess

Dan Cole running Squaw Creek Rapid.

he had gotten into a fracus over his wife in California, shot his uncle, then came north by horse to the mouth of Pine Creek, Oregon, where he had spent the winter. He said it was so cold that January that his mare's ears froze.

Dave Vermillion disappeared during the winter of 1915. He was last seen in the vicinity of Steamboat Creek and many believed he was murdered for his gold. "Oh lost and by the wind grieved ghost."

Squaw Creek spills off the Oregon cliffs and drops to the reservoir over basalt ledges. In the spring three waterfalls can be seen from the scenic pullout to the west of the highway.

There was a rockshelter in the cliff on the Idaho side, about 125 feet from the river, which had been occupied, according to the stratigraphic occurrence of faunal remains and artifacts, from 4500 B.C. The site is now under water.

Perry Gregg had a homestead at the mouth of the creek, according to Gerald Tucker, and starved to death in his cabin in 1923.

Squaw Creek Rapid was located below the bluffs that flanked the river. It was a difficult and impressive rapid, ranked just behind Buck Creek by those fortunate enough to run it.

Dan Cole running Buck Creek Rapid on a medium stage of water with a 33-foot pontoon. Note front of the raft poking out of the exploding wave. Cole is using an extension handle from the motor and holding a "bucking rope" with his other hand.

Buck Creek enters the reservoir from the Oregon canyon slopes a mile downstream from Squaw Creek. Buck Creek Rapid interrupted the river's flow at this location. "Big, Bad Buck" was the most awesome rapid on the Snake. Veteran and unperturbable river-runner Don Hatch described it as "the damnedest thing I ever saw." The river went off a ledge and there wasn't any way to cheat the rapid at most flows. Many river parties portaged Buck Creek.

Thirtytwo Point and **Sawpit Creeks** enter the reservoir opposite each other about a mile north of Buck Creek. Thirtytwo Point Creek on the Oregon shore is considered by students of the matter as the furthest point along the river reached by Captain Benjamin Bonneville in 1834. Sawpit Rapid was a rocky obstruction encountered by river runners at this point. Boatmen compared it to Hance Rapid in Grand Canyon.

Schoolmam Gulch, indicated by a roadside sign about a mile below Squaw Creek is named for Olive Addington. She taught school by the gulch at a site now covered with water. The Red Ledge miners at

Eagle Bar built the frame schoolhouse in the 1920's. They made the desks and chairs as well. The schoolhouse was located here because the mining company didn't want to pay the taxes which would have been assessed against the building had it occupied Red Ledge property. Olive taught about 10 students in the classroom.

Red Ledge school at Schoolmam Gulch

Eagle Bar and the **Red Ledge Mine**. About a mile and a half south of Sawpit Creek is a wide area to the left of the road. It is what survives of Eagle Bar. The site was used for trailer offices, tool shops, and a first-aid station by Idaho Power during construction of Hells Canyon Dam.

Morrison-Knudsen constructed a road to Eagle Bar from Ballard's Landing in 1926 for the Butler Ore Company. Though the road is now under water, it was built to give the Butler interests access to a copper prospect about five miles above the road end, on the forks of Deep Creek. The prospect is known as the Red Ledge because oxidized pyrite colored the ore mass.

Eagle Bar on the Snake River as it looked in 1925.

Tom Heady staked the first claims in 1894, at the time copper deposits were being worked near Landore and Helena. Heady eventually interested Robert Bell, Idaho's state mining inspector, in the property and he leased it with some other men and did considerable prospecting. World War I suspended all activity on the claims, though there had been at least a thousand feet of diamond drilling done by that time.

The Idaho Copper Corporation, controlled by George Rice, Dr. Walter Weed, and associates, took over the deposit in 1925. Three years later, Rice and the corporation were convicted of "using the mails to defraud" in connection with their promotion of the property. The claims were then acquired by Cooley Butler and Butler's company is the owner at this time (1979).

The Red Ledge consists of 23 patented claims and a large number of unpatented lode and millsite claims covering 1500 acres. No ore has yet been produced but 2,400 feet of underground work has been done and about 16,000 feet of diamond drilling which brings the estimated amount expended on the ledge close to a million dollars.

John Mullins and Charlie Spain rafting lumber down the river from Homestead to the Red Ledge mine.

Harold Burns freighting a diesel engine to the Red Ledge at Eagle Bar in 1927.

The known ore bodies are confined to an area 2,000 by 3,000 feet, with copper reported to run as high as 3.6 percent over a 60-foot width in the zone of enrichment. From incomplete data it appears about half a million tons of ore contain 1.4 percent copper and 3 percent zinc. In other words, it is a large low-grade deposit. The red building which can be seen above the road from Eagle Bar is part of the Red Ledge holdings.

Steamboat Creek is the last creek on the Oregon side of the reservoir before Hells Canyon Dam. The name is derived from the winter layover of the paddle wheeler *Shoshone*.

Fred Salisbury had a cabin, garden and peach orchard at the mouth of the creek in the 1890's. He placered during the winter and supported his family by doing ranch work outside the canyon during the summer.

Jack Fisher lived on the bar in the early 1900's with his wife and son. Sometimes his brother, Ed, stayed with them. Jack was buried there, according to Paul Butler.

Gabe Teeples was once arrested at Steamboat for "extracting a controlled substance out of fermented peaches."

Johnny Mullins, who is mentioned in the "boatmen" section with Amos Burg, was the last resident at Steamboat Creek. The property was purchased at a tax sale by District Ranger Grady Miller and resold to Idaho Power Company.

Even before Oxbow Dam was in its terminal stage, the final phase of the Hells Canyon development had commenced just above Deep Creek. The bridge, which was to retire the one at Ballard's Landing, had been strung across the river below the Oxbow. A 23-mile access highway was cut along the cliffs on the Idaho side of the river to the site of **Hells Canyon Dam**.

Once the road arrived, crews drilled and blasted a 40-foot-diameter tunnel 1,800 feet through the mountain on the east side of the river and a moveable form lined its interior with concrete. An earthen weir was pushed across the river below the tunnel's intake in 1965 and the river was thus diverted through the tunnel, away from the location of the dam and powerhouse. Temporary cofferdams were then constructed to isolate the upstream and downstream reaches of the site.

Substream strata were excavated to a depth of 100 feet. Mass placement of concrete began in March, 1966. Pours continued around the clock, as 700,000 cubic yards, heated or cooled to suit the season, were placed by rail-mounted cranes operating over the dam. Engine-drawn shuttle cars delivered the buckets of concrete from the mixing plant at the Idaho end of the trestle. A quarter-mile conveyor belt brought aggregate to the mixing plant. Aluminum tubing with temperature sensors circulated water through the dam in order to limit the curing heat of the concrete to 75 degrees — higher temperatures can cause slips and cracks.

Sand and gravel for the concrete was hauled from Big Bar upriver. Some sand from the mill tailings at the Cornucopia mines was used to

Dredging lower end of the diversion tunnel for Hells Canyon Dam at Copper Ledge Falls.

Hells Canyon Dam, with concrete batching plant on the right and cofferdam with diversion intake tunnel in the lower foreground.

Hells Canyon Dam under construction, looking north downriver.

reduce the amount of cement and lubrication needed in the mixing process. Tailings from the mercury mine at Weiser were also used. The tailings were ground fine as talcum powder and added to the cement in order to accelerate the curing reaction.

Eight hundred men labored on the 320-foot dam. Four of them were killed on the project. The dam began withholding water in 1968. Its spillway, like those of Brownlee and Oxbow, is designed to handle 300,000 c.f.s. Hells Canyon Dam has three generating units, with space for another. The short peak flow through an added turbine could be tolerated only if a reservoir below the dam absorbed the sudden release. Since Mountain Sheep Dam was never built, it is unlikely an additional turbine will be installed.

Hells Canyon Dam is an impressive edifice and the tri-dam complex represents one response to energy demand. But the dams were built with a number of costs never computed by accountants or engineers and such costs must be balanced against the benefits. On one hand, we obtained a peak generating capability in excess of a million kilowatts an hour, 39 permanent jobs, some recreation facilities and flood control, and $250,000 a year in taxes for the state of Idaho. On the other hand, thousands of acres of ranch land and wildlife habitat were lost forever, as were a town, salmon and steelhead runs, archaeological sites, and singular whitewater recreation. In addition, sand entrapment and daily flow fluctuations destroyed beaches, waterfowl habitat and spawning beds for 60 miles of river below this dam — with no mitigation whatever.

The Writhing Snake:
Deep Creek to Pittsburg Landing

"History is a cyclic poem written by Time upon the memories of man."
— Shelley

Mile 1 **Hells Canyon Dam.**

Mile 1.3 **Deep Creek** on the Idaho side of the river just below the dam. This stream was known as Copper Creek and contributed to the rapid known as Copper Ledge Falls before the dam was built. The name change was necessary because there is a Copper Creek upriver a dozen miles and another downriver 43 miles. Deep Creek drops over a mile from its source to the river. The Red Ledge mine is located 2½ miles up the creek and prospectors were aware that water from the creek was sufficient in flow and fall to power a substantial mill.

Mile 2.2 **Hells Canyon Creek** is the drainage in Oregon which can be seen above the U.S. Forest Service administrative site. Manley C. "Gabe" Teeples took credit for naming this creek after he tried to bring some horses down it. Idaho State University's museum field school conducted an excavation at the mouth of the creek in 1967, and artifacts recovered indicated the site was occupied in 1600 A.D.

The students unearthed a coffin pinned with wire nails, suggesting its age was 60-80 years. The box contained a skeleton, without its skull (which had been taken by amateur looters). The arms and legs of the victim were apparently bound with rope before burial and the man had worn calked logging boots. The identity of the remains was never established.

Ralph Barton showed his son, Ace, the grave of a surveyor for a railroad crew who supposedly drowned in Copper Ledge Falls. Paul Butler said his name was Adkinson and that he was from Massachusetts. There was a pair of standing oars crossed over the grave, which was located under the overhang at the entrance to Hells Creek canyon.

Mile 3 **Stud Creek** on the Oregon side. Gabe Teeples spent a couple of winters on this bar in 1910-11. (There was a cabin here.) He had a stud horse that wandered off and successfully eluded recapture. It fathered colts along the Summit Ridge country until it winter-killed — hence the name.

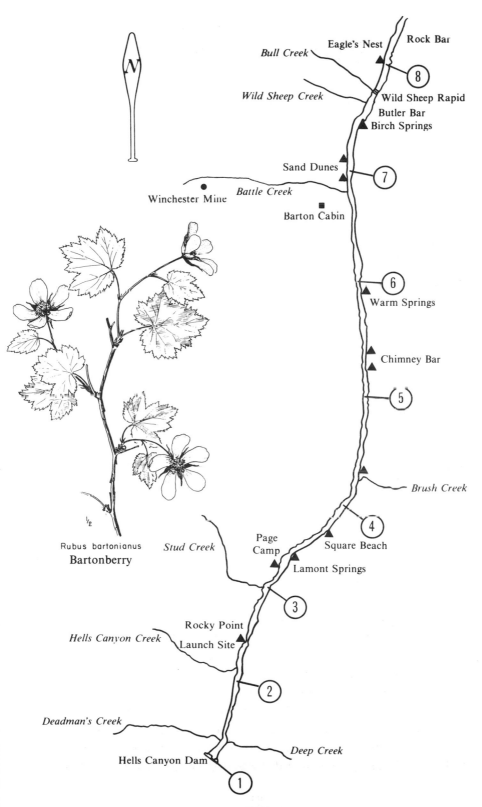

Rock Bar

Eagle's Nest

Bull Creek

⑧

Wild Sheep Creek

Wild Sheep Rapid

Butler Bar
Birch Springs

Sand Dunes

⑦

Winchester Mine

Battle Creek

Barton Cabin

⑥

Warm Springs

Chimney Bar

⑤

Brush Creek

Page
Camp

Square Beach

④

Rubus bartonianus
Bartonberry

Stud Creek

Lamont Springs

③

Rocky Point

Hells Canyon Creek

Launch Site

②

Deadman's Creek

Deep Creek

Hells Canyon Dam

①

155

Mile 3.3 **Lamont Springs** on the right supports a pond surrounded by a stand of thriving cattails.

Johnny Lamont had a tent-cabin on the site in 1905-06. He was a drifter who rode the grub line from Barton's, to Hibb's, to Hiltsley's. Lamont kept a few horses and placer mined the riverbanks. Bill McLeod at Sheep Creek was his best friend.

The Bartons wintered their calves along this bar. When they gathered them in April, they often saw 200-300 deer on the slopes between Lamont and Granite Creek.

The bench is sometimes called Lake Bar, and marks the north-south boundary between Payette and Nez Perce National Forests.

Mile 4.3 **Brush Creek** comes in on the right. Stock from this area could be taken by a rough trail up Chimney Bar drainage and over to Granite Creek. A forest fire in 1949 burned from Oxbow and Deep Creeks down to this point.

Mile 5.4 **Chimney Bar** on the Idaho side. Frank Hiltsley saw the bar in the 1890's and said at that time there was a stone chimney and fireplace on one side of a collapsed dugout cabin. Only the name survives.

Mile 5.9 **Warm Springs** on the right. Considerable placer mining has been done on the bench. Ernest Hutton was working the ground from 1914-18 and wintered here. Two Finnish brothers, Ed and Eno Latai, mined it during the 1930's. They put in a wooden pipe, a length of which can be found at the base of the rocks that wall the spring. The brothers kept a 20-foot scow for use on the river.

The slope at the upper end of the bar is pocked with pits where Indian dwellings once stood. The structures had a framework of upright posts thatched over with grass and rush mats. Dirt excavated from the interior was heaped against the outside perimeter of the lodge. Smoke from warming fires was vented at the roofline. These lodges, which antedate buffalo-hide tipis, are described in the journals of explorers, and recent archeological excavations have revealed base-stones set for the vertical posts. (This location is protected by federal and state antiquity acts, as are all native-American sites in the canyon.)

Looking downstream from Warm Springs, the peak which appears to straddle the river is 6,800-foot Black Mountain.

Mile 6.8 **Battle Creek** on the Oregon side. There is a legend that this stream's name commemorates a fight which took place at its mouth between Shoshone and Nez Perce Indians. The incident is so lost in time that it is difficult to believe the name now affixed to the drainage recalls that event.

A more plausible tradition was conveyed by Martin Hibbs and Ralph Barton. Two men were known to have lived at the mouth of the creek around the turn of the century: Christopher Smith and William Hazel. Both were bachelors and neither seemed interested in mining, but not much else is known about them. They had a falling out and while dividing provisions Smith grabbed an axe and halved a sack of flour which made Hazel mad enough to paw sod; the contest that ensued named the creek.

Ralph Barton, born in Moscow, Idaho, of parents from Illinois who eventually settled in Oregon, bought squatter's rights to Battle Creek from Bill Hazel in the fall of 1905. Barton had become interested in Snake River canyon and learned of the Battle Creek location from Martin Hibbs, who had recently moved to Granite Creek.

The groceries for Barton's first winter at Battle Creek cost $43.75. He had a grazing permit from the Forest Service for 20 head of cattle in 1906. At times he worked on Imnaha ranches, and occasionally at the Cornucopia and Landore mines.

In the spring of 1909, Barton pushed some of his cattle up a steep slope on the south side of the creek. He was tossing rocks and sticks to get them started toward fresh grass when he noticed wire gold matrixed in the stone he held in his hand. A short search revealed the source ledge. Ralph ran down the creek and tore a hole in the river as he took the boat across to share his discovery with Mart Hibbs.

The two men returned and staked the mine, about a mile up the creek. Barton then walked to Homestead to record his claim. There was no trail below Thirtytwo Point Creek, so he had to scramble along benches and cliffs, up ropes and across logs. Ralph made the trip in one day.

Ralph's brother, Guy, became a partner in the venture. They persuaded some men from the Rapid River and Cuprum mines to come examine the Battle Creek prospect. The lead looked promising and eventually John Sennett, an eastern promoter who was in the Cuprum country, became interested in the mine. Sennett formed a corporation called the Emnaha Gold Mining Company, which purchased Barton's claim for $12,000. Papers were filed in Boston; Sherman Winchester from Cuprum was hired as manager. While Sherm moved up the creek and began building a sawmill, Sennett went east to sell stock in the company.

BATTLE CREEK MINE 1910

The Battle Creek mine drawn from memory by Ace Barton. Top to bottom: root cellar, bunkhouse and cookhouse, Winchester's house, blacksmith shop, stampmill and sawmill (with circular saw), mill shop opposite the mill. The trail came down the creek and between the last two buildings. About 600 feet of pipe brought water to the flume which emptied onto the waterwheel. The ore tramway was operated by a power-takeoff from the mill.

158

*Goldie and Sherm Winchester and their children on the right
and Lenora Hibbs on the left, at the Battle Creek
bunkhouse/kitchen.*

*Battle Creek gold mine in 1910. Left to right: Carrie Barton, Ed Fisher, Goldie and
Sherm Winchester.*

Winchester fashioned a small undershot wooden waterwheel which
powered a whip saw that could cut an eight-foot board out of a log in
about 20 minutes. The lumber was used to make two bunkhouses, a
blacksmith shop, a mill building and tool shed.

Some of the stock sold by Sennett in Boston was purchased by a
woman named Mrs. Turner. She sent her son, Ed, who was about 15
years old at the time, out west to inspect the mine. He stayed and
worked at the Winchester for almost three years. The company bought
six small ore stamps, packed them to the site, and Sherm constructed a

water-powered mill with a main shaft to run the stamps. The ore was first crushed by sledge hammer, then carried under the stamps with a small stream of water. A tedious process, but enough gold was produced to enable Sennett to sell more stock on the east coast and even in England.

In 1913-14 a larger mill was built. The apparatus had to be packed in on the company's 11-horse string from the Himelwright ranch on the Imnaha River. The iron wheels for the crusher were a heavy load for a Percheron mare. The packers would back the animal's rear heels into

Battle Creek crew: left to right rear: Faye Barton, Glenn Hibbs, Ernest Hutton, Ralph Barton, Sherm and Goldie Winchester, Ellen Hibbs.

the center of a wheel placed on the ground, then use block and tackle to lift it over her croup so she could carry it around her girth padded by a saddle. A tripod with pulleys was used to lift the weight at intervals, allowing the mare some rest during the trip. Much of the equipment was assembled at the mine. Over 600 feet of six-inch pipe was brought in to operate a Pelton wheel which powered the new mill.

Ore was brought down the hill in buckets on a cable. It was dropped through a crusher above the mill and then fed into a narrow trough in the edge of a large horizontal iron ring. Vertical steel wheels, attached at their hubs to axles running from a shaft in the center of the ring, traveled in the groove around the ring's circumference. The wheels gradually pulverized the ore. Water washed the fines out across a coppered apron where the gold was collected with quicksilver. Including labor, Fred Himelwright estimated that $75,000 was spent on the operation.

Sherm Winchester was something of a recluse and seldom left Battle Creek after he arrived in 1909. Everyone connected with the mine was surprised to learn he had a family. The way of discovery was this: Sherm's attractive 24-year-old wife and boys, about two-and-a-half, and four years old, appeared in a hired livery rig at the

Himelwright ranch one morning. They had come from Weiser to Joseph by train. Fred took Mrs. Winchester to the mine, each of them carrying a boy cushioned by a pillow on front of the saddle. Their arrival startled Sherm, who borrowed the Barton cabin by the river until quarters at the mine could be arranged. Winchester's wife remained for nearly three years. Sometimes she rode alone to Imnaha to attend Grange gatherings and dances.

In the fall of 1912 Goldie Winchester became quite ill. She went out to the Himelwright ranch, then to Joseph, and from there by train to Weiser in order to see her doctor. Sherm went cross-country to Weiser and met her there. The boys were left with their uncles, Sy and Tracy Serrard, at the mine.

A few nights later a message came to Fred Himelwright that Mrs. Winchester's condition had worsened and that she would like to see her children. Fred took a lantern and walked four hours to the mine. While the Serrards bundled the boys, he went down to the Barton cabin and

At the mouth of Battle Creek: standing, left to right, Ed Fisher, Ralph Barton, Sherm Winchester, on horseback Goldie and Lenora.

Ralph and Lenora Barton in April, 1911, at Joseph, Oregon.

Haying on Battle Creek in 1910.

The second cabin at Battle Creek, built in 1931.

163

caught a gentle old one-eyed horse. The boys were placed in the saddle and Fred and Sy on foot led the horse back to the Imnaha. Frank Shevlin was waiting with team and buggy. He took the children to Joseph where they were placed on the train for Weiser. Despite this effort, Mrs. Winchester died before the boys reached her.

The gold vein pinched out after another couple of years and the mine was abandoned in 1916. The Emnaha Mining Company left unpaid debts of $1,500 to the McCully Mercantile Company at Joseph and $700 to the Himelwright family. Frank Shevlin packed the sawmill out to his place on the Imnaha. A caretaker named McManus remained at the mine for several years. The buildings endangered curious cattle and were therefore destroyed. Until 1978, a quantity of milling machinery was still visible, but that fall a waterspout came down the creek and buried most of the site beneath tons of mud. Only the tunnel, cable, and a section of the iron mill ring can now be seen.

Ralph Barton obtained a homestead patent on the Battle Creek land in 1910. He married Carolyn Lenora Hibbs, Mart's daughter from the ranch just downstream at Granite Creek, the following year. He sold the homestead to the Emnaha Company and moved to the mouth of Grouse Creek, but the corporation never paid for the land, so it reverted to Barton in 1916. In 1929 he packed an English lady over the trail from Imnaha because she had purchased stock in Britain and wanted to see the mine. He said she dismounted at the old mill with the words, "Well now, Mr. Barton, that was a bit of a go."

Barton, Dick Fisk and Pat Ahalt packed lumber and shingles from Imnaha to the site by the river in 1932 to build a new cabin. They also hauled some timbers down from the mine for the project. There was a barn on the upriver end of the field, and a root cellar for storage. The original Barton cabin, built in 1909, was located on a diagonal about a hundred feet uphill from the present structure. That cabin, and the second room of the cabin now present on the slope, were burned for firewood by sheepherders.

In 1938, Allen and Hazel Wilson had the place. They sold it to Vern Colvin, who transferred it to Lou Warnock. Ken Johnson purchased it from Lou, and then the government took title from him. The ground has now gone full circle: from unproductive land to flourishing homestead, and finally back to public domain.

The basalt ramparts on the Oregon side, a mile upriver from Battle Creek, are known as Barton Heights. Originally the 5,700-foot butte was called Dizzy Heights. There are shelves on the mountain known as

164

"relic areas" — ledges inaccessible to grazing animals where botanists can determine the composition of native grasses before white men arrived in the canyon.

A one-stamp mill at Battle Creek. The stem, stamp, tappett and pulley are missing. The mill was manufactured by Moyle Engineering and Equipment Company of Los Angeles. Amalgamation plates were used below the discharge weir.

Mile 7.1 **Butler Bar** on the Idaho side. This site is named for B. Lee Butler. According to his brother, Paul, in the winter of 1923 Lee and Jack Keener were staying at Battle Creek to trap fur and look after the Barton cattle. Mart Hibbs returned from Imnaha on business, and had them ferry him to the Idaho shore with the boat kept at the creek for that purpose.

While ferrying back across the river, Butler lost an oar, the boat overturned in the riffles downstream, and though Keener made it to the bank, Butler did not. Lee reached a rock near shore, then exhausted himself attempting to climb its slick surface. He was burdened by a heavy overcoat and a pistol. His body was never recovered.

Mile 7.8 **Wild Sheep Creek and Bull Creek** on the Oregon side. This area was known as Two Creeks until the Forest Service, whose prerogative was questionable, changed the name. The bar contained evidence of early Indian habitation.

For many years the lower end of Two Creeks bar was honored with a stately ponderosa whose crown supported a bulky nest used by bald eagles. Tree, nest, and eagles have long since gone to earth.

Wild Sheep Rapid is formed by the outwash from the basin drained by the twin streams. It is one of two major rapids left in the canyon. Depending on the water flow, there are runs left and right of the center hole. Most professional boatmen scout the rapid each trip. It can be studied readily from a trail along the Oregon bank.

Wild Sheep Rapid at 17,000 c.f.s.

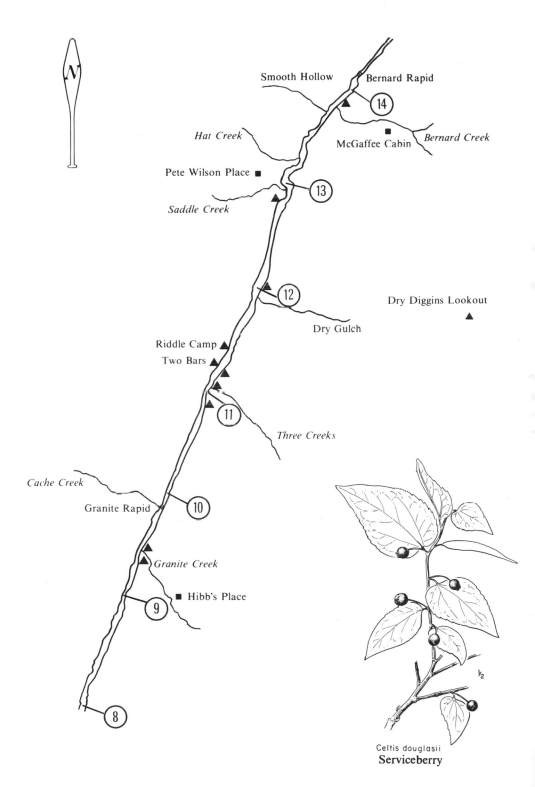

Smooth Hollow   Bernard Rapid

⑭

Hat Creek

McGaffee Cabin   *Bernard Creek*

Pete Wilson Place ■

⑬

Saddle Creek

⑫

Dry Diggins Lookout ▲

Dry Gulch

Riddle Camp ▲

Two Bars ▲

⑪

Three Creeks

Cache Creek

Granite Rapid

⑩

Granite Creek

■ Hibb's Place

⑨

⑧

Celtis douglasii
Serviceberry

½

Mile 9.4 **Granite Creek** on the Idaho shore. This healthy stream drains the western slope of the Seven Devils and becomes a boulder-rolling torrent in late spring, often overflowing its banks. The name is derived from the igneous exposure at river-edge — one of the few areas along the river where the mineral composition of the Devils is revealed. There are campsites above and below the mouth of the creek.

A hay meadow is located up the creek, slightly short of a mile. It is known as the Hibbs Place — when any voice is there to say its name. Cliff Mountain indents the eastern skyline and in the field below it a barn founders by a grave overgrown. A cabin stands empty and open. Visitors drawn to the clearing sense a story and it's there to be told — though particulars lie lost beyond any man's unriddling.

Martin Riggs Hibbs was rough as barbed wire, an Irishman who had spent time in Illinois and Missouri before coming round the Horn to Oregon. He was living with his wife, Ellen Francis, and children Glen, Lenore, and Milt at Horse Creek on the Imnaha River when he staked copper claims with M. E. Barton at Eureka Bar. Hibbs and Barton sold their claims, and Mart packed for the new mining company at the bar during the winter and spring of 1899-1900. Then he moved his family to Joseph, Oregon.

Mart was a mountain man, and the summer of 1902 found him in Council, Idaho, looking for a spot less civilized than Joseph. He rode back through the Seven Devils, spending a night at Rankins Mill on Rapid River. Unhappy about backtracking to Cuprum in order to reach Wallowa County, he was told by a miner of a shorter route down Granite Creek and across the Snake at Saddle Creek. While returning in this way, he saw Granite Creek and it suited him longways and sideways.

He talked with the Hiltsleys down at Three Creeks and learned that a brother, Dave Hiltsley, had lived at Granite and built the log cabin there. Dave had moved out and the land was available. When Mart reached Joseph he broke the news to his family and they began preparations for the pack trip to the canyon.

Hibbs trailed his horses and cattle by way of Freezeout Saddle down to Saddle Creek. With the help of Jensen, McCarty and Hiltsley, he swam the stock across the river and pushed them up to Granite Creek.

The Hibbs were caught between the bark and the sap when their cabin burned in January of 1909, but neighbors arrived to help square a new two-story log house. A blacksmith shop and root cellar were eventually added.

At the Granite Creek homestead in 1905: left to right, the Hibbs: Martin, Ellen, Glen, Mary, Hilton, Earl and Edna.

Hibbs children: rear, Lenora and Glen, front, Mary and Milt.

In 1911, Mart filed a homestead entry for the site, but instead of the allowable 160 acres, he settled for 153 because he didn't want to pay taxes on the rimrocks. He was ten years getting the entry patented.

Though none of them were born on the location, three sons and three daughters were raised at Granite Creek by Ellen and Mart. On slopes as steep as the road to hell, the family fattened cattle with summer grass in the Seven Devils. The stock was taken to market in the fall, to Grangeville, or more often to the railhead at Council or New Meadows. By 1925 the Hibbs had added Three Creeks and Johnson Bar to their holdings.

The Hibbs' cabin at Granite Creek.

If history, as Hendrik van Loon wrote, is "the record of a man in quest of his daily bread and butter," then events which illustrate the resolution and ingenuity of canyon families deserve recording. When someone has a serious problem in the backcountry today, he summons a government helicopter. Another generation has nearly forgotten the time when people extricated themselves from difficulties by their own efforts. One such effort was recalled by a friend of the Hibbs, Iphigenia "Gene" McGaffee. Gene spent 20 years in the Snake River Canyon as ranchwife, mother and cowhand. Her vignette concerning Ellen Hibbs conveys a sense of those people, their mettle and fortitude:

I should be able to tell this just as it happened, since I lived it over in my dreams last night, and so vivid does it seem that I feel I am still in the saddle, riding behind that strange caravan. I can almost believe that it was just yesterday that we took her out, and that I, with the children, hers and mine, am hurrying back to take up life again where we left off to make this emergency trip, and my thoughts are with her, as then were my hopes and prayers that she might come back too, strong in body, as she had always been in spirit, to carry on, free from the malady that took her down, but could not dim the courage of one of the pluckiest women I ever knew. We, the children and I, had followed them to the end of the trail, and had choked back the tears to face her brave smile and cheerful 'goodbye' to us, as we helped tuck her into the car. Then they drove off, with my husband at the wheel, and her Mart, tense and anxious, doing what he could for her comfort.

This event stands out in bold relief against the background of twenty colorful years on an isolated cattle ranch in Idaho, on the Snake River.

It was August, time to gather the beef, but Fred came back to our cow-camp late that night, saying that Ellen Hibbs was sick in bed at their camp, with no one in attendance except her young daughter, Edna. Mart and Earl, her husband and son, had gone to their ranch two days before she took down, to put up the hay, and this sudden return of an old ailment meant that she must get to a doctor very quickly if her life were to be saved. I was all for going right up

171

to their camp that night, but Fred said, 'No, wait till I tell you my plan.' He had already gone to their ranch to get the men, and they would be at their camp that night.

Now, as I look back over the years lived in that strange but fascinating bit of country, I can see my Fred, meeting every emergency with extended hand, and leading always to a safe stretch along the trail. I wanted to feel that he could do it this time. But we had to reach a doctor soon, and all thought of her riding a horse was out, as was the vision of three men carrying her over 25 miles of narrow, steep rocky trail. So I listened to his plan with fear. But every day of life in that country meant facing danger in some form, so I was more than willing to do what I could to help, and he was glad to see my faith in him revive.

As you can imagine, I slept little that night, and welcomed the first glimmer of dawn. Then, while Fred wrangled the horses, I hastily prepared breakfast, packed a few necessities into our saddle bags, and we were off, Fred and I, with our nine-year-old boy Everett. Ellen had been my friend for many years, and I was impatient to reach her side, anxious to give her a bit of encouragement for the proposed undertaking, so I urged my horse ahead for the last mile, and was off and into the cabin and at her bedside before I realized that I should have prepared myself for the sight of her, lying there so pale and, as I thought, helpless. I feared, "She can never go through with it!", but she looked up and actually smiled a little and said, "Mart is scared to death, but I'll make it all right."

The men were soon out looking for poles suitable to make the conveyance that was to carry her over two mountains. It was to be a sort of stretcher. They lashed lodgepole pine together to make it long enough to accommodate a bed for her. And it was to be slung, tandem style, between two sure-footed saddle animals.

After building the carrier, next thing was to accustom the animals to such an unusual requirement. This strange, long thing following the lead animal frightened it into a desire to run away, while the one in the rear rebelled even more at being attached to something in front of it. They decided on two mules. One of them was Ellen's own little gray saddle mule, very sure footed and fairly gentle. Now they must be handled carefully to acquaint them to this new role. In that country we used our horses and occasionally a mule to ride, to rope off of, and to pack. Sometimes they were used to drag a stubborn critter to the branding iron, or a log or pole to the cabin for wood, but this was an entirely new contrivance, and shafts were unknown to them, so it took much patience and strength of will to break them in. Everett was very excited over the whole affair, as most any nine-year-old boy would be, and quite agreeable to the idea of being the one to 'try it out'. He got dumped more than once, but determination and the knowledge that this was not intended for entertainment, but was deadly serious, and just had to work, brought the desired results. After they had the animals under fair control, and Everett riding on the bed, they paraded by the open cabin door so that Ellen could see, and we were soon on our way.

The front shafts were fastened to a pack-saddle on the gray mule, which Fred led for miles. After that, he and Mart took turns leading her, seeing that she followed loosely behind the saddle horse. Earl rode Kate, the brown mule that carried the back shafts, adjusted to the rigging of her saddle so they could be easily removed at points where the trail turned too sharply to accommodate such a long equipage. At such times he dismounted and carried the shafts of the stretcher himself as gently as he could, the brown mule following till they reached a place where it was safe for Earl to re-insert the shafts into their improvised sockets, and ride on. Edna, Everett and I followed on our horses, leading a pack horse or two.

Ellen knew I was tense with anxiety, although for years I had ridden these trails with no thought of danger. But today those crags and deep canyons terrified me. Any one of so many things could happen to frighten the mules, and a lunge off of that trail would have sent them crashing down, down to the bottom of the canyon. But I could see the men, and knew that never for a moment did they relax their firm hold on the reins, so gradually I gained confidence and, as we travelled slowly along, my thoughts drifted back through the years that our families had lived as neighbors in that silent country, working and playing together. Our cattle ranges joined, and we had never taken much care of the drift fences. What did it matter if these white-faces chose to visit back and forth in friendly fashion? They were equals, and met each other on common ground, just as did we, their owners. Beef gathering time was one long picnic for the children, as it was our custom to attend to this before time for them to go away to school. The start was made from Ellen and Mart's cow camp, and as the men gathered and separated the beef from the stock cattle, they drove them in onto fresh range around the lakes, there to be held through the day by the 'women and kids,' till they bedded down at night. But that was usually a leisurely task, and gave us time to visit and maybe crochet; sometimes to hunt huckleberries. I smiled as I recalled the year those little red huckleberries were so thick on the bushes that they lay flat on the ground, but were so tedious to pick that Edna and I got the brilliant (?) idea of combing them off. That night our combs were scrubbed to a fare-you-well, and every night thereafter we picked leaves out of those berries till our patience gave out, and we threw the rest of them out for the squirrels.

'Ellen and I.' On every page in that book of memory of her family and mine.

Most of those trails are steep inclines, and when we were going up the hill, her pillow faced the lead mule. Then going down the other side, we reversed her position, moving the head shade, and she always greeted us with a smile and some witty remark about the elegance of her equipage, or how extraordinary such a procession would surely look to an observer. And it did too. Unknown to us at the time, we were the source of great wonderment to the occupants of a lookout tower in Oregon, just across the river from Idaho. Our progress was necessarily slow, and a strain on those mules, so it called for frequent stops on long climbs. One such climb was up a long, open hillside, and attracted the attention of the lookout at that tower. The lens of his telescope was not powerful enough for him to identify us, but he could see that someone was being carried on this stretcher. And the unusual proceeding aroused his curiousity and concern. He saw we were headed toward a lookout station on our side of the

174

river, so he telephoned to our lookout, and when we appeared at that station late that afternoon, we were greeted with an unexpectedly cordial welcome.

We had stopped along one of the creek bottoms for lunch, and Ellen had slept a little while we rested. We were surprised and very pleased when she said she didn't feel especially tired, and that she thought this was the easiest way to travel that she had ever tried, so we started on, and that night she was hungry enough to eat a bit of the good sourdough biscuit that Lookout boy made for us. He also insisted that she take his bed, and Edna stayed with her mother, while the rest of us slept in another cabin close by. I was tired that night, but devoutly grateful for the day's success. However, we still had another half-day of it, but over better trails, and those gallant little mules had settled down to commendable conduct.

Next morning, Ellen was ready to resume the journey. It was a faultless August morning in the mountains. Even the murmur of the pines was a song instead of a sigh, and mingled with the riotous chorus of bird song. Also the youngest member of our party, our boy Everett, had a birthday, and Ellen promised him a 'Good licking' upon her return.

The route we had chosen would bring us to a road, and to the home of a friend, 15 miles from the town where we kept our car, and the men decided it would hasten matters for Fred to go on ahead of us, and get the car. He could be back to meet us by the time we reached the end of the trail. So Mart took over that morning, and there was a ring of confidence in his voice when he spoke to Kit, the little gray mule. And Ellen's cheerful 'Toot-toot' started us off with a gaiety born of gratitude and faith, quite unlike the forced smiles with which we had started out on this venture the day before. Just one day! I had lived a lifetime in that day and felt very humble as I climbed onto my pony and fell into line.

Between three and four o'clock that afternoon, we reached the road where we found the car waiting. It was Ellen's desire to go on after a short rest, so the children and I bade her as cheerful a good-bye as we could muster, then I went back into the friend's house and took comfort in her hospitality.

Fred's plan had worked. Once again his ingenuity had saved the day.

Next morning Earl, Edna, Everett and I started back into the mountains, and was I glad of the company of those children! Happiness and gaiety are natural to a child, and the light of it carried me through the dark loneliness of that day. Then Fred's return bringing good news of how well Ellen had stood the trip made our hopes rise high for her. And soon we were busy gathering the beef cattle, preparing to take them to another range. That took us into country new to me, but that is another story.

Ellen died in 1926, and was buried in Enterprise. Mart, and his youngest son Earl, were the only people left on the ranch — the other youngsters had grown up and moved out. The two of them worked the place; they had a large garden, fruit trees, and fields in hay — the lower one was on the south bench just above the mouth of the creek, and is used today as a campsite.

Gathering at Granite Creek in 1930: left to right, Earl and Lenora Hibbs, Lou Knapper, Mart and Glen Hibbs, and a doctor friend.

In June of 1935, Earl went out to Pullman, Washington, on a short vacation. Martin had to attend a Forest Service range meeting in Riggins. He needed someone to look after the cabin and irrigate the garden and hay fields while he was gone.

There were two prospectors skim-digging upriver at Warm Springs. Both were crazy as popcorn on a hot stove, but Joe Anderson, of Tennessee, was friendly, while the other fellow would fight a rattlesnake and give it first bite. There had been threats and arguments between them. Hibbs asked Anderson to come down and caretake the homestead during his absence.

After the meeting, Mart was anxious to get back to his place, a little concerned that Anderson might have bungled the chores. He spent the night of June 23 at "Old Timer," a cabin built by Ralph Barton halfway between Riggins and the head of Granite Creek. Cleo Patterson and Don Stroup were there, building fence on Baldy Mountain for the Forest Service.

The next day he rode down the creek to his ranch. He dismounted by the large cherry tree near his cabin, removed his spurs and dropped them next to the door, and went back to unsaddle his horse. At that moment someone shot him from behind. Mart Hibbs was murdered in his 71st year.

Five days later, his daughter, Lenora Barton, came up from Imnaha by way of Saddle Creek to see how he was doing and to gather some fruit while she was there. Horrified by her discovery, she rushed back to Saddle Creek to tell the Pete Wilson family.

Pete Wilson, Charlie Marks, Cleve Lloyd, Dick Fisk, Max Walker, and Mervin Horner went to Granite Creek. They found Hibbs lying face down where he'd been shot, the cabin burned to ground, and the bones of a second man in the ashes. There was a .44-caliber revolver near the hand of the charred skeleton. From teeth in the skull and overall buttons on the floor, the men determined the bones were those of Joe Anderson. His remains were committed to a grave by the creek at the upper end of the field, now marked by a wooden headboard.

Mrs. Wilson called the sheriff, W. E. Aultman, from Idaho County, and he came in with the coroner. Permission was given to take Hibbs' body to Enterprise for burial next to his wife, Ellen.

The men decided that Hibbs died shortly before the cabin was burned. There were cinder holes in his shirt. Ordinarily, the burning cabin would have started a grass fire, but rain had drenched the area. Jimmy Wilson had been hunting horses in the high country and had looked down at the storm moving through Granite Greek on the afternoon of June 24, so the day of the shooting was settled.

Tracks were found behind the cherry tree where someone had hidden while waiting. (That tree toppled in 1977.) There were cigarette butts on the ground and tracks led upriver. The principal suspect was the other prospector, but when Fred McGaffee, and Pete and Jim Wilson followed the trail, it was soon obscured by the effects of the storm. A check of Brush Creek and Warm Springs revealed no trace of the miner. Many were certain he was the culprit.

Wilson and McGaffee often discussed the killing, and a young Jim Wilson remembered their theory of the crime. It turned on some additional pieces of evidence: Anderson was shot in the head. There was a bullet hole in the stovepipe inside the cabin, two cartridges from the pistol were found near the skeleton, and all the rifles in the cabin were stacked in one corner with a shell in each chamber.

Fred figured Anderson became worried that his old prospector pard was coming down the river to kill him. Alone and a bit drifty he became paranoid. He started up the river to see if the other man was there, then returned to the cabin. His tracks were muddled by the rainstorm. While Anderson was in the cabin, Hibbs returned. Hearing the noise, the miner thought his partner had come to get him. He went to the door and shot Mart from behind, but the report of the pistol brought him back to his senses. Realizing what he had done, Anderson then shot himself. The bullet passed through his head and knocked the pipe off the stove. The ensuing fire consumed the cabin.

Whether Joe Anderson was murdered, or a murderer, is now a mystery past any man's solution. But there is no doubt that Mart Hibbs' untimely death was lamented by many. Since Hibbs and his homestead have an important place in the history of Hells Canyon, it seems appropriate to include here another remembrance written by Gene McGaffee.

'You'd be jogging along the trail, and your horse would prick up his ears. Then just coming around the next turn, you'd get a sight of the old man's dog, tail up, care-free, wagging you a friendly welcome, matching old Mart's greeting as he pulled up his pony, lighted his pipe anew, and shifted his position to one more comfortable for the 'get acquainted chat,' or just neighborly visit he seemed always to have time for. Most cowboys train their dogs to stay behind, but old Mart liked his dog for its company, and he wasn't much of a cowboy anyway, albeit he was a good judge of cattle, and had been "hyin" the dogies around for many years when I first ran into him.

We had bought a little cow outfit on the Idaho side of the Snake River, and our range joined his. We knew we were getting into a lonely, untamed region, but it was good cow country, and we never regretted the move. We prospered, but I often think that one of the richest gains from the years spent in those mountains came from our association with and friendship for old Mart Hibbs. He was "old Mart" to everybody. A tough old Irishman; not morally, though he had a line of persuasion in his language that would surprise a sailor, and, like his advice, it always fit. I can't number the times when a light jest or an old saw from his lips eased a tension in camp that could have brought about murder. He had some hot-headed sons (not bad boys), and my husband was no angel. We were good neighbors and good friends, but in the fall beef round-up, when we roughed it in the raw, riding, eating, living together, shifting from one camp to another for a month of fitful fall weather, homesick saddle ponies and beef critters obsessed with a wanderlust or a determination to hide, which the contour of that country surely encouraged, some tempers were whetted to a dangerous edge.

When we women were able to go up and cook for our cowboys, life became a shining joy. They were conscious of the beauty about them, the songs of birds, the melody of the mountain streams. And as they filled their lungs with the sweet, fresh pine-scented air, their hearts responded, 'This is the life! Let the critters hide, we'll find 'em. We know just what pockets to ride out! Jungle Park holds no terrors for us!' What they were really seeing was the picture they knew would present itself to them when they reached camp that night, tired but expectant. Cheerful women, happy kids! *And a good supper!* Then the bonfire after dark. The flickering flame shadows, the tall dark pines all around, and the little creek babbling along just below camp. They're not tired now, they're happy, with a sleepy youngster snuggling up on one side and a contented wife on the other, while the younger members of the group dream dreams of future bliss. And it feels good to stretch and listen to old Mart. He's telling about that time his old dog Buck jumped the cougar and put it up a tree, then he disrobed and spread his garments (hat, coat, shirt and pants) round on the branches, as one of the youngsters said, 'Just like a Christmas tree.' That ruse kept the cougar up the tree too, till he made the two mile trip back to his cabin for a gun. I can see the picture he made, streaking it down the mountain trail, gray hair, gray undies, and on a gray mule; a ghostly figure, and a sight to terrify any family except his. And I can see Ellen, his wife, handing him his gun without question, and speeding him on his way back.

But maybe tomorrow would also be the day when we women would have to go back to the ranches to can peaches or something. That night they would realize that they were tired, whether their day's luck had been good or bad, and each of them would want to delay his return to the lonely camp, hoping one of the others would get there first and have supper started. I said 'each of them,' but I should not include old Mart. He would be there if he could, and I can see him now, bending over the fire, emptying the coffee can into the pot. When old Mart made the coffee it was at least plenty strong. He always said it didn't take all the water in the 'crick' to make good coffee. But they were apt to be a pretty silent bunch while preparing supper, and of course, hungry, so if they hurried the bannocks too much or if the beans rattled as they rolled off of the spoon onto the plates, someone might snort, 'To hell with such an outfit! This grub would kill a dog!' Then they'd hear something like this, 'Done or raw, it'll fill the craw.' And suddenly they would realize that 'filling the craw' was, after all, the main thing. What they were eating was food, and their stomachs could take it. This was not a vacation camping trip. They were there to get those beef cattle to market.

They weren't conscious that they had heard words of wisdom, but I have been in camp on some such occasions, and I have caught myself letting go of a breath as I would have a life-line after reaching safety. And pretty soon someone would say, 'I'm thinking now right where we will find that old line-back cow and the spotted steer tomorrow,' or he would make a joke of the doughy bread by calling it marsh-mallow biscuit. Neither would old Mart feel that he had done anything of merit. I am sure if someone had told him that he was a peacemaker, he would have thought it an accusation. He never talked religion. Lived at the foot of the Seven Devils mountain range, and liked to tell about the Portland doctor inquiring as to the health of the 'other six.' He had been bitten twice by rattlesnakes and recovered. One time he just 'slapped a chaw' onto it. Didn't seem to bother him. He said he didn't know what it did to the snake.

He had a great love for dogs, but never tried to train them. Joshed my husband because he generally had his dogs under pretty good control. Said all one had to do was 'set' on his horse and tell his woman and dog to 'get wide.' But Fred got back at him; told him he couldn't get either his woman or dog to work for him. We used to just smile when he said anything about being the boss in his family, and I am sure he never thought he was, but as I recall those years, I am not so sure he wasn't. Only it was never done in a bossy way.

He had a great capacity for enduring discomfort without complaint, and for making the best of a situation. I recall the time blackleg got into our herds. Big fat calves dying right and left. Looked like we might be going out of the cow business. That was in June or July. Branding done and cattle spread out all over the range. But we got some help from the Salmon River country, and rode, corralled, rowelled and vaccinated for a week on both ranges. It was a disheartening job. The boys would come into camp tired, dirty, bloody, discouraged. They'd fill up their plates, but wouldn't be hungry. Maybe drink their coffee. Then the old man would say, 'Well, boys, I'm goin' to eat just like this was the last meal I ever expected to get.' An innocent enough remark, but a lecture in good sportsmanship, accompanied as it was by a look of mock solemnity on his face, which we knew was intended as a reflection of the doleful countenances of some who were not such good losers. Anyway, everybody would grin and clean up his plate and be ready for the next move.

He called an extra hard winter an 'equalizer' and when a stretch in the trail was so bad it was best to dismount and lead your horse over, old Mart called that 'takin' it by hand.'

I could fill pages with his unique sayings, but his chief talent lay in knowing when to say them, and I will always believe that many times he averted a tragedy by so doing. With all my heart I have wished that he could have had a little time to do something to avert the tragedy of his death. It does seem unfair that he was denied to use for himself the ability that had brought calm out of threatened storm for so many others. But after all, death must have come to him quickly, by the evidence, and its messenger surely repented his act, as he took his own life too. This man was a stranger in the country; claimed to be a prospector, and old Mart had befriended him. But his peculiar conduct showed him to be an escapee from some corrective institution. Thus, his last act will remain a mystery, as there was no witness save the silent sentinels of the wild that had been old Mart's companions for so many years I feel they will always miss him.

But I have no desire to write a story of his death. This is intended as a tribute to his life, and my appreciation of what it still means to me.

The cabin which now stands at the edge of the clearing was built by Earl Hibbs and Cal Davis in 1934. Some of the boards were brought by mules from Hiltsley's place at Three Creeks, 1.5 miles downriver; the rest were packed in from Rankin's Mill on Rapid River.

Earl married Esther Leonard, of Pullman, in the fall of 1934, and she joined him at Granite Creek. They had two children while living there. In 1940, Lenora Barton bought the ranch from the Hibbs, and a year later she sold it to Pete Wilson's son Allen, who was married to her daughter, Hazel. Allen and Hazel had worked at Saddle and Battle Creeks before buying Granite Creek.

The Wilsons sold the homestead to George "Bud" Wilson (no relation) who integrated it into his sheep operation. A sheepherder, "Granite Creek Rose," and her husband, wintered in a tent on the creek and, until interrupted, used the cabin as a source of custom firewood. Half of the original cabin survives. The stove inside the building was packed down from Battle Creek in 1941 by Ace Barton and Allen Wilson. (The Martin Hibbs' cabin occupied a site about 50 feet northeast of the present cabin.) The barn disintegrating at the top end of the field was constructed by Earl Hibbs and Ben Ashbaugh in 1937.

Livestock used the area until 1976. The ranch was acquired from Bud Wilson through condemnation proceedings by the Forest Service as part of the Hells Canyon National Recreation Area.

Mart Hibbs' homestead entry survey marker can be seen on the north side of the trail coming up from the river. It is chiseled into the flat face of a large granite boulder about 20 feet off the trail in the grove of old yellow pines on the lower end of his acreage.

At the Granite campsite, on the downstream side of the creek, there is a rock and earth enclosure against the bluff. This was a storage depot for black powder. Across the river from the magazine is a basalt overhang known as "Powder Rim." The Bartons kept a gunny sack of dynamite there. Mart Hibbs was somewhat deaf, and when they wanted him to bring the boat across the river they set off a couple of sticks to get his attention.

The trail which follows the river on the Idaho side below lower Granite camp was cut with drills and powder by the Forest Service in 1930. It is known as the "tight squeeze" and required two winters to complete. Ace Duncan, blacksmith and miner (from Mexico to Canada), sharpened the steel for this job and said it was the hardest rock he had ever encountered. The old trail took off round the rim about half a mile up Granite Creek and dropped back down near Granite Rapid. In low water, stock could be moved along the river's edge without resorting to the high trail.

Mile 9.8 **Cache Creek.** This Oregon stream was known as Divide Creek for 40 dozen years before the Forest Service was created. The change was introduced because another tributary downriver carried the same name. The line separating the Battle Creek cattle range from Fred Jensen's Saddle Creek range was just below Cache Creek.

Mile 9.8 **Granite Rapid** is about 400 yards below the "tight squeeze", and can be seen from the trail. It is the second rapid of consequence and should be scouted at any water stage. Depending on the flow, it can be run right or left of the center boulder.

Granite Creek Rapid at 20,000 c.f.s.

Mile 11 **Three Creeks** enters on the Idaho side. There is a short, steep trail below the creek which angles up to a bench about 75 feet above the river. In December of 1899, Frank E. Hiltsley and his wife, Alberta Pike Hiltsley, moved to Three Creeks. They fashioned a 14 by 20-foot log house, which served until Frank could build a frame house of similar size. He cleared stones and trees from five acres and planted the ground to hay which he scythed. Their garden was above the creek, from which water was ditched to irrigate the hay. Hiltsley went into a cattle partnership with his brothers, William and Dave.

Calamity overtook Frank in mid-July of 1912. He was rowing a wooden boat down to Saddle Creek when the craft struck a rock 20 feet from the Idaho shore, about 300 yards below his homestead. The rowboat sank and Hiltsley drowned. Mrs. Hiltsley moved out that fall to homestead Race Creek on Salmon River, but Frank's patent was issued to her in 1915. She sold the place that fall to Martin Hibbs.

Earl Hibbs inherited Three Creeks after his father's death. He sold it, along with Granite Creek, in 1940 to Mrs. Lenora Barton, his sister. Allen Wilson purchased the homestead from her three years later and kept it until 1952, when he conveyed title to George "Bud" Wilson. Wilson sold the acreage to the Forest Service in 1974, under duress.

The house occupied the far end of the field, along with the barn. It was dismantled for the lumber that was transported to Granite Creek. Now some fruit trees, grape vines, and an irrigation ditch are the only reminders of the labors expended here.

Hiltsley's place at Three Creeks in 1915. The barn is on the right. Ralph Barton holding his daughter Hazel. The Bartons wintered here before moving to Johnson Bar.

Mile 11.1 **Two Bars** opposite Three Creeks. Ralph Barton was leading his saddle horse by hand on the "coyote trail" around the bluff 200 feet above Two Bars when his pack horse pulled back and lunged off the ledge to the river, taking the saddle horse with it. It was January and Barton was on his way to Battle Creek to check his cattle. He walked on upriver, inspected the livestock, then went back to Saddle Creek where the Wilsons loaned him another horse.

Mile 11.9 **Dry Gulch** on the right. This drainage was known as Blind Creek. There are mountain goats and sheep in the rims above it. The fence here prevents domesticated sheep from mingling with the Rocky Mountain bighorns.

Jack Hastings in 1902 at his Dry Diggins cabin.

Dry Diggins. Set back about two and a half miles from the river, the pine-dark flanks of Dry Diggins Ridge rise to a peak with an elevation of 7,828 feet. This mountain, on the Idaho side of the river, visible between Dry Gulch and Bernard Creek, is 6,400 feet above the water — the highest point in Hells Canyon. Its name is the result of mining activity by Jack Hastings. He staked claims on the ridge in 1903.

Hasting's father was an English cobbler who emigrated to New England. When Jack was 15 he ran away from home and joined the Union Army. He fought in the Battle of Shiloh, but when his father learned his whereabouts, he followed Jack and demanded his discharge. On their walk back to Massachusetts the son carried a Colt revolver in his waistband. At one point, when they stopped to drink, Jack bent over and the pistol discharged, removing three fingers from his left hand.

At age 17, the young man again left home, prospecting through the south and southwest. He said the Apaches were on the warpath most of the time. Mart Hibbs asked if the Indians ever troubled him. Hastings replied, "No, but I helped bury quite a few that did have trouble with them."

He tumbleweeded into the northwest, then to the mines at Eureka Bar on Snake River, and finally to Dry Diggins. Hastings built a small cabin on the ridge, just big enough for his pole bed, table and chair. It had a shake roof and a stone fireplace.

There were no streams on the Diggins, so each fall the miner constructed earthen dams across several gullies. These dams impounded water from melting snow and gave Jack a means of placer mining along

186

the draws. He could trap the water for multiple sluicings as he worked his way down various arroyos during the spring and summer.

In the fall he would go to town and trade a little coarse gold for warm clothes, then return to Snake River. He wintered on a bar just above and across from the mouth of Saddle Creek. Hastings had a tent pitched behind a large boulder that sheltered his supplies. He panned for gold along the river, ran a trapline, and was available to caretake any canyon ranch while the owner was absent. The ranchers packed supplies for him in return. He rescued boards from the backeddy for firewood. Everyone was fond of the little miner. The Hibbs children remember that he baked clay marbles for them.

At times he wintered in a tent just above the lower field on Granite Creek. He became ill there, and stayed with the Hibbs; but his condition deteriorated. They took him out to Joseph, Oregon, where he died in 1925.

The years have caved in on Jack Hasting's cabin at Dry Diggins Mountain, but the dilapidated remains may still be seen.

The first lookout on Dry Diggins.

Mile 13 **Saddle Creek** on the Oregon side, so called for Freezeout Saddle eight miles up the creek. The trail to Freezeout goes across the divide to the Imnaha.

Families involved with the history of Saddle Creek have kept, like heirlooms, the story of events there. Fred Jensen and Tim McCarty were the first to settle the area, in 1895. Fred homesteaded at the mouth of the creek and Tim chose a bench at the head of Rough Creek, which enters Saddle less than a mile from the river. He spent most of his time at Saddle Creek.

Jensen's cabin was on the north side of the creek, back against the bluff. It was constructed from cottonwood and alder logs. The floor consisted of rounds cut from alder and embedded in the ground like flagstones. Alder pegs were driven into the dirt between the pies. Another room with a fireplace was eventually spliced onto the back.

Pete and Ethel Wilson arrived on the site in 1916. Since they are dominant figures in the saga of Hells Canyon their biographies are recounted here.

Pete was foaled Leonard William Wilson in 1884 at Benson, Arizona. His parents moved to Monument, Oregon, in the Blue Mountains, before he was a year old. Jim and Eliza ran cattle there four years, then moved to Imnaha and seven years later went into the sheep business. Pete was herding stock by the time he got out of three-cornered pants.

At age 15, he was breaking horses and riding range for various stockmen. The young man had a knack for it that was nine-tenths hard work. His father died in 1905, while Pete was running and breaking wild horses in the John Day River country. He returned to the Imnaha to help his older brother with the sheep for three years. On the Fourth of July, 1908, in White Bird, Idaho, Wilson made his rodeo debut, winning the saddle bronc contest and wild horse race. They were the first of many rodeo conquests.

Pete went back to Oregon and began riding for the well-known Miller and Lux Cattle and Land Company, south of Burns. He trailed cattle from Silvies Valley south to Winnemucca, Nevada. Then he drifted on down to Camp Verde, Arizona, and ran wild horses in the Mogollon Mountains of Yavapai County for Walker and Keel. They ran the horses from Camp Verde into Oak Creek Canyon and Tonto Basin, then trailed them up to Flagstaff where they were shipped to Kansas.

While in Arizona, Wilson made a deal to ride for George and Buzz Casner in return for half the unbranded horses he could catch. One morning he jumped a legendary black stallion with its band of mares, and managed to maneuver him into a log corral by a water hole. Pete broke the outlaw stallion and used him as his saddle horse for a year. He sold the animal to a cowboy-rider named Whitie Montgomery for $150 and used part of the money for a boat ride from San Francisco to Portland. The summer of 1911 found him back in Oregon's Harney Valley, riding for the W. W. Bill Brown Horse Shoe Bar outfit which had 11,000 horses and 16,000 sheep on the Wagontire Desert. That fall he met 18-year-old Ethel Belle Couche, the sister of one of his best friends.

Ethel was born on the Texas plains and had done many of the tasks at home because her father's hands were largely disabled. She had been sent to Oregon by a doctor who suspected she was suffering from tuberculosis.

Her health returned and she began to train as a nurse under her sister-in-law, who operated a small hospital in Burns. Student nurses worked at all the chores: milking the hospital's cow, cleaning, cooking, and patient care. Ethel met Pete in Burns; they were married in the fall and moved to his homestead on the eastern side of Wagontire Mountain.

The following summer, Wilson helped drive a herd of 300 wild geldings from Wagontire Mountain to the Sycan Marsh, east of

Pete Wilson (center) at the Klamath Falls rodeo.

Klamath Falls. The men went on to town and entered the Elk's Rodeo. Pete won the saddle bronc contest on a famous bucking horse called "White Pelican," placed first in the wild horse race, took a first in the mule race, and was the only rider able to stay aboard the Loosley Fort's Holstein bull. His performance was the feature of the show and several cattlemen stated he was the best rider they had ever seen. Bronc ridin' over, the men went back to the marsh and saddle broke the 300 horses. That fall, Wilson went to the Pendleton Roundup and competed against another fine rider: Jackson Sundown.

Jim Wilson in 1934.

Pete worked on a friend's ranch near Harney City, Oregon, feeding stock and milking cows for $60 a month. The Wilson's first child, Jimmie, was born in January of 1914. In the spring, Pete and his neighbor took work horses down to the Double O ranch on upper Harney Lake and contracted to cut and stack a thousand tons of hay.

The following spring, the Wilsons sold their homestead, piled their belongings in a farm wagon hitched to a four-horse team, and Pete, with one arm in a cast, drove toward the Imnaha. Ethel followed with a spring wagon carrying little Jimmie and their camp outfit. Pete's brother, George, herded their cattle and extra horses. They settled along the Imnaha River, on a place they purchased from Pete's brother.

During the summer, Pete and his younger brother, Tom, rode down and crossed the Snake to enter the Grangeville rodeo. As usual, Pete won the saddle bronc event and returned home with a prize saddle.

In August, the couple sold out to Clem Marks. They acquired the McCarty cabin at the head of Rough Creek, which runs into Saddle

Ethel Wilson at Saddle Creek.

Creek. Ethel said the cabin was built by Andrew Funk and was "big enough for a bachelor if he left his dog outside." Pete packed 90 horse and mule loads of furniture, implements, groceries and grain to the site. The first winter they received newspapers on New Year's Day; then it snowed and they didn't see another until the 16th of April. Mrs. Wilson didn't encounter another woman for five months.

The Wilsons bought in with Pete's stepfather, Fred Jensen, at the mouth of Saddle Creek in 1916. They quilted a couple of other ranches

Pete Wilson ranch at Saddle Creek in 1923.

onto the spread before Jensen sold out, going back to Arizona. For the next 20 years, the Wilsons were examples of the labor canyon life could demand.

They raised enough children to start a school: Jimmie, Allen, Marjorie, Violet, Charlie, Don and Dan (twins), and Katherine. Sometimes Murrielle McGaffee would teach at the ranch; other times Ethel would winter on the Imnaha so the children could be taught there, and one year Jimmie and Allen (seven and five) rode horseback down to Sluice Creek where they were schooled by Mrs. Winniford.

The Wilsons ran 400 cattle and hayed their fields for supplemental feed because winter ice could make the slopes slick as a scalp. They had a barn on the lower flat down next to the creek. There were high pegs for the saddles and harness since all the Wilson men were taller than doors.

The Jensen cabin burned, but the Wilsons replaced it with a spacious lumber house just south of Jensen's site. They had a large garden: tomatoes, potatoes, carrots, onions, peppers, melons, plus apple, apricot and peach trees. There was a root cellar, storehouse, chicken house and blacksmith shop as well.

In 1917 a telephone line made of twisted-pair wire with rubber insulation was strung by the Forest Service from Silvers Ranger Station on Rapid River to the Seven Devils Station, Dry Diggins, down Bernard

Creek to the McGaffee Ranch, up to the Hibbs Place and across the river to Saddle Creek. This line was used for reporting fires but it also facilitated communication between neighbors. Unfortunately, it was so weak that animals and falling limbs broke it faster than it could be repaired. By 1932, the standard "ground return line" of galvanized wire had replaced the first line. This new line was extended from Saddle Creek to Hat Point and connected with Riggins, Idaho, on the other end. Radio communication has now replaced the telephone wires.

Family reunion at Bernard Creek: left to right, back row, Charles and Allen Wilson, William McGaffee, Violet and Marjorie Wilson, Mable and Gene McGaffee, Ethel and Pete Wilson. Front row, Don Wilson, Fred and George McGaffee, Katherine and Dan Wilson.

A difference sloped between Pete and Ethel in 1937 and they separated. The cattle ranch was sold. Ethel worked in state hospitals at Salem and Pendleton, on a sheep ranch, as a cook for a railroad repair crew, and in the shipyard at Vancouver during World War II. She helped deliver several of her grandchildren. After arthritis confined her to a wheelchair, she ran the telephone office in Riggins until dial phones became common.

Ethel Couche Wilson was always busy as a little dog in tall oats. She was a competent nurse and a loving mother with time and concern for the people around her. On her death, she was buried in Riggins.

After leaving Saddle Creek, Pete Wilson went back to riding for cow outfits in Idaho, Oregon, Montana, and Washington. In the fall of

1948, he took second money bronc riding in the NezPerce, Idaho, rodeo at age 64. He was still riding for the Star Lane Ranch near Santa Ynez, California seven years later.

Pete was employed in 1959 by the C & D Cattle Company in Joseph, Oregon. Its cowboys were riding herd on some 3,000 head of cattle. Mike McFetridge, the foreman, remarked, "If cow sense and horse sense would get a man in the Cowboy Hall of Fame, Pete Wilson should be in there. Handling stock he was always in the right place at the right time."

Pete sacked his saddle in October of 1968, the victim of a heart attack. He was buried in Riggins, Idaho — a Snake River cowboy by anyone's definition.

The Wilson house at Saddle Creek burned in 1939, while Violet and Buster Shirley were living there. The place was acquired by Kenneth Johnson as part of his sheep ranch. With Forest Service purchase, the land returned to the public.

The lower field holds a walking plow, spring tooth harrow, mower, and hay wagon. These implements were disassembled and packed in 13 miles from Imnaha, over Freezeout Saddle. Stained now by time's disfiguring touch, they weather quietly, silenced instruments that once played out the rhythms of the past.

Mile 13.5 **Hat Creek** is the drainage on the left. It has its start on the slopes of the 6,982-foot ridge visible from the river. J. H. Horner asserts the name originated in the 1890's when Alex Warnock's horse began bucking close to the creek and Alex's hat flew off and couldn't be found. Later his stepfather, Jonathan Armintrout, found it and fastened it to a bush where it hung for over a year.

The Forest Service built a 60-foot lookout tower on Hat Point in 1931, and all materials had to be packed up by horse. A road was constructed to the lookout from Joseph and Imnaha by the Civilian Conservation Corps in 1932-1935. In 1948, the old tower was replaced by the present 90-foot fire lookout, which can be seen from the river.

View from Hat Point Lookout.

Mile 13.7 **Smooth Hollow** on the Oregon side. Grass covered hills form the upper reaches of this draw, where Andrew Funk patented a homestead in 1908. Funk raised hogs and Percheron draft horses. How he managed to ride and pack those frying-pan hooved horses in such steep country is more genuine mystery than the pseudo-enigma of Bigfoot. In 1927, Pete Wilson bought Funk's farm.

Mile 13.8 **Bernard Creek** flows in on the Idaho shore. This stream was called Squaw Creek when God was a boy. Since another Snake River confluent carried the same name, the Forest Service commemorated Captain Reuben F. Bernard, an officer active in Idaho's Indian wars, by renaming the creek.

William "Bill" Hiltsley, together with his wife and two children, arrived at the mouth of Bernard Creek in August, 1901. They erected an alder and cottonwood log bunkhouse about ten feet from the location of the present cabin. The Hiltsleys packed some lumber from Imnaha via Saddle Creek, boated it across the river and trailed it down to Squaw Creek. They salvaged driftwood along the river as well.

Left to right: Mr. Bennett, Bill, Frank and Mrs. Hiltsley, and Mr. Johnson (for whom Johnson Bar may have been named).

A second cabin was constructed with boards and batten. Much of its lumber was packed from a sawmill on Rapid River. This is the two-room house, with front and back porch, which occupies the site today. The inside was lined with burlap. Water was ditched out of the creek and flowed past the rear porch. Since the nearby creek could be dangerous in the spring, Mrs. Hiltsley built a wire pen in front of the house to keep her children from straying. The log bunkhouse was converted to a saddle shed.

Bill cleared about seven acres and set out an impressive orchard that included apricots, peaches, cherries, apples, walnuts, plums and pears. He irrigated an acre of garden and a berry patch, too. They had several horses, a couple of dozen steers and nearly a hundred chickens. Their homestead patent was approved in 1909.

Bill's brothers had followed him into the canyon, but Dave left Granite Creek and Frank drowned below Three Creeks. Bill and his wife decided to sell the place in 1915 to Alfred and Iphigenia McGaffee.

Fred and Gene McGaffee.

Fred McGaffee was born in northern California, but moved with his parents to Grangeville, Idaho, in 1883, while still a young boy. Fred took a homestead on Slate Creek, a tributary of Salmon River, but sold that land in 1915. He had met and married a young New Meadows, Idaho, school teacher, Iphigenia "Gene" McCorey. Gene was the youngest of a large family, raised on Craig Mountain. She had two children by

197

a previous marriage, Katherine and Charlie Gordon. Among other abilities, she had a fine hand with horses.

After selling his homestead, Fred and Gene were in the market for a new place. They went into the Snake River canyon to look at the Hiltsley ranch on Bernard Creek. In recalling this trip, Gene mentioned she had only one spur, so going upriver she put it on her right foot (outside), and coming back she put it on her left. They bought the place, with Fred's brother Billy as a partner. But Billy kept his job at Tom Pogue's store in Riggins, Idaho, to help support the place until it could be fully stocked with cattle.

Fred and Gene moved to the river in February. They had a few purebred cows and sold bull calves for their cash the first few years. The opportunity came to buy a good herd of "grade" cows; from that time on they sold steers. Fred knew how to manage stock and more than once his cattle topped the market in Portland. On one occasion top price was five cents a pound!

Summer range was on Dry Diggins, but McGaffee's cow camp was on a ridge just below the Diggins — they said it was about six miles down the creek to the ranch from there and 16 miles back up. Fred built a cabin and some log corrals by the spring at the camp. The couple spent much of the summer there, going down to the ranch, where it was hotter than a burnt boot, just long enough to water the orchard and hay fields and put up the ripe fruit. Some years they would have a cow who gave a little more milk than her calf really needed, so she would be kept around camp for a month as a source of fresh cream and butter. But the calf's needs came first, and if feed got short the cow was driven up on the Diggins with the others, and the family went back to using canned milk.

The McGaffee cow camp.

198

When the McGaffees moved into the Hiltsley cabin, Billy tore the burlap out of the interior and pasted old magazine pages over the boards to give a more pleasant light — Hells Canyon wallpaper. He removed the ceiling from a cabin down at Bills Creek and packed the lumber to Bernard Creek. The boards were used to make an attic floor in the two-room cabin, thus creating a storage area and spare bedroom. The house interior was always clean, and hop vines around the porch lent a welcome exterior shade.

Fred's father, John McGaffee, came down to the canyon for a visit in 1924, when he was 80-years-old. He spent the winter helping Si Bullock construct the root cellar behind the cabin. Fred brought in the trees, planks, and stone for the project. Bullock did the rock work and Mr. McGaffee built the framework for roof and door and made the bins and shelves, as well. He left by boat from Johnson Bar at the end of his stay.

A pole barn covered with pine shakes was built on the little flat at the edge of the creek just below the field. It was placed against the slope so that hay could be forked into the mow with greater ease.

Fred had a blacksmith shop adjacent to the saddle shed, containing a forge and anvil. He made repairs on what machinery they owned and shod his own horses.

He was a competent animal doctor and a proficient packer. Billy and Mabel McGaffee boated a Monarch stove upriver in 1927. It had to be packed to Bernard Creek from Johnson Bar. The stove proved to be the only load that ever baffled Fred — it had such a heavy fuel box it couldn't be balanced on a horse. They had to make a travois with poles, and while Billy led the animal, Fred guided the rear of the load around curves in the trail. The stove that was dragged six miles in this manner still sits in the cabin. Hopefully, no one with a power boat will attempt to steal it.

Among the luxuries at Bernard Creek was a small sewing machine which Gene owned. It, too, was brought in on the back of a horse. The machine was powered by a hand crank, and in the evening Fred would often furnish the power while Gene steered the fabric. They made clothes and quilts in this way.

Medical problems were frequently self-solved. Gene said the hardest thing she ever had to do was cut a sturgeon hook out of her husband's hand. A doctor did ride in from Pittsburg once, to help Gene when she suffered a gallstone attack.

Fred McGaffee packing furniture to Sheep Creek in 1927.

Although the area between the Salmon and the Snake where the McGaffees lived was part of the State Black Lake Game Preserve, they discretely butchered a deer or grouse when necessary. No meat was wasted. If killed in the summertime, what venison couldn't be eaten was canned or shared with neighbors. It was customary to air meat at night after the flies were gone and sack it at dawn, before storing it in a cool, dark place. Cut into pieces, and placed in lard buckets in the creek, it could usually be kept for a week. An amusing story was related by George Behean at the Pittsburg ranch. A little girl saw a cowboy kill a deer near the house and she was repeatedly cautioned against mentioning the incident. After all evidence of the violation had been cleaned up, a Forest Service employee stopped by. The Forest Service men doubled as game wardens. The little girl, wanting to visit, said to the Forest Service officer, "Do you know what we did this morning? We . . . ." then stopped, realizing her mistake, and finished, "Oh no, we didn't kill no deer this morning!" Behean laughed, while the forester pretended not to understand.

Sturgeon, salmon and trout were caught from river and creek. Huckleberries were gathered in the mountains and blackberries at Granite Creek. Staples such as flour, sugar, coffee, and tobacco were brought upriver by boat from Lewiston in the spring and fall.

Lenora Barton traded the McGaffees her Imnaha ranch for the Bernard and Sheep Creek places in 1935. Her son, Ace, packed cabinets to the house, and brought the wagon and Champion mower up from Sheep Creek. He even plowed the field once, despite all the rocks. Mrs.

Barton sold the place to George "Bud" Wilson in 1952, and he surrendered the property to the Forest Service in a condemnation proceeding, so it is now federal land.

A contemporary view of the McGaffee cabin at Bernard Creek. Powerboaters, running a winter trapline in 1979, burned the front porch for firewood.

Mile 14.5 **Marks Creek** drainage on the left, takes its name from Alfred Marks, who patented a homestead in the basin above the river in 1909, and ran cattle there with his brother until they sold out to Pete Wilson in 1918.

Mile 15.3 **Waterspout Creek and Rapid.** This stream enters the river from the Oregon side. A waterspout is a tornado occurring over water which becomes a tubelike column of air carrying spray. But in parts of the west, the word describes a summer flashflood, usually in a narrow canyon. The creek was named by Grady Miller who witnessed such an incident here. Waterspout Rapid has impressive waves in high water, but the run is obvious to anyone who has gotten this far.

On the Idaho side of the river, about 300 yards above the rapid, there are some interesting potholes alongside the trail. Cobbles and silt, set whirling by pre-dam high water, bored them into the rock.

Mile 15.9 Bills Creek on the Idaho side. Bert Weinheimer was the first white man to live on the bench below this creek. He was here in 1905, and filed for a homestead, but withdrew the application six years later. Bert had packed for the mines at Eureka Bar with Mart Hibbs, and ran horses from Oregon into Idaho. He planted an acre of the bench in alfalfa and built a cabin so small even the mice must have been hunchbacked.

201

The man whose name is better remembered in connection with Bills Creek was Si Bullock. Murrielle McGaffee Wilson, who knew him, as did her parents, contributed the cordial sketch which follows:

Silas Bullock came to the Snake River canyon in the spring of 1912, looking for better health. He was a brick layer, and a good one, but he developed asthma which grew worse. It became all but impossible for him to work. He tried various communities at different elevations, but it was all the same. Finally someone suggested the Canyon. Perhaps the summer heat there would help.

He borrowed a horse and rode down Saddle Creek, since he was an Oregon resident. He visited the various ranchers, 'riding the grub line' as they used to say. Most of the people he visited were enthusiastically 'proving up' on land, homesteading. It occurred to him, that even if he could not work at his trade, he could spend three years and have something to show for his time.

He chose Bills Creek, a very small stream, coming from a spring not so high up on the mountain. Beside the creek were two long flat bars, admirable farm land, except for the rocks, which almost covered them. Bills Creek did not offer enough water to irrigate, but bunch grass and hackberries covered the flats, making good pasture.

Si went back with his borrowed horse, and bought a young bay mare that he named Maude. He arranged with Fred Jensen to pack in some belongings, a tent, tools, a little food. Jensen put it across the river, and Hibbs packed it down the river to Bills Creek. So began a fifteen year interval in a man's life.

He set up his tent, and began to clear a spot for a garden. The rocks he removed were set up for a fence. That first spring he planted onions, beans, potatoes, corn and watermelons. He was to find that the warm water from his short creek made his garden a good spot for watermelons, and he packed them to his neighbors with great pride.

Once he had a little garden growing he turned his attention to a permanent shelter. Rocks were plentiful, so he planned to build from rocks — he chipped them so that they fitted like bricks. He built a rectangle about 12 by 20 with walls two feet thick. The floor was dirt. He left apertures for windows on three sides, and space for a door. On the fourth side he constructed a fireplace. He had discovered a big eddy in the river just upstream from his house. This was his lumberyard. There was flotsam deposited from years of high water. He found boards of all sizes, plus trees eddied out for firewood. He framed his doors and windows, then shuttered the glassless windows for winter.

Si Bullock with a sturgeon at Bills Creek.

Not far from his cabin site stood one lone white pine. Like most men his age he knew how to make shakes. This pine tree became his roof. By the time cold weather arrived he was snug and warm. Early in the winter he spent days and days dragging logs from the eddy with Maude and cutting them for firewood. Then he borrowed some traps from his neighbors and during the coldest months he ran a short trap line. The mink, marten and muskrat he captured were his dollars for those things he could not make or raise — flour, pipe tobacco and clothes. He was always available to look after his neighbor's dogs and cats, or irrigate their fields while they took a brief vacation outside. In return, since money was scarce with all, they did his packing, or paid him with canned fruit.

He soon discovered he had the best sturgeon hole in the river, and would put out a 'set line' tied to a stake on the sandbar. When he had a sturgeon he would share with his nearest neighbors. They in turn shared with him when they got a deer, or sturgeon. In summer he could shoot a grouse, almost anytime, close to his cabin. But best of all, he was free of asthma. Never once did a fit of this choking ailment visit him.

Gradually he improved his cabin. First, a floor was made from the bridge timbers that a raging river had swept down to Si's eddy. Sometimes he dragged the lumber up with a rope from Maude's saddle horn. Sometimes he packed it with a wonderful squaw hitch.

Once he had the floor in, he turned his attention to a ceiling, which would reduce the amount of wood needed to heat his little cabin. It also gave him storage room in a low attic, so he nailed a ladder at the back of his room, leading to a trap door. Here he could store his dried corn and beans in coffee cans, or fruit jars, safe from mice. He never had a dog, but always an old gray tomcat. Every rancher had to have a cat, else the rats and mice would have put him out of business. He had gradually built his furniture: a chair, a table, a bed. He saved cornshucks for a mattress after the first year. Gene McGaffee made him a tick to put the cornshucks in when she moved to the river.

When the McGaffees moved to the Squaw Creek ranch (renamed Bernard Creek), which was about two-and-a-half miles upriver, they were happy to continue the trading of work with Si. And when they bought the Brown cattle to increase their herd, Si bought one of the heifers. She ran with the McGaffee cattle, was bred to their bulls, and in return, late in the winter, some years, the McGaffee cattle could graze on the Bills Creek flats. Then each year there was a

Silas Bullock's stone house at the mouth of Bills Creek.

two-year-old to sell. If it was a heifer, McGaffee bought it to add to his growing herd; if a steer, it was taken to market with the McGaffee steers. But Si had his own brand, and the calf was so marked. Even though a two-year-old steer didn't bring much, it still gave Si a larger income, and with his few furs, he did very well. Eventually he bought a small cook-stove from Montgomery Ward, which used less wood and gave as much heat as the fireplace, and bricked off his fire-place. He also bought small glass panes for his three window openings.

Si was not a big man, rather short and tubby in build. He wore a full beard, which was curly and brown, streaked with gray, as was his hair. He had a great sense of humor, and twinkly eyes. He would tell of the size of his watermelons, and if Gene McGaffee would brag of a bigger one, he would tell her in mock humility, 'You must remember Mrs. Mc, I told my story first.' She recognized this as his joke, but she wished just once he would admit she had grown the biggest melon.

In the summertime, travel almost ceased along the river. The ranchers were 'on top' with the cattle in their summer pasture. They returned to the river only to irrigate and can fruit, then back to their cooler cabins high in the mountains. Si wore only his long-handled underwear and shoes during this time. His hair grew long and curled at his neck. One year the railroad companies sent a young engineer up the river to look for a site for a railroad track. Ken Taylor was not really familiar with horses, and when his horse grew lame, as they approached Bills Creek, he just got off and led the limping horse. When he came in sight of Si's cabin, Si came out with a shotgun in one hand, and a huge butcherknife in the other. He greeted Ken, 'You're just the guy I'm looking for.' Ken said later that he was outright terrified, thinking Si was a lunatic, but to keep the peace, he asked how he could help.

'Get on your horse and follow me.'

'My horse is lame, and can't carry me.'

Si examined the bad foot, found the shoe was loose enough to let a small pebble get between the shoe and hoof. Setting his knife and gun down, he went to the cabin for his horseshoeing outfit, picked the gravel out, and tightened the shoe again. The horse was as good as new.

Again he ordered 'Follow me,' as he picked up gun and knife and started down a little trail to the river sandbar, where a rope was tied to a stake driven in the sand. Now Ken had never heard of sturgeon — he did not know there were any freshwater fish of such size. The problem was Si had caught one too big to pull in by hand, and he did not want to go and hunt Maude in her big pasture. He tied the rope on Ken's saddle horn, then told him to ride back up the trail. At first the rope followed easily enough, then as the fish neared shallow water, it tightened across Ken's leg, and when he looked back to see a seven-foot sturgeon, wildly thrashing in an attempt to stay in the water, he was amazed. He later said 'I decided I was the one that was crazy, not Si.'

Once the fish was on the sand, Si shot it in the head with his gun, then with Ken's help, he butchered and dressed out this huge fish. Ken stayed for a lunch of fried sturgeon, then carried the word on to the McGaffee ranch, and that evening Fred was down with a packhorse to take what Si couldn't use, to share with the neighbors. The next morning, Si was up early to can a part of the fish for winter use. He would boil it in fruit jars, in a wash boiler for 4 hours, and when cool it would be tucked away in his little rock cellar. All he could eat fresh would be placed in ten-pound lard buckets, sliced ready for frying, and salted lightly. The buckets were placed in the creek, in a shaded spot, and weighted down with rocks. The fish would keep this way for two or three days.

One year he thought he would keep his cow during strawberry season, so he could have a little cream to go with his berries, but it involved building a pen to keep the calf away from the cow during the night, and then when the pasture turned dry with summer's heat, he alone would have to drive her and the calf to the summer pasture, so he gave up that project. Besides he was used to canned milk.

He took great pride in his strawberry patch, and in May lived almost exclusively on the berries.

He held housekeeping chores to a minimum, and even caring for his garden and berries did not take a lot of time. During the hot summer afternoons, he would sit in the shade near the creek and read. He collected all magazines and books the neighbors could spare, and read them avidly. All the cast-off magazines were stored in his attic, and were often reread when he ran out of new material. Once or twice during the summer he would arise at daybreak and ride slowly up Squaw Creek to the McGaffee cow camp to visit a day or two, then journey across Dry Diggins to the Hibbs Cow camp, spend a day or two with them, come down Granite Creek to their ranch, and so down the river again, to his own little domicile. The garden would be sadly in need of water, and as soon as Maude was unsaddled, he would turn the water in, greet his cat, who had fared very well in his absence, but welcomed his company and a dish of canned milk for a treat.

In the spring of 1926 two female cousins from California with whom Si had been corresponding for some time, decided to pay him a visit. They drove to Lewiston, rode the boat to Sheep Creek, and walked the three miles to Bills Creek. Fred McGaffee offered to loan them horses, but after a look at the trail, they thanked him, and forcefully refused. Si came down to meet them with Maude. McGaffees loaned some bedding, and a pack horse to carry it, and his extra groceries. The cousins stayed a week. Apparently they had a good time, as the following spring they came again. But this time they were determined that Si should move to California. They had been writing, urging this all winter.

So suddenly Si's life on the Snake River was over. He sold his one cow and horse to the McGaffees, along with his half a homestead, which he had long since proved up on. He left with his cousins, going down river on the boat, taking only his bedroll and a few clothes.

After a short time in California, he wrote that he had gone back to laying bricks. There was a shortage of bricklayers there, and he was much in demand. After a year he hired his own crew and was contracting brick-laying, amazed at how much money he was making. And then one day, only a little over two years after he left Snake River, he died on the job, from a heart attack.

The cat moved to Sheep Creek to continue his mice patrol for the McGaffees when there was no longer any need for him to protect the Bills Creek cabin.

As mentioned earlier, the ceiling from Bullock's cabin was taken for the McGaffee house at Bernard Creek. An example of the mason's stone work can be seen in what remains of the walls that constituted his dwelling. They stand on the river side of the trail that passes through his field. The other rock structure along the path is what survives of Si's cow corral. His garden was about 50 feet downriver from the house.

Mile 16.5 **Winehammer Gulch** on the right. Bert Weinheimer's name was simply misspelled on the U.S.G.S. map.

Mile 17.3 **Sluice Creek** twists down from the Oregon side of the river. The name is believed to result from some sluice boxes found by the first stockmen on the stream. It is among the oldest ranching areas in the canyon.

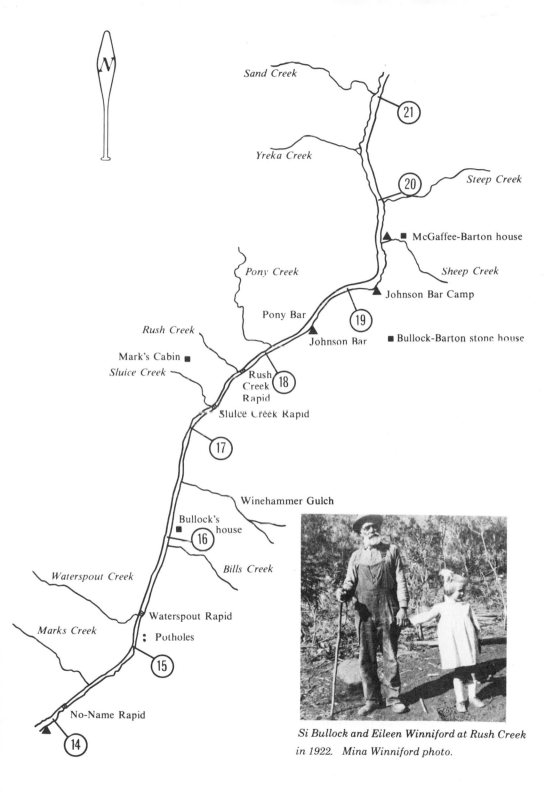

N

Sand Creek

21

Yreka Creek

20

Steep Creek

▲ ■ McGaffee-Barton house

Pony Creek

Sheep Creek

▲ Johnson Bar Camp

Pony Bar

19

Rush Creek

▲ Johnson Bar

■ Bullock-Barton stone house

Mark's Cabin ■

Sluice Creek

Rush
Creek
Rapid

18

Sluice Creek Rapid

17

Winehammer Gulch

Bullock's
house

16

Bills Creek

Waterspout Creek

Waterspout Rapid

Marks Creek

⫶ Potholes

15

No-Name Rapid

14

*Si Bullock and Eileen Winniford at Rush Creek
in 1922. Mina Winniford photo.*

209

Alex Warnock had a cow camp on Sluice Creek in the early 1880's, according to Kit Warnock. They had a dugout cabin cut into the bank, logged up on three sides, with a rear rock wall that encompassed a fireplace. There was a sod-covered pole roof which one could walk onto from the embankment.

One evening Alex, Bob, and Kit rode up to the cabin and found the door ajar. No one had been there for several months, and Alex went in to check for rattlesnakes — a customary Snake River precaution. He was startled to find a mountain lion in the room. Alex stepped back, closing the door, and told Kit and Bob what he had seen. They persuaded him to have some fun, rather than shoot it. There were half a dozen cow dogs along, and Kit got up on the roof while the men handed him dogs to tamp down the chimney. After the fourth dog was dropped through the smoke hole, Kit said the chimney began spewing dogs like a volcano, followed by the cat itself, which dashed up the creek faster than hell could scorch a feather.

The winter of 1886-87 was so severe that it became the one against which all other western winters were measured. Two feet of snow windrowed the ground along the river. Though the men cut willow and cuttonwood trees on Sluice and Rush Creek in order to give the cattle some browse, they still lost half their stock. The Warnocks shared the range after George Denny moved in around 1889.

Denny worked out a cattle raising agreement with Clem Marks, son of Ben Marks, who lived on the Imnaha.

The Marks brothers, Clem, Jake, Charlie, and Alfred ran sheep and cattle in the area during the early 1900's. In 1909, Clem patented his homestead entry on the creek. The Marks dragged fir and alder logs four miles down to the flat, located about a quarter mile above the river. These were used to make twin cabins which faced each other beneath a common roofed entryway. They still occupy the site close to the creek, shaded by a grove of black locusts that were planted in 1918 by the Winniford family.

The Marks sold their interests to the Winniford brothers: William, Walter, and John Franklin. Billy and his wife Stella lived at Sluice Creek, Walt was at Rush Creek, and John had a place on Homestead Ridge between Pony and Yreka Creeks downriver.

The Winnifords put a second roof over the twin cabins which made them cooler in summer and warmer in winter. Water was ditched from the creek to irrigate the fields, where alfalfa was grown.

The Marks/Winniford cabin as it looks today.

Billy and Stella Winniford on their 50th wedding anniversary.

The Winniford men were from Oregon, and all three married school teachers. Billy and Stella Winniford had four daughters. Stella taught school in a walled tent at the creek in 1922; two of the Wilson boys from Saddle Creek were students, along with six Winniford children.

211

The winter of 1918-1919 was colder than frog legs — its disastrous effects on livestock and game were compared with the winter of 1886-87. Then after World War I, livestock depression struck in 1922-23. Billy and Stella moved out of the canyon in March of 1924, and it was eventually acquired by the Johnson sheep outfit.

When the Wisenors ran sheep in the Sluice Creek country their summer range was around Quartzite Butte and Bull Creek on Salmon River. Looking downriver from the flat at Sluice Creek, one can see the Snake River Divide on the Idaho side. The sheepmen would trail their bands down to the ferry at Pittsburg Landing, cross the river and ride over to the ferry crossing at White Bird on the Salmon, then travel by way of Grangeville to the Bull Creek drainage. On the way back, they would leave their spring lambs at the railhead in Grangeville and trail the ewes back to Snake River canyon for the winter.

Sluice Creek Rapid is not considered difficult by boaters and can be read from the river.

Mile 17.7 **Rush Creek** streams in from the Oregon shore. Walter and Mina Winniford had a log cabin at Rush Creek from 1920 to 1924. They had homesteaded at Pony Bar, a mile downriver, but creek water proved unreliable, so Walt took the cabin apart, log by log, and reassembled it at Rush Creek.

The couple had five children. Walt had been a teacher in the Willamette Valley for several years, before moving to Snake River. Mina taught school in her house during the spring and fall, and Walt would take a turn when activities were slow in the winter. Jim and Allen Wilson rode down by mule, stayed during the week, and returned home for the weekends. One year there were a dozen students, aged four to ten.

The Winnifords left in the spring of 1924 and the cabin remained until 1948 when it caught fire during the lambing season.

Rush Creek contains a serious hole at the head of the rapid. There is ample room to avoid it on the right.

There is a bench with a spring up the north fork of Rush Creek. A cabin was built there by Walt Brockman. The site is known as Dead Failure because his Grazing Homestead application was disallowed by the Forest Service. During the protracted winter of 1918-19, Gene McGaffee's son, Charlie Gordon, used the cabin while running a trap line.

In mid-December, Billy Winniford stopped overnight at the cabin but found no sign of Charlie. There were dishes on the table but only a little coffee and three frozen potatoes on the shelf. He went down to the Wilson ranch at Saddle Creek and then he, Pete Wilson, and Jack Titus decided to conduct a search. They called across the river to Fred McGaffee to tell him of their concern, though he couldn't cross the water because it was running ice. They covered the snowy slopes without finding any clues.

With the coming of spring, another effort was mounted. This time Charles was found, by Milt Hibbs, sitting against a tree where he had frozen with his rifle across his knees. Half a deer was hanging in the tree. The men buried him there and erected a small pole corral around the grave. It is located by the trail, a quarter mile north of the south fork of Rush Creek.

Mile 18.5 **Pony Bar** on the left. This bar was homesteaded by Walt Winniford, his wife and two daughters in 1913, before he moved to Rush Creek. His brother, John, was district ranger for the Forest Service on the Oregon side of Snake River from 1911 to 1918. He then quit to ranch with his brothers. He took over the Homestead Ridge place, north of the bar, and got his water from a spring at the head of Pony Creek. Eventually he had to dig a well by the spring at the head of Yreka Creek downriver.

Mile 19.3 **Johnson Bar** and camp, with a small beach on the Idaho side. This bar, which extends upriver from the campground, is the stopping point for Army Corps of Engineer's navigation markers. It also represents the traditional end of the Snake River mail route.

Johnson Bar was probably named after Johnny Johnston, who placer mined the site with a rocker in the early 1900's. Johnston lived in a rock-walled dugout near the north end of the bar during his stay.

Frank Johnesse, a mining entrepreneur, was aware of the bar in 1910, while working on the Blue Jacket mine in the Seven Devils. But there was not sufficient interest to attract a homesteader to the location until word of the Union Pacific railroad survey began to circulate. Then Johnson Bar became a desirable piece of real estate because it was one of the most extensive flats on the river between the Red Ledge mine and Pittsburg Landing. Johnesee filed on it in October of 1911, requesting that it be opened for entry.

Ralph Barton became interested in the property and wrote Johnesse about it. Frank replied that it was a valuable piece of land if the railroad materialized. During the next couple of years, five other men requested applications. Johnesse had not done anything with his application, but he had a "60-day preference right" to file for homestead entry.

After talking with Johnesse in person, Barton gave him $200 for his entry right. When the preference expired, Ralph made entry on the bar in 1914. That winter, with the assistance of Si Bullock's talents, a rock and mortar house was constructed on the flat, rumped against the hill. It was 12 feet by 14, with an unusual corner fireplace and a sod roof. Ralph, his wife Lenora, and their baby daughter, Hazel, moved into their new home in February of 1915.

The first house on Johnson Bar built in 1915 by Barton and Bullock.

The Bartons constructed some fences, planted a garden, and built a rock corral — rocks were thicker than meadow muffins on Johnson Bar. Ralph helped McLeod farm Sheep Creek, the next stream downriver, and considered fluming water five miles from that creek to Johnson Bar. He built the cabin at "Old Timer" during the summer, then moved to Grouse Creek on the Imnaha in the fall. In 1916, he relinquished his homestead entry right to Glenn Hibbs, Lenora's brother.

Glenn and his wife proved up on the bar, building a one-and-a-half story frame house with a "lean-to" kitchen. The lumber was boated upriver on the *Prospector*. Hibbs had 20 acres in dryland rye hay, and grazed over 200 head of cattle and 30 horses.

Glenn sold out to his father, Mart Hibbs, in the 1920's and left to run a ranch in Nevada, where he was killed.

Johnson Bar in the spring of 1915.

In 1935, Ralph and Mary Stickney and their sons inherited the property. Mary was one of Mart's daughters. They ran cattle for a couple of years, before switching to sheep. Stickney worked many years for the Dobbins and Huffman sheep outfit on the lower river. Their sheep were wintered on Johnson Bar. The Stickneys sold the land to Lenora Barton in 1942, after she had acquired Sheep Creek. Bud Wilson purchased the location from her ten years later, and he was eventually bought out by the Forest Service.

The Barton/Bullock cabin at present.

The ruins of the Barton-Bullock stone house can still be found on the bar, as well as the cellar hole for Glenn's house. The ancient Adriance Buckeye mower with chain drive, rusting in the field, belonged to Glenn Hibbs.

Incidentally, the Johnson Bar boat landing at the lower end of the bar had half-an-acre of sand before Idaho Power built its dams.

The silver cylinder on the bank across the river from Johnson Bar camp is a U.S.G.S. water level gage which automatically transmits flow information to Lewiston.

Mile 19.6 **Sheep Creek** trails out to the river on the Idaho shore. William McLeod, a Scotsman and Civil War veteran, followed his friend George Reid into the Snake River country and selected the bench at Sheep Creek for his homestead in the spring of 1884. He made an excavation in the streambank, just a short distance above the mouth of the creek, on the north side, which is still visible. McLeod's stone cabin was recessed there, with shake roof, rock fireplace and dirt floor. Over the years, he managed to clear about four-and-a-half acres, though he didn't file on his claim until 1913 and received his title two years later. He had a few cattle and a couple of horses.

In 1888, McLeod traded a rowboat to the Warnocks, across the river, for a sow and boar. He released the hogs up Sheep Creek and they soon went feral. The offspring were wilder than their parents. A wild boar disturbed in his lair in uglier than galvanized sin. Before long, travelers began complaining to McLeod. The prospect of riding up Sheep Creek was enough to turn a man's guts to fiddle strings. After Jim Clark was treed, McLeod finally appealed to the Warnocks to help him round up the porkers.

Alex, Dan, and Kit Warnock swam their horses and cow dogs across the river. They were joined by several other men and rode up to the mouth of Lightning Creek and up Clarks Fork. The Big Hog Roundup began. They headed downhill, with an avalanche of sound: whoops, yells, and barking dogs. When they arrived at McLeod's there were two dogs dead and three horses crippled — but they had killed enough hogs to feel it was worthwhile. Kit said some of the boars had six-inch tusks.

Bill's rock house held a table, a straw tick, a wooden bench, and a large iron pot that hung in the fireplace. He did most of his cooking in this pot, making a mulligan of onions, potatoes, carrots, rutabagas and dried sturgeon. He would ladle the stew into wooden bowls for his guests. The pot was never washed. When the stew got down to a critical level, he would add the same ingredients again.

McLeod dried sturgeon on willow sticks in his fireplace. Sometimes fish oil would drip on the floor until it ran out the door.

He had a sturdy pole barn covered with shakes. Peach and apple trees provided fruit. Bill made just enough gumboot juice to ward off the "chills" — with a little left over to share with friends. Mart Hibbs said it was pretty good stuff after you strained the flies and yellow jackets out of it. A friend, Ed Fisher, came by and talked about the possibility of getting a small still — that would produce just enough for home consumption, of course. McLeod's still was up on the rim past the first ridge behind Sheep Creek. He had heard there might be a revenue agent in the area, so he sold his rig to Ed. Fisher packed it in pieces on his back all the way to Steamboat Creek (above Hells Canyon Dam).

Bill McLeod was a good neighbor. One evening, Jim Clark, who lived up Sheep Creek on Clarks Fork, came down saying he was very sick. Bill was convinced from Clark's appearance, but he couldn't diagnose or alleviate the ailment. He saddled his black mare, Bess, rode downriver 16 miles to Pittsburg and another 16 miles out to White Bird where he aroused Dr. Foskett. The two arrived back at Sheep Creek early in the morning — a 64-mile round trip.

Dr. Foskett found that Clark's trouble was caused by an impediment in his intestines. The situation demanded an immediate operation.

The cabin's interior was dark as the inside of a cow because there were no windows. Bill cleared his table and Doc lighted an oil lamp. The lighting was still insufficient, so Foskett had McLeod cut a hole in the roof about the size of the table.

The doctor performed the surgery successfully and remained another day, before leaving Bill in charge. Bill nursed Clark back to health. The amusing aftermath of this story is that McLeod never got around to repairing his skylight. He didn't seem to mind the weather falling on his table; perhaps he enjoyed the moon as a chandelier.

Age made its inevitable wintry push against Bill McLeod. He suffered burns in a fire at his cabin. Taken out to Riggins, it became apparent that he could not return to the canyon. Mrs. Holbrook cared for him until his death.

The county sold his place on Snake River and it was purchased by Fred and Billy McGaffee. Since Fred and Gene already had their hands full with the ranch at Bernard Creek, Billy and his wife Mable, and their young daughter, Murielle, moved to the river at Sheep Creek.

Mable Holcombe McGaffee was born in Wisconsin, in 1879. She

taught school for a few years there; then came west. In Idaho, she taught at Slate Creek and on the Doumecq Plains before she married Billy. They settled in White Bird, where he freighted for the Salmon River Stores. He managed one of the company stores in Lucile, and another in Riggins for a dozen years. With the acquisition of the McLeod ranch, the couple and child left the mercantile business for ranch life in Hells Canyon.

Billy and Fred McGaffee had lumber boated to Sheep Creek and constructed a house which occupies the site at present. The brothers also had the mail boat haul tin upriver to sheet a pole barn they erected. McLeod's cabin was converted to a blacksmith shop. Billy was the builder and farmer, while Fred concentrated on the stock, but obviously much of the work was shared.

Mable was never comfortable with horses; she was an avid gardener and preserved their food production for the winter. She studied Spanish in her spare time.

Bill and Mabel McGaffee at White Bird six months before the birth of their daughter.

Sheep Creek as it looked in 1925.

Their daughter, Murielle, went to school in Riggins during the winter. She attended high school at Clarkston, Washington, and advanced to teacher training at Lewiston Normal School. Then she returned to teach in the canyon, at Saddle Creek and Kirkwood Bar. She had certificates for Oregon and Idaho.

Murielle gave this account of her trip for instruction materials to be used at Saddle Creek:

In August of 1933, Marjorie Wilson (14 years old) and I went to Pittsburg Landing to get the school books and materials. I had long looked across at that straight ridge on the skyline and wondered if it was as straight as it looked, but this was my first chance to ride it. We went up to Hat Point the first night, delivering a watermelon and other fresh fruit to Jim Wilson who was on the lookout. Next morning we rode to Mormon Lookout, where Lawrence Potter and his wife were stationed, and delivered the rest of our mule-load of fresh produce. The following morning we went down the hill to Pittsburg and loaded our pack mule with one globe, an unabridged dictionary, a blackboard cloth (which we folded together), erasers, chalk, and various books. Neither of us

219

had learned to throw the diamond hitch, each supposing the other had this handy information. Well, we threw a squaw hitch, and threw a squaw hitch, again and again. We weren't very proud of our pack at the time, but since the globe turned and the dictionary squirmed, I'm not so sure we didn't do pretty well. Anyway, we made it to the Kirkwood ranch to have supper and stay the night with Ms. Anna Maxwell, and then home the next day.

Murielle McGaffee married Jim Wilson a couple of years later — the two had shared a canyon childhood.

Left to right: Murielle and Gene McGaffee in the fall, 1930, at Sheep Creek.

The McGaffees traded ranches with Lenora Barton in the spring of 1935. Billy and Mable moved to Lenora's place on the Imnaha. While Mabel had enjoyed aspects of Snake River life, she was pleased with the switch. There was a rough road to the Imnaha ranch and a car to travel it with.

Lenora Hibbs Barton was a woman of unhaltered ability who could be kind as the Samaritan and as salty as Lot's wife. She could ride anything with four legs and a tail. Lenora hopscotched Sheep Creek, Johnson Bar and Bernard Creek into one large cattle operation, with most of the grazing land under permit on National Forests.

Christmas, 1932, at Sheep Creek: left to right: Dick Maxwell, Len Jordan, Billy McGaffee, Murielle McGaffee, Fred and Gene McGaffee and grandson, and Herman and Mrs. Trappier.

Her son, Ace, rebuilt the two-bedroom house at Sheep Creek. (A pitcher pump provided water at the kitchen sink.) He had a Pelton wheel in the creek to charge wet cell batteries. The cellar was added after World War II. The house had a washing machine, a phonograph to play classical music, and a library, which included the complete works of Dickens, shelved in the front room.

The McGaffee barn collapsed, and Ace skidded rafter poles down from the point above Johnson Bar for a new barn. The Bartons usually got four cuttings of hay off their field and put up about 35 tons each year.

The huge rock between the shop and the barn fell from the bluff behind the barn one night. It raised nearly as much dust as the startled horses.

The pieces of iron between the barn and the river are part of a Model T Ford that was brought upriver on a boat. It was used for chores, particularly for sawing wood. This car was intact in 1952, but power boat operators and tourists over the years have carried off all but the chassis.

On November 7, 1952, Ace Barton loaded three pack horses, belted on pistol and chaps, hung the two house cats in gunny sacks on his saddle horn, went over and closed the door to the house, mounted his horse and called his dog. He took the lead rope, turned through the gate and never looked back. The sun had dropped behind the Oregon rim and the flame-edged cliffs rose in front of him. Ace had a heavy heart and a knot in his gut as he rode down the trail. After 17 years, Lenora

Barton had sold out to Bud Wilson. The Forest Service would eventually obtain the land from Bud for the National Recreation Area.

A fascinating, if insignificant, story concerning Lenora Barton's sheep dog "Spike" can be appended to the history of Sheep Creek. Lenora left her saddle and Spike with Johnny Carrey one fall on Rapid River, across the divide from Snake River. She intended to winter in Lewiston and told Johnny the animal would stay with her saddle.

The little Australian shepherd remained with Carrey until the first of April. Then it howled all night, and in the morning Johnny found it was gone. He followed the dog's tracks up to the snow line and then figured it was headed for Sheep Creek, 25 miles across the divide. He went back and telephoned word to Lewiston, but Lenora had left for Sheep Creek by boat the day before. When she arose the first morning after her return to the creek, there was Spike, resting on her front porch.

Mile 20. **Steep Creek** on the right. Named "creek" by an optimist. An interesting feature of this gulch is that it contains the northern-most examples of a thornless raspberry that grows only on the slopes of Hells Canyon between Hells Canyon Dam and Steep Creek. It was discovered in 1933 at Battle Creek by Lenora Barton and identified by an Oregon botanist who came to the canyon at her request. The plant was named Bartonberry *(Rubus bartonianus)* in her honor. When not in bloom, the plant could be mistaken for a ninebark, but in spring its showy, white flowers are present; and in the late summer its brownish raspberries can be detected. This plant is proposed as a "threatened" species in the Federal Register "Endangered and Threatened Plant List," and the Idaho Rare and Endangered Plants Technical Committee has recommended that it be kept in that status because of its limited distribution. *(See drawing page 155.)*

It was at Steep Creek, as she left in a boat after a two week stay at Sheep Creek one summer, that Ace Barton's young niece remarked: "Uncle Ace, this place sure has a rocky climate."

Mile 20.5 **Yreka Creek,** a pine and hackberry-masked gully on the Oregon side. The beach suffices as a camp in low water. Ace Duncan said he named the place because it reminded him of the Eureka mine formation on the lower Imnaha.

The trail climbed over the rim below Yreka Creek and then dropped back down to Sand Creek. Tom Rayburn, Jess Poulson, and some other members of a Forest Service trail crew cut a new trail through the rock overhang above the river in the winter of 1947-48. That stretch of trail is known as "the Eagle's Nest."

Mile 21. **Sand Creek** comes in on the left. This is the bench where Kyle McGrady, mentioned in the "boatman" section of this book, had his tourist lodge. It was equipped with a generator, and had facilities for 50 people. The lodge, which was built in 1946, was sold to the Inland Navigation Company at the time it acquired the mail contract, but Inland never used it, and the building fell into disrepair. Since it was situated on National Forest land, under special-use permit, the Forest Service burned the lodge in 1962.

Ace Duncan had a mine up the north fork of Sand Creek, which he worked at times. When Ace Barton asked him what he had up there, Duncan replied, "She runs about 2000 pounds to the ton."

The sage-colored cabin that is now located on the flat serves the wardens and biologists of the Oregon State Game Commission.

Kyle McGrady's lodge in 1960 at Sand Creek.

Mile 21.5 **Willow Creek – Pine Bar** on the Idaho shore. A sand beach extended almost to the pair of rocks in the eddy off Pine Bar, before the dams were built. The erosive effect of staggered water releases from Hells Canyon Dam has reduced the extent of the beach, and it continues to shrink.

An insurance broker in Lewiston, Floyd Harvey, held this site under a Forest Service special-use permit during the 1960's and early Seventies. Harvey was a power boater on the Snake River and became concerned with rescuing Hells Canyon from the dams proposed by

223

power companies. He worked against overwhelming odds from 1960 to 1965, speaking out on a matter of principle when it was unpopular and discouraging to do so. Floyd was spending so much time on the river that he started a business there, Hells Canyon Excursions, which boated guests to his camp at Willow Creek. Harvey deserves credit as the founder of the Hells Canyon preservation movement which eventually gathered the public support necessary to save the canyon.

During the night of January 31, 1974, an undetected arsonist used charcoal briquettes to set fire to Harvey's seven buildings on Pine Bar. The main lodge and tent cabins were destroyed and the Forest Service refused to renew his use permit, so Floyd Harvey was put out of business.

The ocher-hued gash on the bluff behind Pine Bar is a natural formation and contains an alum deposit.

Mile 22: **High Bar** on the right. Ralph Stickney, who married Mary Hibbs, filed a homestead entry in 1920 on this bench. But because there is no water available to the site, except from the river, it was found to be unqualified for a homestead and classified as non-agricultural land.

Mile 23.3: **Hutton Creek** on the right will never wet its bed. On the upstream side of the gulch, next to the trail, is a root cellar and a small collapsed cabin. They can be seen from the river. Ernest Hutton lived here, placer mined, kept a little garden, and worked at times for C. J. Hall, McLeod, Barton, and others.

Harlan Clark, skim-digger and trapper, took up the place in the late Thirties.

The body of Frank Hiltsley, who drowned below Three Creeks in 1912, was recovered here. The location of his grave is marked by a headboard on the gully just above the trail.

Mile 24: **Caribou Creek and Little Bar** on the right. Caribou is reputed to be old-time slang for lodgepole pine — slender trees good for cabin logs and fences.

Little Bar was withdrawn from public entry in 1909 by D. W. Arrison, the ranger at White Bird.

In 1921, a special-use permit was granted the Nez Perce Sheep Company to use the site as the location for their shearing shed. Lumber was hauled from Lewiston, appropriately enough on the *Clipper*. A one-lung gas engine, with a shaft running the length of the 60-foot shed, provided power connections to the shears. The building was on the flat and a bunkhouse and cellar were located among the hackberry trees.

Bud Wilson removed the lumber in the late 1940's.

The Nez Perce Sheep Company was one of the largest outfits in the country, running up to 200,000 head of ewes. It was owned by the Swift & Co., meat packers, and their Snake River holdings were managed by Updike and Clinton whose headquarters were at Pittsburg Landing.

Mile 24.5: **Myers Creek and Big Bar** on the Idaho shore. This stream was first known as McClaren Creek, after an early settler. Its present name recalls a man involved in tragic circumstances.

Myers had a rock cabin on McClaren Creek just above the spot where the river trail crosses the stream. (Evidence of the foundation is still there.) County records show Myer's Christian name to be Joseph, but newspaper clippings of the time read Thomas. Those who knew him called him Mac. He first appeared in the Meadows Valley of Idaho where he worked for Charley Campbell on what was to become known as the Circle C ranch. Campbell liked Myers. Others thought he had a disposition sweet as sour milk.

After Myers moved to McClaren Creek on Snake River, the only person he neighbored with was McLeod at Sheep Creek. Mac ditched water south toward Little Bar, where he grew fruit and alfalfa.

The C. J. Hall cattle outfit was using water from McClaren Creek on Big Bar, just over the rise from Myer's place. Their cattle were often in Myer's garden and field and he tangled horns with the Hall cowboys over creek water rights and livestock trespass. He was probably subjected to some harassment because he closed the trail to Eph Holbrook and John Fallon when they tried to bring a pack train through to supply Jim Remington's sheep camp. Mac warned Hall's men they would be grabbing the branding iron by the hot end if their cattle entered his garden again.

In May of 1904, Wallace Jarrett and George Brownlee were moving Hall cattle from Kirkwood up Myers Creek toward Low Saddle. They ate lunch at Big Bar with Ernest Hutton, while their cattle had lunch in Myer's garden. Mac returned from a visit to McLeod and saw what had happened. He was madder than a bull in bumble bees.

The cattle were being driven up the ridge between Myers Creek and Caribou Creek. Mac grabbed his rifle, went up Caribou Creek and waited for the cowboys and cattle to come into what is now known as "Brownlee Saddle."

The Brownlee shooting is a well-known incident in Snake River history. There are many versions of the event, and irreconcilable differences exist among them. Mark Twain wrote, "It isn't so astonishing the things that I can remember, as the number of things I can remember that aren't so." In light of the contradictory accounts of this event, it seems safest to rely on the *Grangeville Free Press* version. Newspapers can be as mistaken as human memory, but in this case, the contemporary, local account seems less vulnerable to the discrepancies which arise from lapse of time.

MYERS CAPTURED
Further Details of the Killing at Crooks Corral

Thomas Myers who shot and killed George Brownlee near Crooks Corral last week was captured Thursday at George Behan's ranch on Snake river by Roy Gordon and Fred Ried as he was coming to White Bird, so he said, to surrender himself to the authorities.

The details of the trouble as near as can be learned are that Brownlee and Jarrett were taking a bunch of cattle to the summer range and, as had been the custom for years, drove team through Myers claim. They were some distance past the place and had stopped to rest the cattle when Myers who had evidently followed them came up from behind and shot Brownlee with a .30-30 rifle using a soft-nosed bullet. The ball entered the side of his back passing through his back bone and must have caused almost instant death. When Jarrett heard the shot he looked around and saw Brownlee fall from his horse and saw Myers just as he fired the second time. This shot struck Jarrett in the fleshy part of the forearm, passed through, cutting his bridle reins and piercing the ears of his horse. This so frightened the horse that Jarrett was thrown to the ground and fell down the steep hill side. Myers fired six more shots at him but none took effect. After running about two miles Jarrett secured another horse and made his way to the ranch of C. J. Hall from which place Richard Crooks carried the news to White Bird. When the news reached there Roy Gordon and Dr. Foskett left for the scene of the trouble and in the morning captured Myers just as he was passing George Behean's ranch. At the time of his capture Myers carried a .30-30 rifle and three boxes of cartridges but offered no resistance and said he was on his way to give himself up.

The remains of Brownlee were taken to White Bird where an inquest was held and then to Cottonwood where they were interred Friday afternoon by the Odd Fellows of which order he was a member. Jarrett's wound is not serious and he will soon be from under the doctor's care.

Myers was brought to Grangeville Friday evening by Sheriff Seay and his preliminary hearing is set for June 1st. He refuses to make any statement regarding the shooting or offer any excuse for the rash act. As far as is known there had been no trouble between the parties and it had only been a few days since he had told Brownlee and Jarrett where they could find his keys in case they wanted to enter his cabin during his absence.

Wallace Jarrett, rear left.

Jim Remington's yearling wethers which were moved up Snake River despite Myer's hinderance of the packers.

MYERS LYNCHED
Came to His Death at the Hands of a Mob

Thomas M. Myers, who killed George Brownlee and shot Wallace Jarrett near Crooks Corral on May 18, was taken from Deputy Sheriff Seay last Thursday morning on the road from White Bird and hanged. Myers had been taken from here Wednesday to White Bird where he was given a preliminary examination before Judge F. Z. Taylor who held him to appear at the district court. After the trial he was taken to W. A. Newman hotel and later that evening rumors reached Deputy Sheriff Seay that an effort would be made to lynch the prisoner that night and that a posse was already organized for that purpose. This he soon found to be true and what was worse the feeling against Myers was so bitter that it was impossible to get anyone to take any active part in his protection. Armed men paraded every street and no one was permitted to leave or enter the town who was suspected of wanting to interfere with their plans. It was expected that the attack would be made about midnight but several ladies were stopping in the hotel, two of whom were ill, and it was feared an attack might cause serious results. Through respect for the ladies the mob agreed to postpone their job until the next day but declared that it would be useless to try to get the prisoner away.

The next morning the streets were practically deserted but no one suspected that the mob had abandoned their purpose. About 8 o'clock Mr. Seay with Constable Roy Gordon started with Myers for Grangeville but when this side of the Hawley ranch about two miles this side of White Bird they discovered men on horse back at several points in front of them and knew that the critical moment had come. Getting out of sight of the watchers Mr. Seay got the prisoner on a horse and turning the buggy over to Constable Gordon determined to make a run through the hills in hopes of escaping in that way. They had gone but a short distance until they were again confronted by the mob who with drawn guns demanded the prisoner. Seay begged earnestly for his prisoner but resistance was useless as there were about 30 men in the mob and nothing could stop them in their purpose. They ordered Seay to return to town and the crowd started toward the mountains with their man. As soon as the news became known, searching parties started out and Myers was found hanging to a tree near where he was taken from the deputy sheriff. The body was taken back to White Bird where it was buried after a coroner's jury was empanelled and although the inquest is being held today it would be easy to guess what the verdict will be.

All during the trouble the lynchers were orderly and quiet yet in their every action they showed a grim determination to make the wretched prisoner expiate the crime he had so recklessly committed."

Myers was hung from a cottonwood on the George Bentz ranch on White Bird Creek. Bentz was not home at the time, but when he returned and learned the story from his wife, he went to White Bird and made the men come out and cut the body down. George later felled the tree as well. It is hoped there were some saddle-sore consciences along the river in the years that followed.

In early 1910, Matilda H. Hall, wife of C. J., applied for a Desert Patent on Big Bar. Her husband had already used his eligibility. The patent was granted four years later. The Halls constructed a ditch to carry water out of Caribou Creek into Myers Creek. Myers Creek was flumed and ditched to bring irrigation water to Big Bar. A water-powered whipsaw at Sawpit Saddle provided the lumber for the flume.

Len Jordan had Big Bar as part of his sheep operation in the 1930's. Ken Johnson had run a pipeline around the rim from Myers Creek to the bar for hay irrigation.

George "Bud" Wilson and his wife, Helen, of Nyssa, Oregon, acquired the site from Jordan in 1943. Bud quilted most of the private holdings from Pittsburg to Granite Creek into one large sheep ranch. For 32 years he and his wife struggled to develop and improve the operation.

The Wilsons spent $34,000 on Big Bar alone. The Johnson pipeline from Myers Creek was subject to frequent fractures. Ace Duncan, a renowned blacksmith from Cambridge, Idaho, was hired by Jordan to drive a tunnel through the ridge that separates Big Bar from the creek. Duncan single-jacked powder holes, with an eight-pound hammer and drill steel, into rock so dense his drills had to be sharpened hourly. He placed small flags on the overburden to determine his distance and direction and worked from both sides of the ridge. Ace put in eight-hour days over a two-year period to complete this tunnel. Ace Duncan was 81-years-old at the time!

A pipeline was run through the finished tunnel and the 13 acres on upper Big Bar were planted to high quality, imported alfalfa. Lumber was boated from Lewiston in order to build a barn on the lower bench, and hay was dropped down a chute from bluff to barn. When work got tedious, the men loading the chute would put a rattlesnake on the load and send it sliding down to the fellows forking hay into the mow below.

Lambing sheds were also constructed on Big Bar. The place was busy as an anthill most of the year. Haying, shearing, lambing, and feeding were cycles regular as phases of the moon.

The Wilson holdings were taken under eminent domain proceedings by the Forest Service for the National Recreation Area. Under the settlement, the Wilsons received enough money to burn a wet mule, but considering the years they contended with unimaginable vicissitudes — weather, stock, transportation, government regulations — they earned every cent of it and maybe more.

Ace Duncan at 80 years of age. He weighed 81 pounds when he was pounding drill steel on the tunnel.

The tunnel can be seen as a dark spot just below the notch in the ridge in the lower photograph. Big Bar is on the other side of the ridge.

Today Big Bar is lonely as an unmarked grave. Only the time-stained wooden cook shack remains on the flat. A poem by Johnny Carrey is a fitting conclusion to the story:

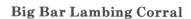

Big Bar Lambing Corral

It's empty and silent a-sagging and creaking
With windows a-gaping
To the high wind that blows.

The rafters are cobwebbed
The hinges are squeaking,
As idly the wind swings the door to and fro.

The camp stove is cold, it is cheerless and strange.
Vainly I search for the honest, old faces
Of herders I worked with while out on the range.

I listen for the voice of the old herder,
But out of the stillness none do I hear.
Nothing but grim desolation is found there,
The place is abandoned to silence and gloom.

The empty corrals have no dust clouds arising
With dogs and the pack string astanding outside.
No loud swearing herders vainly devising
Some means of subduing the boss and the ranger.

The long trailing bands
Of sheep have all vanished;
The draws and the hillsides are empty and lone.
I see the old saddles, that hang in the bunkhouse
Each, one time or another, was a sheepherder's throne.

A sheepman these days is only a relic,
A silent reminder of the days they were King.
I picture the lantern as it hung from the ridge-pole;
The bell on the lead sheep —
I can still hear it ring.

And as I awaken, I find I've been dreaming
Of the life I once lived out on a sheep range.

Sheep sheds and corrals on Big Bar in 1952; looking north downriver.

Big Bar, in the foreground, as it looks at present. Hay was slid down a chute to a barn on the lower flat. When things got dull, the haying crew on the upper flat would sometimes put a rattlesnake on the hay load and watch the boys in the barn loft below scramble out of the way. Ken Johnson's Temperance Creek ranch occupies the bench across the river in the photograph.

233

The Brockman cabin at Temperance Creek.

The Great Eastern mine is located on the slope above the lower end of Big Bar. It was a gold and copper lode discovered by Ezra Baird and Jack Eckerts, sold by them in 1901 to Captain J. R. Woods, of Chicago. Several hundred feet of twin tunnel were driven and Captain Ed Mac-Farlane hauled about 150 tons of ore to Lewiston in 1913 on the *Prospector.* The ore was shipped to a Tacoma smelter where it returned $52 per ton. There was a mill on the site, but it burned at an early date.

Ace Duncan and Jimmy McCalla mined the claim later, and Frank Sotin worked for them there one year.

Mile 25.3: **Temperance Creek** rivers out on the Oregon bank. In the mid-1880's, Alex and Bob Warnock came to Temperance Creek to do some placer mining. While bringing in their winter supplies, they rolled a packhorse with their quota of whiskey. As a result, their winter camp was dry as buffalo jerky and the creek's name is a reminder of that memorable drought.

The Warnocks were brothers from a Kansas family of nine children. Their father had drowned in a flood and their mother supported the family by renting rooms to boarders. The boys helped her by herding cattle that were driven through Abilene, and by gathering wagon loads of buffalo bones from the prairie which they sold at $3.50 a ton.

The oldest boy, Tom, went west with a wagon train in 1878 and filed a homestead claim where Joseph, Oregon, now stands. He wrote his family, asking them to come for a visit. Mrs. Warnock had remarried,

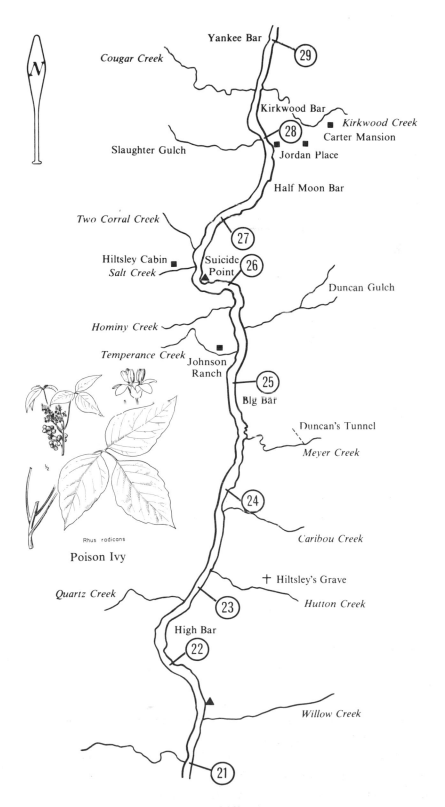

N

Yankee Bar

Cougar Creek

(29)

Kirkwood Bar

Kirkwood Creek

(28)

Carter Mansion

Slaughter Gulch

Jordan Place

Half Moon Bar

Two Corral Creek

(27)

Hiltsley Cabin

Suicide

(26)

Salt Creek

Point

Duncan Gulch

Hominy Creek

Temperance Creek

Johnson
Ranch

(25)

Big Bar

Duncan's Tunnel

Meyer Creek

(24)

Caribou Creek

Rhus radicans

✝ Hiltsley's Grave

Poison Ivy

Quartz Creek

Hutton Creek

(23)

High Bar

(22)

Willow Creek

(21)

but her husband sold his homestead and the whole family arrived in Wallowa Valley in the summer of 1879, with three covered wagons and a few saddle horses.

The Warnock brothers split fence rails all winter and traded them for beef cattle. In the spring they moved to Enterprise and milked about 85 cows from which they produced 19,000 pounds of butter. A team hauled the butter to Baker, Pendleton and Walla Walla where two-pound rolls were sold for 35 cents each.

In the fall, the Warnocks camped at the head of Wallowa Lake and seined the mouth of the Wallowa River for redfish (Kokanee salmon). It required a team of horses and eight men to haul in catches of 1,500 fish — averaging about five pounds a fish. The salmon were split, brushed and packed in 60-pound kegs, then transported to the nearest towns and sold.

The three oldest boys, Tom, Alex and Dan, invested their earnings in cattle for four years. In 1884, they divided the herd and moved to ranches of their own.

In the fall of 1886, Tom and his wife, his brother Billy, and John Veits and his wife brought 275 head of horses to Temperance Creek for the winter. They found Ezra Durham and Frank Hoover camped on the spot. The Warnocks built a fir bough lean-to and lived on venison. Evening entertainment consisted of conversation and card games with Durham and Hoover.

The Warnock party killed five cougar and 105 deer that winter. The venison was cured and packed out to Imnaha in the spring. The hides were traded for Indian ponies.

Alex and Bob Warnock began using Temperance Creek as a base for their cattle operation. When Walter Beith spent ten days working with Alex on Snake River in 1893, he recorded the following conversation. Alex said:

> When I first came to Snake river I had 150 head of cattle, a wife (Ellen), a few horses and a pretty tacky outfit of rigging and household goods. If I had known what I do now I would not have had the guts to come in. The first two years were hard. The bears killed our cattle, the cougars got our colts, we couldn't keep a chicken or a cat. I don't know how many times we packed in a dozen hens and a rooster and had bobcats, coon, mink or owls catch the last one. We would bring in a pair of house cats, then the first time we were away

from home, which was soon, because it seemed we were on the range or trail to the valley most of the time, something would catch them.

Now we have the varmints killed out of this canyon until we can keep chickens and cats. Most of the big grizzlies are destroyed, and the cougars are much reduced in numbers. I remember a trick a family of coons played on us. We had put up a lot of fruit and berries which we had raised or packed from over in Idaho. There must have been 100 jars or more, mostly quarts. A prospector had dug a short tunnel into the solid rock hill near our cabin, so we used this for a cellar. We left the fruit in the back end of this tunnel while we went on the fall ride. When we returned there was not a jar left. Broken glass and fruit stains on the rocks told the story. We tracked the robbers three-quarters of a mile up a dry creek bed where we found a great hollow cottonwood, the den tree. The route was marked at intervals by broken jars. The surprise, however, was not that they were broken but that any were carried that distance over the rocky way without being broken. Apparently the coons could not take the jars up the tree, for nearly half of the fruit was found and recovered, jars intact. The coons had buried them near the tree with a covering of dirt and leaves.

A hay chopper for feeding sheep, with the cook shack in the distance, on Big Bar.

Alex and Bob were joined by three of their brothers on Snake River in their cattle venture. They obtained lands along the Imnaha, Fence Creek, and in the Chesnimnus country for summer grazing; wintering their herds on the Snake from Pleasant Valley Creek to Saddle Creek. Summer range was in the high country, spring and fall range lay on the slopes, and winter feed was found on river benches or south-facing slopes.

The winter of 1886-87 was colder than an icicle's backbone, and taught western ranchers the importance of a hay harvest. The Warnocks built a mile-long irrigation ditch from Temperance Creek and began growing hay on 90 acres of the bar.

The sturgeon, and stories concerning it, are embedded in Hells Canyon lore. Since Beith also recorded some of Warnock's sturgeon stories, this seems an appropriate point to introduce the famous fish.

Sturgeon are the largest present-day fresh water fish known. They have a fossil history reaching back about 300 million years. The fish have four sensory barbels near their mouth to aid in locating food on the river bottom, and their sides are armored with five rows of bony scutes.

Adult sturgeon migrate into fresh water to spawn in the spring, and a large female may lay 3 million eggs. The young stay in fresh water about a year before they go to the sea. The fish may live 75 to 100 years.

Dams obviously block the sturgeon's route to the Pacific and destroy food production and spawning areas. A few green sturgeon were taken by commercial fishermen on the Snake River prior to construction of Bonneville Dam in 1937. They have not been observed in Idaho waters since that time.

The white sturgeon has survived in the flowing portion of the Snake, between Lewiston and Hells Canyon Dam, and appears to have adapted to a fresh water existence. Since the fish has to reach a length of about six feet before it is capable of spawning, and because that process requires almost 20 years, the sturgeon is now protected by law. The population was over-fished in the past, and while fishermen may still hook the creatures, they must release any they catch. The tasty, white fish was a useful source of food to canyon homesteaders, particularly since a line with multiple hooks could be left in the river and checked once a day.

In 1893, Walt Beith asked Alex Warnock about his encounters with the big fish. Beith recalled:

I brought up the subject of sturgeons by asking Mr. Warnock how big they grew. He said:

It's a God's fact, there are sturgeon in this river as long as my boat and that is 16 feet. I have caught scads of small sturgeon up to 250 pounds by using a hook and line and baiting with eels. My ambition is to catch a whopper, but I never yet have landed one. I tried bait-fishing with a hook fashioned out of the steel of a hayrake tooth, a two-pound chunk of beef with a barbwire leader and a half-inch rope for a line but I never could get the big ones to bite. There is an eddy at the mouth of Temperance Creek where I have seen a lot of big sturgeon from time to time. I have kept after them off and on. They have a habit of stopping for days in this eddy, swimming up along the bank with a foot or two of thin tail and dorsal fin showing above the water. Slowly they move along until they reach a point where the current leaves the bank; then they drift over sideways into the current and drop back to the foot of the eddy, only to repeat the process. I have known them to do that time and time again. One can only see their fins when they are swimming up, at other times they are submerged. I made myself a strong four-pronged spear, mounted it on a peeled pole handle and attached 40 feet of one-half inch rope to the handle. There was a hackberry bush growing in the rocks close to the eddy. Tying the rope end securely to the hackberry I was all set.

I watched that eddy for a week, and finally a big sturgeon was circling lazily as I had seen others do. Watching my chance for a sure thrust, I socked the spear into him. Say, he shot broadside into the current, rip went the bush torn out by the roots. Mr. Sturgeon started for Lewiston spear, rope and all, and towing a sizable hackberry bush at the end. That held me for a while, but finally I rigged up another spear with a new plan of modus operandi.

I had a good strong saddle horse that could pull his weight by the saddle horn. A young man was working here. We had to wait some weeks before the next big one was sighted. I speared him as before. The boy on the horse had the

A Snake River cowgirl, mounted on a sturgeon.

rope end securely snubbed to the horn. Well, I thought that horse could walk up the bank and drag any sturgeon out of Snake River, but he couldn't. When that fish got into the current and made a lunge the horse's feet began to slip. The bank was loose dirt, a little sloping, and darned if I didn't almost lose horse, boy and all. The boy cut his rope but not before he was so far in that he got a bath.

My third attempt was made alone. I buried a log deep in the sand with a chain around its middle, with a new spear, a new sea grass rope attached to the chain. I figured the next one was surely my meat. With the rigging all attached and the spear stuck in the sand I waited a long time for the chance. Finally one morning my wife called to me that there was a sturgeon in the eddy. It looked like the biggest one of all.

I rammed the spear into him, thinking I had him this time, but the rope tore loose from the spear handle — the fish was gone, tho I saved my rope. Do you know that bird never left the eddy for days. I could see the spear handle weaving around in the current with a foot or two of the end above water. I thought maybe I could get him yet.

240

Two men came over from Idaho on an errand one day, whom I pressed into service. I had a plan which we undertook, that was to swim out and attach the rope to the spear handle. As a safety precaution I buckled on a belt to which another rope was tied. The men were to hold this rope and pull me in when the time came. Carrying the first rope with a double half-hitch all prepared, I swam it gently over the spear handle drawing it tight without disturbing the fish. Not being able to hold myself in the current any too well, I suppose I splashed water some. I had just got out there and finding myself drifting down I instinctively grabbed the handle. Like a flash it started for China. I was six feet under water before I could even let go. Just as I started under I opened my mouth to yell "Pull", and strangled on river water.

They snaked me out, darned near drowned. Yes, I have had a grand time with the sturgeon, but my batting average in landing the big ones is 0000.

With competition for range from other cattlemen, such as the Marks brothers at Sluice Creek, the Warnocks finally sold their holdings in 1904 to Frank Wyatt. "Bow" Wyatt, as he was known for his bow and arrow brand, headquartered on Deer Creek of the lower Salmon River, and was running cattle in Idaho from the mouth of the Salmon up to Pittsburg Landing. By adding the Warnock range on the Oregon side of the Snake, Wyatt was able to graze about 2,500 head at one period.

Bow Wyatt sold his Oregon range to Walter Brockman in 1908. Walt obtained a homestead patent on the land at the mouth of Temperance Creek in 1911. He and his wife worked it as a cattle ranch, and annexed a mining claim upriver the following year, which was purchased from Iva Millen, the wife of Brockman's foreman.

In the fall of 1916, Walt was packing supplies from Imnaha down Temperance Creek on the Zig Zag trail, when death put the running iron on him. The tail-mule's pack turned and Brockman stopped to adjust the load. The next to last mule in the string was something of a renegade, and Walt untied him while he worked on the pack. The renegade spooked, mules and man fell to their death.

The rest of the string trailed down to the ranch where their appearance alarmed Mrs. Brockman. She telephoned the neighbors at Pittsburg and Saddle Creek for help. Jack Titus and Pete Wilson found her husband in the morning. Wilson said the tail-mule was loaded with dynamite boxes which never exploded.

Hulda Brockman was pregnant at the time, and suffered a miscarriage. She moved out, and later worked as a housemother for a fraternity in Pullman, Washington.

Jack Titus supervised the ranch until it was sold to satisfy the bank note. The buyer was a veterinarian, Dr. Herman Trappier. He sold out in the mid-Thirties to Leonard Johnson and his son, Kenneth. The elder Johnson was a native of Wallowa country who had been in the sheep business since the early 1890's, becoming the biggest operator in his area.

Ken Johnson enlarged the Temperance Creek Livestock Company by welding into one operation land that was once under 18 separate ownerships in 15 tracts. The holdings extended upriver to Battle Creek. This deeded grazing land was complemented with substantial summer range allotments on the National Forest.

Ken married Hazel Welsh of Lewiston, and the couple lived in a log cabin at Temperance Creek until their modern house was constructed. They had two sons.

The Johnsons ran about 3,600 sheep. They got three cuttings of alfalfa, about 150 tons a year, which was stacked against a severe winter.

A barn, shearing sheds, airstrip, and hanger are located on the bench. A 32-volt Windcharger can be seen from the river, though it no longer functions. Propane and diesel fuel proved more reliable.

There is a grave on the flat, on the upriver side of the creek at the north end of the landing strip. It holds the remains of Louis Shields, employed by Alex Warnock around 1895. He shot himself; whether accidentally or intentionally is unknown, since there were no witnesses. The Shields' family were neighbors of the Warnocks in Indiana and Kansas.

The Temperance Creek holdings were purchased by the Forest Service in 1974-75. At the time of this writing, one of Ken's sons, Greg Johnson, continues to operate the ranch under permit from the Forest Service.

Mile 25.5: **Duncan Gulch** on the right is a tribute to Ace Duncan.

Mile 25.7: **Hominy Creek** empties into the Snake on the left. J. H. Horner told Grace Bartlett, of Oregon, that this stream is so named because Alex Warnock was camped there with his brothers and spilled a kettle of hominy in the cooking fire. The Warnocks placer mined on the bar.

Hazel and Kenneth Johnson.

Mile 26.2: **Suicide Point** makes a rocky thrust from the Idaho shore. The histrionic name focuses attention on a Forest Service trail that clings to the point, passing along the river a couple of hundred feet above the water. Before this trail from Big Bar to Kirkwood was built in 1926, the traveler had to climb through Half Moon Saddle and around into Kirkwood Creek, then down that drainage to the river.

Forest Service crew cutting the trail up Suicide Point.

Mile 26.4 **Salt Creek** flows in on the Oregon bank. It is a popular and convenient campsite for boaters.

Frank Somers said he was the only man on a 100-mile stretch of the river when he placer mined the bar in the 1870's. He noticed a sizeable apricot tree growing on the bench at that time and wondered who might

244

have planted it in this back-neck of the world. District Ranger Grady Miller cut a section from one of the trees that died in 1937 and obtained a ring count in excess of a hundred years. Apricot trees originated in western Asia, moved to Europe and then to America. The nearest trees in the 1830's would have been in California — so how in the Hells?

Chinese miners worked the placer ground around Salt Creek in the winter of 1886-87.

The Hiltsley/Wisenor cabin at Salt Creek as it looks today.

Arnold Hiltsley, related to the Hiltsley brothers mentioned earlier, settled at Salt Creek in the 1890's. Hiltsley was probably the builder of the cabin which still abides along the downstream side of the creek, about a quarter mile from the river. Mr. Hiltsley sold out to Jim Wisenor around 1908.

Jim and Stella Wisenor proved up on the place. They had six young children at Salt Creek: Celia, Sallie, Christina, Wesley, Rufus and Melvin. In 1916, the Wisenors sold to Jack Titus. Jack married Celia Wisenor the same year.

Lem Wilson, brother to Bud, was the last private owner of the Salt Creek property. Lem was a sheep rancher, headquartered at Pittsburg Landing. He subdivided the Salt Creek parcel into 39 lots and sold 15 of them to six individuals. Then the Forest Service stepped in with condemnation proceedings under eminent domain and purchased the site as part of the National Recreation Area.

Mile 26.6 **Two Corral Creek,** within a rifle shot of Salt Creek and on the same side of the river. The L. J. Falconer family had a homestead up the south side of this creek, and "Professor" James Kiger, a bachelor with horses, had his homestead on the north side. (Tom Cone gave Kiger his nickname when he started to brag about his grammar school education.) The name of the creek is the result of the Pittsburg Livestock Association's corrals on the bench where the High Trail cuts the stream.

Hells Canyon children received their school lessons in a log classroom on the bench near the High Trail, just north of Two Corral Creek. W. "Willie" R. Davis had filed on the site in 1907, but because it was on a trail and was the location of a school, the Forest Service decided it was an ideal site for a ranger station. So the homestead was cancelled in 1910, and Davis was paid $500 for his improvements, but no ranger station was ever built.

The log school house was known as Pittsburg School #69, and students were taught there from 1908 to 1920. When the one-room log school deteriorated, it was replaced by a frame school house, built about 3½ miles southwest of the first one, on the flats by the north fork of Two Corral Creek, approximately 5½ miles from the river. The school was constructed of lumber from Jim Wisenor's sawmill at the head of Temperance Creek.

Children from the E. B. Wilson, Warnock, Wisenor, Crader, Falconer, Winniford, and Titus families attended over the years. School terms varied from 20 to 32 weeks. Some youngsters, like the Wisenors, would ride to the school, camp for the week, and ride home for the weekend.

Afton Rogers recalled attending the log school in the spring and summer of 1911, when his older sister was teaching there. He was 10 at the time. Every two weeks they would go get their horses, which had been left at Two Corrals, a couple of miles from the school, ride seven miles to the Pittsburg ferry to cross the river, then ride over Pittsburg Saddle and down to their parent's ranch on the Salmon River side, arriving after dark. When the weekend visit was over, brother and sister retraced their trail to the Pittsburg school in Oregon.

In 1920, school shifted to the river, where the Winniford women taught at Sluice and Rush Creeks. Pete Wilson's house at Saddle Creek was the classroom in 1924. That was the last year a school census was taken for the Pittsburg School District; Pittsburg was then incorporated into the Imnaha District. However, classes were held at the Pittsburg ranch home of Mike Thomason in 1927-1928 and then again at Saddle Creek in 1933-34.

The first Pittsburg log school house.

The second Pittsburg school with teacher and students. Photographs courtesty of Florence Smith.

Teachers toil at the arduous task of awakening their students to a choice of worlds. In addition to the teachers already mentioned, the roll call of others who served the canyon's children in that capacity includes: Levancia Holcombe, Hattie Rogers, Iva Jarrett, William Wisenor, Mary Hyatt, Martha Doyle, Blanche McCann and Turner Bond.

Mile 27.5: **Half Moon Bar** on the left. The bar takes its name from the saddle above it on the way to Kirkwood Creek, which in turn carried a Nez Perce Indian's name. Half Moon fell to his death in the bluffs near Suicide Point, probably in the 1870's. His remains were found, along with the skeleton of his horse, in April, 1892, by Dennis Holland, owner of the Kirkwood Bar ranch. Along with the remains, a saddle, sawed-off shotgun and 1866 silver dollar were found. Holland buried Half Moon and told Clark Gill of the incident; Gill conveyed it to the authors.

The Half Moon brothers, Nez Perce Indians. They were sons of Old Half Moon.

In the summer of 1974, Morris Kohlepp, a sheepherder for Bud Wilson, was coming around the Half Moon Trail with a packstring from Kirkwood. He dallied his lead rope on his saddle horn while he rolled a cigarette. One of the mules pulled back, sending Morris and his horse off the brink. The horse rolled to the river, dead as corned beef. Kohlepp dangled unconscious on the bluff while his wife, Carmen, went back to Kirkwood for help. Lem Wilson brought some men upriver with a boat to carry Morris in a stretcher back to Kirkwood. A helicopter lifted off the bar after dark, with Morris strapped in a basket beneath it, and men holding flashlights on the treetops so the 'copter could clear them. The pilot flew to Grangeville and Morris recovered with nothing worse than a scar.

Mile 28: **Slaughter Gulch** on the Oregon side. Jack Titus indicated this gully was the locale where cattle thieves, who had made off with a small herd from the Wallowa Valley country, killed the animals to avoid capture by a pursuing sheriff's posse.

Mile 28.3: **Kirkwood Bar and Creek** on the Idaho shore. Early visitors to this bar found extensive artifacts from Indian occupation. Dr. Jay W. Kirkwood and his wife, who lived in Grangeville, squatted on the bar for a time, going back and forth to town. They salvaged some whipsawed lumber from Chinese mining claims across the river and built two cabins. The Kirkwoods, and their one child, left Grangeville for Lewiston in 1885.

Dennis Holland acquired the site, with a working partner, Louis Termis. They stocked the range with nearly 700 cattle. The animals were eventually sold to Frank Smith and Ed Sweet, who were located on the headwaters of Corral Creek. Holland left for Lewiston, where he bought the DeFrance Hotel.

By 1901, George Brownlee was living on the bar; he had a cabin against the bluff on the lower flat. Brownlee was here between stints as a hired hand for several cattle ranchers. Emma Davis remembered him as being wagon tongue-tall, with a red moustache — in overcoat, a fearsome figure to a little child. After Brownlee was killed by Myers, his brother, Tom, inherited the homestead, which was patented in 1909.

The Brownlee cabin on Kirkwood, which was torn down in the 1950's.

249

Tom and Anna Brownlee.

Snake River rancher C. J. Hall on Rapid River.

Pauline and Mildred Hall, daughters of C. J.

Mae Ballard Carter in the center of the photograph holding a vaccination needle for cattle at the cow camp with Emma Davis and her children.

The Fred and Julia Reid family spent the winter of 1906 at Kirkwood, before moving to Kirby Bar. One of their six children, Goldie Reid (Falin) was delivered at Kirkwood — the first white child born in the canyon.

C. J. "Charley" Hall used the bench as part of his cattle operation. It also served the Nez Perce Sheep Company until that outfit sold its holdings.

Kirkwood Bar was then purchased by Leonard and Kenneth Johnson (father and son). They used it as a base for their sheep on the Idaho side of the river. Anna Maxwell, Ken's aunt, cooked for them while they were there. Johnson built the two-story white frame house that faces the river from the bar. He sold his interest in 1932 to Len Jordan. Len's partner, Dick Maxwell, withdrew after a short while. The Depression had struck the country, but unlike today, when food is so expensive it would be cheaper to eat the money, canyon people had little money but foraged quite well. The Jordans were on the bar for 11 years, and became a prominent Idaho family. They remodeled the frame house. Peter Maus excavated the lower level for them, where an indoor bathtub and basin were added.

They had three children who required an education. Murielle McGaffee taught two of them during their first winter at Kirkwood. The three were taught by their mother after that, using the courses of the Calvert School of Baltimore. When Pat Jordan entered high school in Grangeville in 1941, it was her first encounter with public education.

The Jordan family at Kirkwood: Grace and Len, children, left to right: Joe, Stephen, and Patsy.

The Jordan "home below Hell's Canyon." Pete Maus excavated the area beneath the house.

*The bathtub-basin combination which is discussed in **Home Below Hells Canyon.** A sheet metal form was set inside the tub and filled with sand to hold it in place while the concrete set. The tub was then finished with multiple coats of paint.*

254

Len Jordan with the family cow.

Len riding the mower.

Haying at Kirkwood, Max Walker on the load.

Len sold the place to Bud Wilson in 1943. The Jordans left Kirkwood for Grangeville, where Len eventually became a one-term state Governor and then a U.S. Senator for 10½ years, retiring in 1973. His wife, Grace, wrote a memoir of their years at the bar called *Home Below Hells Canyon*. The narrative of family life on a sheep ranch in this rugged locale sold widely enough to be translated into six foreign languages and has been through 10 printings at this time.

Autograph party for Grace Jordan: left to right, rear, Max Walker, Jim Wilson, Carl Hibbs, Ken Ryan. Front, Esther Hibbs, Murielle Wilson, Grace Jordan, Julie Reid, Fred McGaffee.

As mentioned at Big Bar, the new owners Bud and Helen Wilson, worked sheep in the canyon for 35 years, running 4,800 head. At considerable expense, Bud punched a road down to the bar in 1946-1947. It is six miles by this route to Cow Creek Saddle, and 12 miles to Lucile.

Lambing sheds used by the ranch in the spring are still in place on the bench. A ewe and her lamb were put in these pens during an initial adjustment period, so the mother would not lose or reject her offspring.

Carl Hanna's cabin which is located on the north side of Kirkwood Creek. Len Jordan dismantled the cabin at the Carter place, hauled it down to Kirkwood Bar and reassembled it.

Bud Wilson at Kirkwood Bar.

The Kirkwood ranch hayfield.

Dick and Bonnie Sterling.

The Sterling cabin up to square. Not one nail had been used at this point. Dick built other exemplary log buildings as well. He also worked as a packer on the Bright Angel Trail in Grand Canyon.

Dick Sterling worked as ranch hand and packer for the Wilsons. He built the impressively crafted log bunkhouse that stands on the bar between the frame house and the river. The lodgepole logs were trucked from Lost Valley to the site where Dick prepared them with crosscut saw and axe, fitting them like feathers on a duck. The enduring solidity of the building is a tribute to his skill.

The Sterling cabin as it looks today.

The Wilsons parted with Kirkwood Bar when the Department of Agriculture filed a Declaration of Taking in 1973. It is now included in the National Recreation Area, though the area is still permitted to graze sheep at times.

On the upper end of the bar, within the fenced corral, a tombstone marks the grave of David Kirk: Born Nov. 26, 1852, Died Jan. 3, 1916.

Kirk had proved up on a homestead east of Crooks Corral in Hells Canyon. He had mechanical ability, and constructed a couple of sawmills that furnished lumber for settlers and miners in the area.

Dave worked for C. J. Hall at Kirkwood Bar and handled the irrigation chores.

He jumped his head hobbles one night, went screaming into the dark, delirious from fever, poorly clothed when it was cold as a snowball. Pneumonia followed the incident, and the sand in the hourglass ran out for David Kirk. Clay Davis made his casket, Mrs. Hall and Jenny Smith lined it and sewed a shroud, and he was buried while Jenny read a selection from the Bible. The stone was placed by Tom and Anna Brownlee.

David Kirk in 1910.

The Carter Mansion: About half a mile up the Kirkwood road, the Carter place straddles the stream. D. W. Erler filed on the site in 1910, but his stay was shorter than the tail hold on a bear. Carl Hanna replaced him, building a small square cabin before leaving for World War I, from which he never returned. The ancient log building on the downriver side of Kirkwood Creek at Kirkwood Bar is Carl Hanna's cabin. Len Jordan took the logs from the Carter place and reconstructed the building at its present location.

In the spring of 1920, Elzia Clarence "Dick" Carter settled on the Hanna claim. Everyone lives by selling something, and Dick Carter sold moonshine — famous five-star double-rectified moonshine. National Prohibition went into effect in January of 1920. River people love all things that flow, and though they lived in an arid canyon, few attained a cactus-like indifference to thirst. Without Carter's excellent efforts, some people might have been dry as a year-old cow chip.

Clarence "Dick" Carter.

Carter snaked logs down from Sumac Gulch above Kirkwood, and built the most impressive house of its day in the canyon. The exterior was fashioned with logs set on end and deer hair was mixed with the mortar for chinking. Then the seams were covered with strips of tin. There were cement slabs front and rear for covered porches. Inside: tongue and groove flooring for five ample rooms with plastered lath walls. Doors and windows were framed with wooden trim. The front door opened onto the porch, where one could sit in a shady sanctuary and contemplate the constant inconstancy of Kirkwood Creek.

Dick married Mae Ballard, a lady from Baltimore, with whom he had corresponded. They had a garden and a few horses. A barn was constructed just up the road. With income from his sought-after sideline, and a pleasant house, they could have been comfortable as an annuity. A homestead patent was issued in 1923.

The Carter Mansion photographed from the rear. Note vertical logs with tin caulking.

But the tin-star heel-flies of the Treasury Department paid Carter an unexpected visit. He spent some time in the state do-right, while his wife stayed with the Davises on Corral Creek and carried the mail from Lucile for the neighbors. After Dick returned, they sold their place to Ken Johnson and moved to the old Jarrett homestead on the south fork of Kirby Creek, which had been purchased by C. J. Hall. In 1940, Dick Carter sold his ranch and moved to Clarkston, Washington, where he lived out the days that were given him.

Though Kirkwood Creek has begun to undercut the front porch, the Carter mansion still perches on the edge of the stream. Except for an occasional packrat, it is empty as a birdnest in November. Recently, some greedy clotpoll stole the glass pane from the front door. It was a plate of frosted glass with a bounding stag in the center.

Mile 28.5: **Cougar Creek** is opposite Kirkwood Bar. The stream issues through a narrow notch in the canyon wall and is crossed by a trail bridge, visible from the river. Inviting as it appears, this snake-infested gorge is not recommended to hikers.

C. A. "Dad" Russell. He used to walk the phone line from Pittsburg to White Bird.

Mile 28.8: **Russell Bar.** There is a mine tunnel at the river's edge, just below Kirkwood Bar, on the Idaho shore. It is the result of C. A. Russell's labor. There is a grass and hackberry flat about a quarter mile downriver from the tunnel, known as Russell Bar. C. A. "Dad" Russell lived in a pair of framed tents which faced each other there. One tent was his bedroom and the other was his kitchen, and both were kept immaculate. He cultivated some fruit trees and vegetables and had a small gas pump to put water in his garden. He did some placer mining as well. Mr. Russell always wore a clean white shirt on Sundays.

Russell worked for the Jordans and Bud Wilson as hay hand, irrigator, and caretaker. He finally left the river on the mail boat due to poor health.

264

Mile 30.1: **Kirby Creek** hunts its way down from the hills on the Idaho shore. Jack Kurby floated his stick to this bar and lived in a tent there. The creek carries an altered spelling of his name. Chinese miners had placer-mined the location in the late 1870's and early 1880's before Kurby's residency.

The parents of the next man to take up the place were Texans — George and Sarah Reid. George fought for the Confederacy during the War Between the States and when the issue was resolved, he freed the slaves on his plantation. But feelings ran high, and rather than struggle with the disjointed post-war period, Reid sold his holdings and brought his wife and two sons, Fred and George, northwest to Idaho. He augered around for a place to settle and chose the Crooks Corral Basin, just on the Snake River side of Cow Creek Saddle. When they came of age, each son filed on a homestead close to that of his parents.

Fred Reid married Julia Mothorn, daughter of Oregonians who had settled on the north fork of Kurry Creek. The couple filed a Desert Entry at the mouth of Kirby Creek and moved there in 1907. The ground was patented in 1910. Fred and Julia had six children. Ruth and Orin were born on Kirby Bar, Goldie was born at Kirkwood; the other children were Fred, Della and Gladys.

The *Prospector* hauled lumber for the house the Reids built. They constructed a cellar, planted trees and irrigated alfalfa. Their cattle and sheep wintered at Kirby Creek and were summered out of Crooks Corral.

Norm Riddle's lodge.

At one point, Fred sold the Snake River site to Al Stewart, but Stewart's efforts were unrewarded, and it reverted to the Reids. Fred died in 1934 at age 73. Julia sold Kirby Creek to Len Jordan and the Crooks Corral homestead to Harry Robinson. She moved to Grangeville, where she owned and operated a resthome, brightening the vale of years for many an old-timer.

Kirby Creek is now the only privately held riverfront lot within the N.R.A. The two-story building on the beach belongs to Norm Riddle, an experienced Snake River power boat operator, who uses it as a lodge for his Lewiston-based Snake River Outfitters excursion business.

Mile 30.5: **Muir Creek** on the left. Christened for a Scottish prospector, Silas Muir.

It was approximately in this area, on the Oregon side of the river, that cowboys Walt Beith and Frank Winters got involved in a rather amusing bit of drudgery. The story is told by Beith in one of his "Sketches of Pioneer Life on the Snake River Range" published by the *Enterprise Record Chieftain* in 1930. (The event occurred 36 years earlier.)

A certain young cow of the Winters iron had slid into a pocket close to the river and could not get out. The pocket was a short, steep canyon three miles up stream from Pittsburg. There was a trickle of water always there, also grass and brush enough to keep her. Frank knew about her and said that she had been there three years. It was a place impossible to get to with a horse. George Winters (Frank's brother), proposed that as it was now well along in October that we find a way to butcher her and salvage the meat.

His plan as outlined to us that night was: Frank and myself were to take a gun, knife, some ropes to let ourselves down the cliff to her, some baling wire George had provided, with whatever else we needed, ride as close as we could to her prison, then walk and climb down, butcher the cow, quarter her up and attach each quarter to some kind of float, then dump them in the river. George said we would have to have our watches set together because he had figured out how fast the river ran and he wanted to be at the Pittsburg crossing with his brother-in-law and a boat to catch the meat.

Walter Gray Beith. Born in Kansas, 1873.

Well, it looked to me like most of George's plans, one involving a lot of work for Frank and me and not much for George. Also I figured he would divide the meat like the monkey divided the cheese with the cats in the story.

Frank was persuaded as usual by the sophistries of brother George, and I was eager for whatever adventure might befall. Before George crossed for home we had our plans figured to the smallest detail. The next day, but one, was the day. The intervening time was spent storing away supplies and helping George take some private stuff across the river.

Daylight on the day set for us to go forth and slaughter the cow, found us in the saddle. It was a roundabout ride to the vicinity of her prison pen. Tying our horses a half mile away and working carefully down through the cliffs we came to the very rim by 9 o'clock. On the side of our approach there was a smooth bunch grass slope standing at about half pitch, overlooking the basin. On the other side was a frowning wall of rock literally straight up and down. Upstream from the canyon floor was a perpendicular face of granite down which a small stream of water poured, only to be lost in the rocks and gravel underneath. The lower end next to the river actually leaned 30 or 40 feet out over the water.

The basin itself must have contained 20 or 25 acres. There were small secondary slopes of bunch grass on either side, a few scattered trees, some weeds and shrubbery at the upper end, and a boulder-strewn floor of rock below. We could not see any cow, but thought we could see trails around the upper edge of the basin. Frank had told me that riders on the Idaho side had reported two years ago that a cow was somewhere here.

Finally we found a place where we could descend hand over hand without the aid of ropes as we anticipated. When part way down the cow broke out of some bushes 40 yards from us, snorted and dashed to the extreme upper limit of her prison. We found the bones of two others at the foot of the cliff not far from where we descended. Frank's thought was that three head of cattle had some time worked this way down thru the ruins in search of better feed, had come out on this steep grassy slope, been suddenly startled by a rolling stone or something, started to run and all slid, this cow being the only survivor.

We had little time to conjecture, or stop to enjoy the wild grandeur of the scene. We had contracted to begin dropping quarters of beef into the river at 12 o'clock, after which we were to set others afloat at intervals of 20 minutes. We would much rather have liberated the cow and placed her on the benches with her kind, if that were possible. It was not, and we had given work to do. We climbed up toward her, keeping well to one side until she shot down the other side as far as she could go. Here next to the river was where we wanted the meat.

Frank had little confidence in his small pistol and less in his agility, so climbed to a vantage point on an irregular shaped rock about six feet high. I was armed with the .44 Winchester and was supposed to shoot the cow. To my romantic soul this was a game; here was Spain. The whole basin was a vast amphitheatre. The cow was a black Tyroleanon bull and I an intrepid Matador. Here was the arena! In fancy I could hear a roar of applause! My victim was backed up as far away from me as she could get and stood glaring defiance

As Frank was giving directions, I was edging closer, engaged in a mental calculation: If a gun shot two feet wild in 50 yards how close should one be to the cow to be sure of hitting her between the eyes? I had just figured out that four feet was about right, when she charged like a flash!

Then I forgot the rules of the Spanish bull ring entirely and landed on the rock by Frank with my knees badly skinned. I turned to shoot, but found I had mislaid my gun. She rushed up and almost climbed on the rock. Much to my surprise, and relief as well, Frank shot her in the brain the first pop with his little woodrat gun. He also skinned and quartered the beef while I chopped dead trees as tough as the rocks from which they sprung. Then we would drag a quarter of beef 75 yards and a log twice that distance, another quarter and another log, until we had them all assembled on the iron ledge over the river. We lashed each quarter to its transport log very securely with baling wire, running the wire doubled around the log and deep thru the meat.

Our first float was ready on the dot, and we heaved it over a sheer drop of more than 100 feet. Kerplunk, it went into old Snake. The meat turned under, but the white log showed up pretty well, so we thought George would spot it readily. I wanted to put them in faster, in order to make George hurry a little, but Frank insisted on 30 minutes between sailing dates. It was only after all this was done that I found my gun, still cocked, and sticking muzzle down in a sand-wash.

We gathered our outfit and proceeded home as laboriously as we came. That night we found a quarter of beef with its log tied to our own gate, so to speak. Later we learned that three quarters in all had been recovered. One never was sighted or heard of.

Mile 31: **Durham Creek,** the next stream on the Oregon side. According to J. H. Horner, Ezra Durham was also a Scotsman prospector, a friend of Muir. He moved to Moscow, Idaho, where he was once elected to the state legislature from that district.

Mile 32: **Corral Creek** enters from the Idaho shore. This stream was originally called China Creek. The drainage threads from Crooks Corral placer claims located about three miles from its mouth. Crooks lived on the headwaters and trained horses in the corrals, before taking them out for sale.

Several parties became interested in the gold and bromide of silver deposits on the site around 1890. One of them was Frank McGrane, a rancher from Wolf Creek on the Snake. A water shortage hindered the first attempts to placer the ground.

David Kirk built a horse-powered sawmill on Kirkwood Creek, near Camel Ridge. Boards were cut 24 inches wide to make a flume that carried water out of Lost Valley and Kirkwood Creeks to Corral Creek. This flume gave Kirkwood the early-day name "Canal Creek." Water was flumed and ditched approximately five miles to the Crooks Corral diggings. The wide boards allowed a rider to patrol the flume on horseback. The mines were worked periodically until 1917. Dan Baker and Jim Carr mined the summer of 1903 and removed $3,000 worth of seed gold. Several cabins, including two saloons, were constructed on the site. One building and stretches of the ditch are still visible.

There was a 40 acre hay field on Corral Creek, about three miles from the river. Two bachelors, Bill Petty and Tim Gorrie, arrived there just before the turn of the century. They sold their claim in 1902 to Frank and Jenny Smith for $500. Frank earned the purchase money

Left to right: Frank Smith, Jenny Wagner, Clara Wagner, Oliver Stewart. Photo taken in 1901.

while working in the mines at Buffalo Hump. The Smiths built a six-room house and a large barn and ranged 190 head of cattle. Their three children, Margaret, Harold, and Mel, were born on the claim.

Jenny taught classes in 1911-1912 at the Crooks Corral School, sometimes called the "moonshine school," about three miles from their place. The school was pretty as a heifer in a flower bed: made of lumber and logs, it was larger than most country schools, shaded by magnificent ponderosas and bordered by little creeks on two sides. The playground was acres of pinegrass and wildflowers. A four-room cabin with woodshed was constructed for the teacher. On the same flat stood an eight-horse barn.

The number of students fluctuated, but six were generally required to constitute a district. Children from the Hall, Smith, Stewart, Rape, and Reid families were among those who attended. Some of them walked and some of them rode to school.

"If the student hasn't learned, the teacher hasn't taught," is a common observation. Yet the teachers at Crooks Corral were so dedicated that if the student hadn't learned, he was probably never meant to climb the tree of knowledge. Other teachers at the school who deserve mention are: Cleo Alkire and Frances Stewart.

Cow Creek School: Emma Davis (left rear), Edna Overman, teacher. Note boy in center proudly displaying his double thumb with which he delighted in pinching people.

Dan and Jessie Baker on their ranch at the head of Cow Creek.

Clay and Emma Davis in 1943.

The Smith place was acquired for payment of a store bill, with 40 head of cattle as added security on the mortgage, by Clay and Emma Davis in 1925.

Clay was a brother to Stella Wisenor at Salt Creek. He met Emma Baker at a masquerade dance in White Bird. Clay had borrowed a buckskin coat from Emma's brother and asked her to dance. He got to cutting up and she got out her lariat and roped him. When he removed his mask she was surprised to find he was someone she had never seen before. They were married a year later.

Emma was one of six children. Her parents had homesteaded on Cow Creek above the Salmon River. In hard times she proved to be gritty as fish eggs rolled in sand. No sooner had they taken on the Smith ranch, than Clay was stricken with an ulcer. He had to undergo surgery in Cottonwood, Idaho.

With three children to feed and a bank note to meet, Emma saddled her buckskin mare and sowed the fields with grain as she had seen her father do. The children wrangled horses in the morning while she cooked breakfast. The oldest youngster was ten.

Emma was called to Grangeville to palaver with the bank officials. They wanted her to sell the cattle and replace them when Clay recovered. She said no. They told her it looked bad. She said it could be worse.

Frank McGrane: "I don't see how it could be much worse.".

Emma: "Well, I could be one of those women that don't know a cow from a steer."

They let her keep the cattle. She not only cared for the children and livestock, but with the help of a neighbor she got logs pulled down from the timber so there would be wood for fence posts in the spring. Clay was home by Christmas.

There were two days the Davises didn't worry about: yesterday and tomorrow. When the bank closed in 1929 and it was impossible to get a loan on their cattle, Emma trapped coyotes to survive. Then Roosevelt was elected President and the Pacific Credit Association granted livestock loans that allowed small ranchers to subsist.

Clay and Emma put up all their dryland hay by hand. They met their obligations and increased the herd to 100 head. By the time arthritis in Emma's back forced them to sell out to Albert Campbell after 21 years, they had 150 head of cattle and money enough to buy 1,840 acres at White Bird.

Indian petroglyphs at Pittsburg Landing.

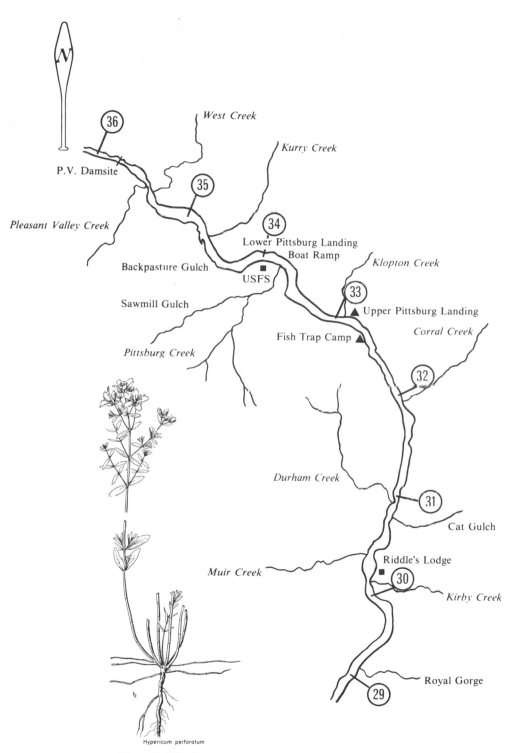

West Creek

Kurry Creek

36

P.V. Damsite

35

Pleasant Valley Creek

34

Lower Pittsburg Landing
Boat Ramp

Klopton Creek

Backpasture Gulch

USFS

33

Upper Pittsburg Landing

Sawmill Gulch

Fish Trap Camp

Corral Creek

Pittsburg Creek

32

Durham Creek

31

Cat Gulch

Muir Creek

Riddle's Lodge

30

Kirby Creek

Royal Gorge

29

Hypericum perforatum

Klamath Weed

Mile 33-34.5: **Upper and Lower Pittsburg Landing, Klopton and Kurry Creeks** on the Idaho side; **Pittsburg Creek and Sawmill Gulch** on the Oregon side.

The history of the Pittsburg area is older than Adam. Lodge rings, petroglyphs, and artifacts found on the benches are evidence of extended use by native Americans. During the 1840-1870 period members of Toohoolhoolzote's Nez Perce band occupied the location as part of their wintering ground. One account indicates the Indians called the area "Canoe Camp."

The origin of the name Pittsburg is obscure — those who might have known its derivation are no longer alive. The name was used in March of 1864 by the Lewiston *Golden Age:*

> Navigation to the mouth of Salmon River has been tested, and the opinion of experienced men, who have been up and down the river in small boats, is, that steamers can be made to run successfully to a point eighteen miles above Pittsburg Landing. The opinion of some others is, that this can not be done.

LaFayette Cartee's survey map in 1867, done for the Surveyor General's Office that year, shows Pittsburgh ending with an "h" in the same manner as the Pennsylvania city.

The writers have spent many hours sifting through the offered explanations. Since the name pre-dates any steamboats on the river, stories linking them with the origin are disputable. Bob Day, who worked for Mike Thomason, stated that the creek, and therefore the landing, were named because of a small seam of coal that was found on the north fork of the stream. Pittsburgh, Pennsylvania, money financed much of the early Idaho mining activity. On the other hand, it is possible a member of the Stubadore party may have affixed the name in 1862 because the area reminded him of the landing in Pennsylvania where the three rivers meet at the city.

Mike Thomason was on the Oregon side of the river at an early date — perhaps by 1885. Other men arrived and patented homesteads: G. B. Robertson on the north fork of Durham Creek, Mr. St. Giles on Pittsburg Creek and J. H. Chatten just downriver from Thomason. As his cattle operation grew, Mike gradually bought them out.

Thomason established a ferry across the river in 1891. He hired men to assist him. One of these hands, Jack Titus, eventually became the owner of the ranch and ran it with his wife, Celia, until they sold in

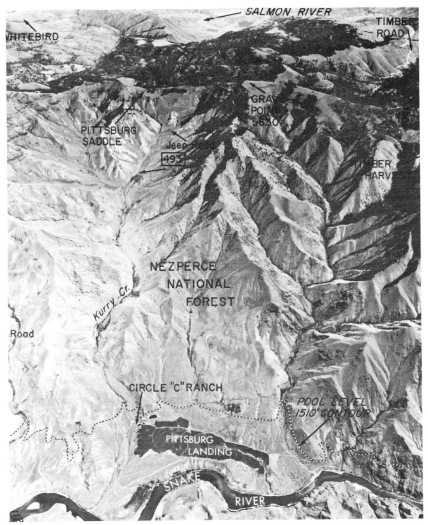

Aerial view of Pittsburg: The road going up Kurry Creek to Pittsburg Saddle can be seen on the left. From the saddle it drops to Salmon River, which can be seen at the extreme top of the photograph.

The dotted line which can be discerned in the foregound paralleling the river represents the reservoir level had the Mountain Sheep Dam been built.

1950 to Lem Wilson. Wilson's property was acquired by the Department of Agriculture for the N.R.A. in 1974-1975. Lem's house is now used by the Forest Service as an administrative station.

The Pittsburg Ferry in 1912. Mike Thomason is on the far right.

"He who comes first to the hill may sit where he will," and the first one down the hill on the Idaho side of the river was Henry Kurry. He arrived from White Bird in 1877 with his wife Mary and their three boys: Henry, Albert and Ira. The Kurrys settled on the high bar, where the present road crosses Kurry Creek for the first time. They built rock houses which were a local landmark until leveled by a Forest Service bulldozer.

By 1896, besides Thomason, the Kurrys had three other neighbors: John Wellman was living at the spring on the head of Kurry Creek, W. W. Johnson had taken a parcel at the ferry landing, and H. Klopton had a cabin at the mouth of the creek that still bears his name.

The wagon road from White Bird ferry over Pittsburg Saddle and down to the Thomason ferry was completed in 1900 and was referred to as a county road a year later. This opened the gate to new arrivals. Between 1904 and 1915, 21 homestead entries were filed in the Pittsburg Landing area. Only eight of them were patented, the rest were rejected or relinquished.

The Kurrys enlarged their holdings when both Henry's and Albert's wives obtained homesteads in 1904 and 1909. In addition to their ranching, Albert ran Thomason's ferry at times.

A post-office was established in May, 1905, operated by Martha Wood. It closed in early 1907, reopened in January, 1910 under Anna Brownlee but closed again three and a half years later.

"Cougar" Dave Lewis, government scout and packer for the Sheepeater Indian War, was running some horses in the Pittsburg Basin and cut trails with the Kurry boys. He told them about the country on the lower end of the Middle Fork of the Salmon River and Albert decided to try cattle ranching there.

He pulled out of Pittsburg around 1915 and bought squatter's rights to Brush Creek on the Middle Fork. There he went into the winter of 1919-1920 with 300 cattle, and in the spring had scarcely enough left to hold a barbecue. Then his wife Loula died. After the funeral in Boise, his older brother Henry joined him on the Middle Fork for several years. Albert returned to Pittsburg in 1926.

The old man with the hay hook came for Henry Kurry, Sr. about the time of World War I. He rests on his homestead in an unmarked grave next to the hill, on the flat where the county road first crosses the creek on the way down from the Saddle. A row of Osage orange trees planted by the Kurrys still grow on the homestead. The trees are a member of the mulberry family, native to southern states, and bear a milky, curiously wrinkled, inedible fruit in the fall.

The main bar at Pittsburg, below the Kurry land, was taken in January of 1896 by George "Long hair" Wood and his wife, Martha. Martha had three children by a previous marriage: Julia, Carl, and Ralph Kennedy. She and George had three children: Lester, Georganna, and Boyd.

George was six-foot-six-inches tall, a prize fighter from Texas. He sold all but a small band of his 3,600 sheep before coming to Pittsburg Landing. After a few years the Woods turned entirely to agriculture. They had a large hewed log house with cellar, a wagon shed and tenant house as well. George and his sons ditched water from Klopton and Kurry Creeks to irrigate over a hundred acres of hay, and an orchard with a couple of hundred fruit trees, plus a 2-acre garden. In 1900, Wood tunneled beneath Kurry Creek in the hope that he could increase the stream's flow, but his efforts failed. Within ten years, the Woods were cutting 375 tons of alfalfa which they sold to neighboring ranchers. They also kept a few horses, cows, chickens and pheasants.

Tom and Anna Brownlee filed on a tract near the mouth of Klopton Creek in 1910, but Wood owned all the land around it and denied them access. Brownlee relinquished the claim and Wood filed on it, obtaining title.

George noticed a seep on the upper bar, in the early Twenties, which he believed was petroleum. He had a steam drilling rig brought by iron-wheeled wagon to the bar and spudded a 500-foot well. It proved to be a dry hole, but the casing is still in place. Rufus Cole bought the rig and hauled it to McCall to run a sawmill.

The grim winter of 1919-1920 caught Frank "Bow" Wyatt's cattle at Pittsburg. There was no fall feed and the hay was all consumed. Wyatt lost over 500 head in one night. When winter finally thinned away, there were piles of bones that remained visible for many years.

The Nez Perce Sheep Company bought the Wood ranch and the Woods moved to Springfield, Oregon. Nez Perce was managed by Charley Finnigan, and Neal Morris was foreman at this time. They used the winter range along the river and struggled with the livestock market during a period when good years were like angel visits: few and far between.

George and Adelaine Behean homesteaded the head of Kurry Creek in 1903, where John Wellman and Tom Jolly had preceded them. The Beheans had five children, and built their cattle herd to 700 head. They eventually acquired Sam Robinson's homestead on the stream. Robinson, who raised barley hay, arrived the same year as the Beheans.

The George Behean family in 1903 at their ranch on Behean Creek.

(He was Mrs. Behean's brother.) Sam and Pathena Robinson moved across Pittsburg Saddle down to Deer Creek, where one of their four children, Harry, still ranches at this writing. The Beheans, along with Wyatt and Gills, controlled most of the open range around Pittsburg and up the ridge to Cold Springs. The Beheans sold their holdings and 1,000 head of cattle in 1916 to Frank Wyatt for $90,000 — a particularly impressive sum for that time.

Sam and Pathena Robinson. Pathena was Dad Wilson's oldest daughter. The picture was taken in 1910.

Another homestead entry was made in 1914 at the mouth of Klopton Creek by William Stockdale, who pursued it with more success than Brownlee had. Bill Stockdale's family had a large six-room house and a log barn.

The Campbell brothers of New Meadows bought the entire Pittsburg area in the early 1930's and made it part of the well-known Circle C ranch. There were 61 people living in the Pittsburg Landing area at that time. As with most of the private holdings along the river, this portion of the ranch was acquired by the Forest Service for the Hells Canyon N.R.A.

Kyle McGrady on the boat and Jack Titus next to the 1941 Chevy. Jack had purchased a new car and was bringing the old one over to Joe Sterling at Pittsburg.

Joe Sterling, who had lost one arm in a shotgun accident, and Frank Wilson, who had lost a leg when a horse rolled with him, at Pittsburg Landing. Both men could pitch hay and ride horses with the best of the ranch hands.

*A 1942 photograph of Kyle McGrady hauling Bob Titus' plane out from Pittsburg on the **Idaho**. Bob wrecked the plane in a freshly plowed field, but was unhurt.*

Looking west down at Pittsburg Landing from the road to the suddle.

The Pittsburg ferry was discontinued in October, 1933, by order of the Wallowa County Court due to lack of funds. Jack Titus was operating it at the time for $20 a month plus crossing fees.

The boat landing where abbreviated Hells Canyon river trips terminate is marked by a cement ramp at Lower Pittsburg Landing on the Idaho side.

Snake River pictographs, done with red pigment.

The Torpid Snake:

Pleasant Valley Creek to Lewiston

"We live in a moment of history when change is so rapid that we begin to see the present only when it is disappearing."

— Laing

Mile 35.5 **West Creek** on the right. The Forest Service set aside 30 acres at the mouth of this creek in 1909 for a winter ranger station, but it has never been so used.

Oscar Newkirk built a small frame house and farmed a half dozen acres of alfalfa at this site. He fought fire for the Forest Service in 1919. Oscar patented his homestead a year later.

Mile 35.6 **Pleasant Valley Creek** on the left. Ben Johnson was a pioneer rancher in the attractive basin located up the creek.

About a quarter mile below this creek is the site once proposed for construction of the Pleasant Valley Dam. Yellow paint marks on both sides of the river indicate the intended location and height. The flat on the Idaho side of the river was used as a camp in 1954-55 by men involved in exploratory drilling for Morrison-Knudsen construction company.

The dam proposed for this site by Pacific Northwest Power Company would have been, at 535 feet, the third highest concrete-arch dam of its time, with the five largest generators in the world. This $495 million impoundment would have backed water to the base of Hells Canyon Dam, flooding 6,600 acres. Construction would have taken four years. Access plans called for a new bridge across the Salmon River near White Bird and a paved road from there over Pittsburg Saddle to the river.

Between Pleasant Valley Dam and the Grande Ronde, five additional Snake River dams were on the drawing board. Details about each will be furnished at their proposed locations, but a brief recapitulation of the 20-year struggle between dam opponents and proponents seems appropriate here. Those who feel the controversy was too recent and political to merit inclusion might bear in mind that, historically, the defeat of the pro-dam forces was the most significant conservation victory of the decade; without that success this guide would be as necessary as a windshield wiper on a submarine.

The events of those contentious years can be most readily comprehended by presenting them in chronological order:

1954: Four private utility companies, Pacific Power and Light, Portland General Electric, Washington Water Power, and Montana Power and Light incorporate in Oregon under the name Pacific Northwest Power Company (PNP) to build, operate and maintain a dam at Pleasant Valley and apply to the Federal Power Commission (FPC) for a preliminary permit at the site.

1955: The FPC grants PNP a three-year preliminary permit. Five months later, PNP files a construction license application with the Commission for Pleasant Valley Dam *and* for Low Mountain Sheep – a reregulating dam 20 miles downstream, just above the mouth of the Imnaha River.

1956: FPC holds hearings on the PNP Co. application.

1957: The Examiner for the FPC recommends that a license be issued to PNP Co. for the project.

1958: The Federal Power Commission denies the license application (and their Examiner's advice) on the ground that any project which includes the 700-foot Nez Perce Dam, a mile below the mouth of Salmon River, will make greater use of Snake River hydro-potential than PNP's proposal. Pacific Northwest Power then files a license application for a 670-foot dam (High Mountain Sheep) on the Snake, a mile *above* the mouth of the Salmon River.

1960-61: Washington Public Power Supply System (WPPSS), a coalition of 18 Washington municipalities, applies to the FPC for a permit to build the Nez Perce Dam under the "public preference" clause of the Federal Power Act. WPPSS also amended its application to include the High Mountain Sheep Dam should the FPC find that project preferable.

1962: Secretary of Interior, Stewart Udall, puts the Department of Interior on record as favoring a *federal* dam at the High Mountain Sheep site. The FPC Examiner issues an opinion in favor of PNP and rejects WPPSS and Interior applications.

1964: The FPC upholds their Examiner's recommendation and issues PNP a 50-year license to build and operate High Mountain Sheep Dam. WPPSS and the Department of Interior file separate appeals in the U.S. District Court of Appeals for Washington, D.C. PNP begins core drilling on the Snake River.

285

1965: The court of appeals hears oral arguments, rearguments, and a rehearing. (Warren E. Burger is one of the three judges to sit at the rehearing.)

1966: The appeals court rules 3-0 in favor of the FPC and PNP. Petitions for review filed by WPPSS and Interior are accepted by the U.S. Supreme Court.

1967: The Supreme Court in *Udall* v. *Federal Power Commission* remands the case to the FPC with instructions to rehear the entire proceedings while considering all issues relevant to "public interest" including "preserving reaches of wild rivers and wilderness areas, the preservation of anadromous fish for commercial and recreational purposes, and the protection of wildlife." Russ Mager and members of the Idaho Alpine Club form the Hells Canyon Preservation Council (HCPC).

1968: Idaho Senators Church and Jordan introduce a bill calling for a 10 year moratorium on Snake River dam building. PNP and WPPSS join forces and file a joint application for the High Mountain Sheep project.

Interior Department now seeks federal development of the Appaloosa site, halfway between Pleasant Valley and High Mountain Sheep.

1969: The new Secretary of Interior, Walter Hickel, announces that Interior has decided to oppose *any* dams on the middle Snake.

1970: Senator Bob Packwood, of Oregon, and Congressman John Saylor, of Pennsylvania, introduce the HCPC's Snake "National River" bill to Congress. The bill and moratorium die during that session. Governor Cecil Andrus writes the FPC, putting the state of Idaho on record as opposed to further dams in Hells Canyon.

1971: The Examiner for the FPC recommends issuance of a license for the Pleasant Valley — Mountain Sheep project to the PNP-WPPSS coalition.

1972: The Senate appropriates $4 million so that the U.S. Forest Service can purchase private land which is being subdivided in Hells Canyon.

1973: The Hells Canyon National Recreation Area bill, with backing from Idaho and Oregon Senators, is dropped in the hopper. Field hearings are held on the bill in Idaho and Oregon.

1974: Senate Interior Committee schedules final hearings in Washington, D.C. A two month delay is caused by the Forest Service announcement that it has no position on the matter and is preparing an alternative plan.

1975: The Senate passes the Hells Canyon bill in June, for the second time. In November, the House passes the bill 342 to 53.

1976: New Years Eve, President Gerald Ford signs the Hells Canyon National Recreation Area Act. Snake River of Hells Canyon has been saved.

Mile 36.7 **Davis Creek** on the Oregon side; named for Ben Davis who had squatters rights here.

Mile 37.2 **McCarty Creek** enters on the left, a compliment to Tim McCarty, early homesteader.

Mile 38.3 **Big Canyon Creek** drains the Idaho hillside. Jimmy Powell settled in Big Canyon in 1892, about three-and-a-half miles from the river, where Bear Gulch comes into Big Canyon. Powell built a comfortable, split-level log house. Visitors entering the front door came down steps through two rooms to the kitchen. Warm air from the kitchen stove heated the higher rooms.

Jimmy Powell's cabin in Big Canyon. His building is on the left and Jones has spliced in the addition on the right.

Powell irrigated 20 acres and raised a herd of cows.

In 1901, Jimmy Powell sold his squatter's rights to Lewis Termis. Termis transferred the holdings to Seth Jones, Jr., a year later, and Jones obtained a Desert Patent for the tract in 1910. Seth's wife, Edna, filed on the Grand Prize mining claim adjacent to their entry. They lived on the land until it was necessary to put their children in school.

Jones sold out to cattlemen Wyatt and Ross. They built corrals and fences in the area.

The Oscar Canfield family were early settlers on the Doumecq Plains at the head of Big Canyon, and one of their sons, Bert, located the Keno copper mine in Big Canyon. The vein was worked by hand and development was never extensive.

Neal Morris had the ranch as sheep range for a period, then it was purchased by Herb Walters in 1935. It remains in the hands of the Walters' family.

There is a campsite on the downriver side of the creek.

Seth Jones (left) and George Behean (right) in 1914 at Border Days celebration in Grangeville. Jones is astride a mule.

Mile 38.9 **Somers Creek** flows in on the Oregon side. This stream commemorates Frank Somers, who was mining along the river in the 1880's from Salt Creek to Somers Creek. Lou Knapper met him in the summer of 1889 and stated that Frank trapped for a living at that time.

Somers homesteaded about three miles up the creek and grazed cattle. In the 1890's he switched to sheep and hired a teen-aged herder, Leonard Johnson, to help him. They became partners for several years, until Johnson decided to run his own livestock business. Frank reverted to cattle ranching until he became too elderly to do the necessary work. At that point, he sold out to F. R. "Dad" Wilson.

Dad Wilson and his wife came to the Snake River from the Sugar Loaf country on the Idaho side. They raised a family of three boys and four girls on the creek. The youngest boy, Frank, managed the place as part of his sheep operation. He and his wife, Minnie, had two children. Frank lost his leg in an accident when a horse rolled on him. Despite this handicap, he successfully handled the ranch and all the chores it entailed for several years.

F. R. "Dad" Wilson, who purchased the Somers Creek ranch from Dad Somers. The girl on the left is his granddaughter, Malva.

Dad Wilson (right) with his children in 1919 at Lewiston.

Anna Wilson (standing with her mother, Mrs. F. R. Wilson).

Frank and Minnie Wilson on Snake River.

Nancy Whittier and her three children, Lela, Howard and Blanche, moved from Spokane to a cabin about a mile up Somers Creek in 1911. Nancy survived by raising a flock of 200 turkeys, which subsisted in turn on grasshoppers and grass seed.

Nancy's oldest daughter, Lela, was married to Frank Raymond. When Frank had been drinking he was the original subverter of "all's right with the world." One afternoon, a well-liquored Frank headed back to Somers Creek after a five-day stay in White Bird. He crossed at the Pittsburg ferry and arrived at the cabin after dark. Entering the cabin, he pulled his pregnant wife out of bed and began to beat her. When Nancy attempted to interfere, he struck her. Lela's brother, Howard, tried to interrupt the battery and was also floored. "The limits of tyrants are prescribed by the endurance of those they would oppress." Howard seized a .45-70 rifle and dropped Raymond, dead as mutton. The man was buried in an unmarked grave by the creek.

Howard, who was 17, was exonerated by a jury in Enterprise the next spring.

Lela's boy drowned in the creek a couple of years later, and he is also buried on the site.

Nancy Whittier moved to Seattle. Lela later remarried, and moved there too.

Blanche Whittier and Iva Jarrett crossing Snake River.

Mile 39.3 **Camp Creek** enters on the left. According to Harley Horner, Nate and James Tryon had a sheep camp here in the 1890's on winter range. The Indian name for the area was Wis-pei-kas-poo-hol.

A rough trail and jeep road lead four miles up the creek and around to the O-O ranch.

Mile 39.6 **Tryon Creek** runs out on the Oregon shore. Nate and Jim Tryon, brothers, homesteaded on a bench about two miles from the river. They had herded sheep for Lou Knapper before developing their own ranch. The Tryons built a two-story log cabin and used the creek water to irrigate their hay crop.

Low stone walls on both sides of Tryon Creek, below the river trail, form a crude "corral." The corral is known to have existed before any white men came to the canyon, but its purpose has never been ascertained.

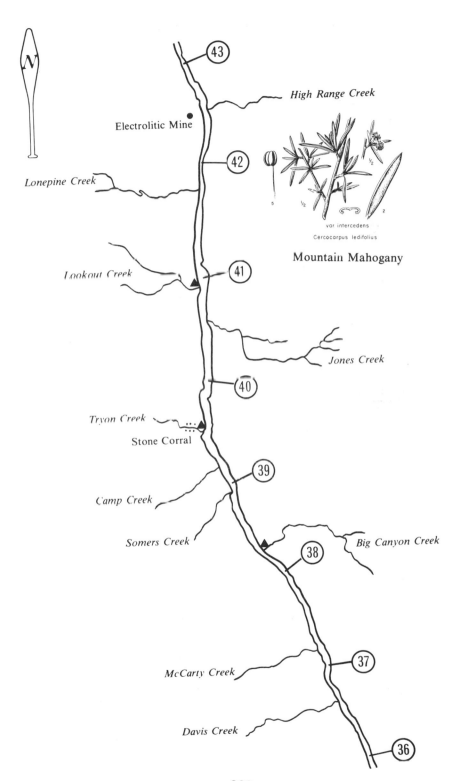

High Range Creek

Electrolitic Mine

Lonepine Creek

var intercedens
Cercocarpus ledifolius

Mountain Mahogany

Lookout Creek

Jones Creek

Tryon Creek

Stone Corral

Camp Creek

Somers Creek

Big Canyon Creek

McCarty Creek

Davis Creek

Mile 40.6 **Jones Creek** on the Idaho side. The surname of Asa "Ace" Jones, son of "Sourdough" Jones, and brother of Seth Jones, has been bequeathed to this stream. Dace Harriman and Carl Henderson took homesteads here.

Mile 41. **Lookout Creek** on the Oregon side. The old stock trail in this vicinity, prior to 1946, crossed slopes steep as a church roof, and in winter the path was slick as soap. The Tryon brothers cautioned travelers to "look out for that piece of trail" and their solicitude is recalled by the creek's name.

There is a limited camp on the bluff, downstream from the creek drainage.

Mile 41.8 **Lonepine Creek** is the gulch on the left. There is a 400-foot mine tunnel just below the creek — the tailing dump can be seen from the river. The copper mine was known as the Electrolytic mine, though a 1917 map shows it as the "Electrolyptic." The mining took place early in the twentieth century. Jim Dorrance removed the steel ore cart rails and transported them to a site above Bar Creek where they were used to make a sturdy corral.

Mile 42.5 **High Range Creek** runs in from the Idaho side. The homesteads taken on this creek were filed on benches several miles from the river. Joe McHenry was the first squatter. He sold to the Poe brothers, Fred and Claude; both Poes married Qualey sisters who were neighbors on the Snake River slope. The Qualey ranch was founded by Earl Brace, who was succeeded by the Hunsacker family.

Mile 43.4 **Getta Creek** on the Idaho shore. John Getta was a Frenchman. He had a cabin by the creek and spent most of his time placer mining on the opposite shore of the river. Getta kept a dog and two white horses.

The first family to settle at the mouth of Getta Creek were the Auchimballes — they had two sons. Mrs. Auchimballe taught school across the divide at Deer Creek on the Salmon.

Jim and Tom Aram, brothers of Mrs. Auchimballe, started a cattle ranch on Getta Creek in 1897, not far from the river. Tom drowned in the Clearwater while moving cattle to market on the Silcott ferry. Jim continued to run the ranch by himself for many years.

Slim and Mary Johnson acquired the Getta Creek Ranch from Mrs. A. S. Hardy after her husband died, and they ran cattle there in 1939. Their oldest boy was a year old when they moved into the house a mile up the creek. Slim had been living on Cow Creek, packing for the Forest Service. Mary had taught school there for four years, and she taught at

Crooks Corral as well. They tried their hand with sheep for a couple of years in the early 1940's, then went back to cattle.

The Johnsons had four children; all of them were born at Cottonwood, Idaho. Life became a little easier when loggers, in exchange for a right-of-way, punched a road down from the Qualey ranch to the mouth of Getta Creek in July, 1945. Supplies could then be hauled with a surplus weapons carrier instead of by horse or boat. The road can be seen from the river.

Their oldest boy, Pete, went seven miles to school at Boles on the Joseph Plains. When all of the children were of school age, the Johnsons moved to Cottonwood. Slim was killed in a tractor-mowing accident on Rice Creek in 1961, but Mary, her daughter Polly, and son-in-law, Lou, still operate the ranch. They graze Santa Gertrudis cattle at the time of this writing.

D. H. Saxby Boles, from the community of Boles, drowned in the Snake across from the mouth of Getta Creek. He and his wife, Hazel, and their two children had come down from the Joseph Plains to can some peaches. They took an afternoon for a picnic and rowed across the river to bathe on a sand bar they had used for that purpose before. High water had undercut the bar and Hazel went in over head. Neither she nor her husband could swim. Saxby went to her rescue, but drowned. She took the boat back across the river and went for help. Jack Brust brought a horse and mule down Wolf Creek the next day and found Boles still clutching a boulder beneath the water. He packed the body out for burial.

Nile 43.5 **Rankin Bar — Dick Rivers Camp — Copper Creek** on the Oregon bank. William "Billy" Rankin camped on Rankin Bar in March, 1900. At this time he discovered what he believed was a significant copper prospect and staked the claim.

Rankin was born in Kansas in 1876 and was adopted at an early age by John and Aseneth Rankin, who emigrated to the Oregon country by wagon train. Most of the information about the old man's life was preserved by Robert Wiggins of Joseph, Oregon, who recorded Rankin's conversation in a resthome a few months before his death in 1967.

Billy exhausted the educational opportunities of the public schools in Joseph, and at the Academy in Enterprise, as a young man. He then taught school during summers in Oregon.

Dick Rivers camp at Copper Bar.

In 1889, at age 23, he decided to try the outdoor life, and began herding sheep on the Snake River for his uncle, Jim Rankin, and his uncle's partner, Jim Lozier. Their winter range extended from Lonepine Creek to Robinson Gulch.

The early 1900's found Billy spending increasing amounts of time on his mining interests at Copper Mountain, behind Rankin Bar. Prior to 1908, he had been herding sheep, doing assessment work, and laboring on his own place at Joseph Creek. Rankin had sold some claims downriver at Eureka Bar to the Eureka Mining Company for $14,000 in shipping credit. The Eureka Company's boat, the *Imnaha,* was to haul

Billy's ore at Copper Mountain to Lewiston for $12 a ton — to be charged against the credit. But throwing your rope before building a loop doesn't catch the calf. As mentioned in the boating section of this book, the *Imnaha* sank at Mountain Sheep Rapid. Rankin's credit went down with the ship.

Billy and his partners tried to haul the ore on their own 20-foot sweepboat. They made several trips, but roping the boat back upstream proved impractical for transporting commercial quantities of ore.

Billy Rankin's mining pump which can still be seen close to the river below Copper Bar. It was powered with a Model-T engine.

Rankin passed the civil service examination for Forest Ranger in 1912, and served as District Ranger for the Burnt River District in Whitman National Forest for three years. When Forest Service policy expanded the job to a full-time position, Rankin resigned because he felt he would have insufficient time to develop his copper lode. The teacher-herder-miner spent most of his remaining years on the bar by the river. He died at age 91 in the Idaho County Nursing Home in Grangeville. Billy Rankin's original stone cabin still stands in the draw up Copper Creek, quiet as the dreaming trees and empty as their shade.

Rankin's second frame cabin on the bar is now part of Richard "Dick" Rivers' Copper Creek quarters. Rivers, discussed in the "Captains and Boatmen" section, runs the mailboat upriver from Lewiston. He obtained a special-use permit from the Forest Service and hauled materials to the site in order to build a dining hall and a dozen cabins. These comfortable facilities can accommodate 24 people. During the summer, Rivers' boats make trips twice weekly, for tourists who wish to stay overnight, or longer, at the camp. Guests can hike, fish, or simply relax, without sacrificing hot water and clean sheets.

Mile 44.5 **Bob Creek** on the left, followed by **Cat Creek.** Named by Lou Knapper and Ed Jennings, according to Harley Horner, for the bobcats they killed while running sheep along the river in this area.

Mile 44.8 **Ragtown Bar** on the right. Dace Harriman and Carl Henderson lived in tents here until David Van Pool bought them out — hence the name.

A three-mile ditch, packed with clay, brought water to the bar from Getta Creek.

Mile 45.5 **Roland Bar — Blankenship Ranch — Roland Creek** on the Oregon side. J. Ray Johnson, Ken Johnson's uncle, owned Roland Bar and Tryon Creek. He went out of business and the Blankenship brothers, Jim and Dick, went partners in the sheep business here. They acquired the Jim Dorrance property on the north fork of Roland Creek as well as Cat Creek and the Tryon Creek land. Jim and his wife Lois lived on the bar for several years. Lem Wilson was the subsequent owner, and the Forest Service acquired the land from him for the Hells Canyon NRA.

Mile 46. **Wolf Creek** drains the country on the Idaho shore. According to John Rooke, an elderly German named "Wolfe" mined at the mouth of this stream for several winters. He was gone by the time Frank McGrane and Louis Belknap came through with cattle in 1880.

Bert Canfield was the first man to settle at the mouth of the creek, about the time the Otto brothers, Newt and Ed, located upstream from him. Ed was killed by a bartender in Riggins; shortly afterward Ollie Canfield and Ed Wyatt acquired the Otto holdings. They brought the first white-faced bulls into the area.

Ed was a son of the "cattle baron," Frank "Bow" Wyatt, and married Mattie Crooks who had land at the head of Wolf Creek. This creek

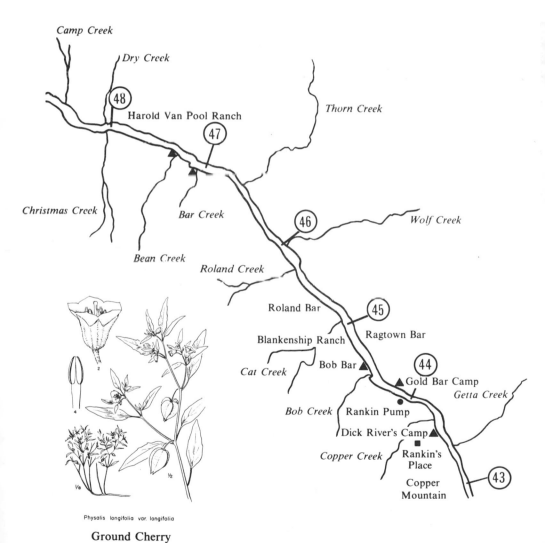

Camp Creek

Dry Creek

48

Harold Van Pool Ranch

Thorn Creek

47

Christmas Creek

Bar Creek

Bean Creek

Roland Creek

Wolf Creek

46

Roland Bar

45

Blankenship Ranch

Ragtown Bar

Cat Creek

Bob Bar

44

Gold Bar Camp

Getta Creek

Bob Creek

Rankin Pump

Dick River's Camp

Copper Creek

Rankin's Place

Copper Mountain

43

Physalis longifolia var. longifolia

Ground Cherry

draws its water from a big country and Mattie Wyatt used to say there was "only one thing wrong with the area" — but she would never specify the defect. A year before she died, Johnny Carrey finally pried the secret out of her. She said, "You know, the only thing wrong with that country was somebody was always gettin' the worst of it."

In more recent years, George and Nan Brust owned substantial acreage on Wolf Creek and sold to the Heckman brothers who have retained it to this time. Clyde and Alberta Morrow also had land in Wolf Creek, though their main ranch was downriver at Birch Creek.

Mile 47 **Birch Creek,** just downriver from Wolf Creek, in Idaho. The first locaters on this stream were brothers and sisters of the Oscar Canfield family, for which a settlement on the Doumecq Plains above the river was named. The father was a survivor of the Whitman Massacre. The Canfield brothers raised cattle and grazed a large herd of horses.

Clyde and Alberta Morrow acquired the holdings in 1927 and ran it as the Flying U ranch. After Clyde's death in Grangeville, Alberta continued to operate the ranch most competently. Her son, Floyd, was killed in a tragic accident when his horse fell in an icy feed yard on the Birch Creek quarters. Two daughters, Grace and Dolores, grew up in the Snake River breaks, and the ranch remains in Morrow hands — for over 50 years at this time.

Mile 48. **Christmas Creek** on the Oregon slope.

J. H. Horner indicates the name commemorates Christmas Day, 1888, when Jim Tryon and Lou Knapper brought their sheep here for winter range. Horner also said that there was an Indian ford across the river at the bar just above the mouth of the creek.

Jim and Elvarre Dorrance bought the location from Homer Hayes in the fall of 1927. Homer was raising cattle there and they moved into the house he had occupied. Their holdings extended upriver to Roland Bar.

The Dorrances ran about 275 Hereford cattle. They wintered the steers along the river and summered them up on Lord Flat. In the fall, the market crop was trailed to Joseph. About 40 acres of hay was raised on the bench — most of it rye, which didn't require irrigation.

The couple had one of the first radios on the river, but batteries were so precious it could be used only for the evening news. They also had the first phone in the area on the Oregon side. Jim stretched 800 feet of #9 wire across the river to connect with the switchboard at Boles, which in turn was linked to Grangeville.

The Dorrances had two children: Jimmy and Phyllis. When their son was ready to attend school, the family moved to Enterprise. They sold the ranch in 1943 to Frank Wilson, mentioned at Somers Creek.

Mile 48 **Dry Creek** on the Idaho side. When Mattie Crooks Wyatt saw Dry Creek as a 16-year old girl there were signs of Nez Perce camp grounds all the way to the forks of the stream.

The Bill Rooke family settled Dry Creek; they farmed rye hay on the dry bar, grazed some cattle, and raised horses — their first love. The Rookes handled a rodeo string, and when they pulled out of Snake River they had 700 head of horses. They followed the Boise Trail out and moved down to Oreana and Three Creeks in the Owyhee country of southeastern Oregon and northern Nevada.

Dry Creek is still called the Van Pool ranch at this writing, after Harold Van Pool who built the white house visible from the river, but the ranch has been sold to Maurice and Catherine Hitchcock, of the White Swan Lumber Company.

At the forks of Dry Creek, less than two miles from the river, was Ed and Mamie Robie's homestead. They ran cattle in the area and their son, Bill, was born on the ranch. After they proved up on the homestead, the Robies moved back to Slate Creek on Salmon River.

There was a brush corral with rock wings at the Robie ranch. This structure was of interest historically. It was built by Little Bear and Half Moon, Nez Perce Indians left behind by Chief Joseph when war broke out in White Bird Canyon. The Nez Perce cattle had crossed the Snake but hadn't forded the Salmon River. Joseph left word with the two Indians to look after the stock. Of course, the situation proved impossible — horses swam the river, steers were stolen by white men and what wasn't caught soon went wild. When Clark Gill first saw the corral there was a sign on the gate which read: Usum — Breakum — Fixum.

Mile 48.4 **Camp Creek** on the right.

Mile 49.2 **Big Sulphur Creek** on the river's edge in Idaho. David and Sarah Van Pool bought Newell Stubblefield's preemption rights on Big Sulphur in 1911. The Van Pools had moved from Missouri to Sterling, Colorado, and then through the persuasion of a cousin, to Cottonwood, Idaho.

They left Grangeville with a wagon and three of their nine children, Hazel, Harold and Heeman. They travelled to the White Bird ferry, crossed Doumecq and Joseph Plains and settled at Stubblefield's place about a mile and a half up Sulphur Creek.

David and Sarah Van Pool.

David and Sarah Van Pool with their children, leaving Grangeville in 1911 for the Snake River.

The Van Pools and their children had the ambition of a beaver colony. They turned Stubblefield's shack into a satisfactory house. Hazel and Heeman took homesteads. As homesteaders acquired patents to their entries and then sought to sell them, David always managed to have the money to buy. He bought land on Sugar Loaf for a song and did his own singing. Their herd of 500 cattle expanded with their holdings. Eventually the Van Pools held title to nearly 18,000 acres.

Hazel Van Pool on Snake River.

*David and Sarah haying their Snake
River ranch. Hazel holding the pitchfork,
Hemman on the left, Harold on the right.
The rake was brought up river by boat.*

David and Sarah left the ranch to their son, Harold, and spent their last years in Lewiston. Harold operated the cattle outfit for several years, then sold to the Hitchcocks.

Thorn Spring Creek comes in across the river from Big Sulphur.

Mile 49.6 **Trail Gulch** on the left. The river trail climbs up this gulch and around to Roland Creek, where it drops again to the river.

Mile 50 **Deep Creek** flows into the Snake on the Oregon side of the river. This stream drainage has been the scene of considerable activity over the past hundred years. It was known first as Dead Line Creek, in the 1880's, because a stockman, T. J. Douglass, would not allow Indians to range their horses north of this drainage.

A massacre occurred at the mouth of the tributary in 1887 — 31 Chinese miners were murdered for their gold. The incident has been ably researched by Robert Sincock and Gerald Tucker, but some background information might add context to the situation.

Thousands of Chinese left their homeland for the goldfields of California in the 1850's; many thousands more came to work in the western railroad construction camps. As the Mother Lode played out and the transcontinental railroad was completed, the "Celestials" moved to the mining areas of the Inland Empire. Indefatigible and frugal workers, they labored as cooks and laundry men, saving enough money to buy exhausted placer claims at exorbitant prices and then reworking them with surprising success.

White prospectors regarded the Chinese as "foreigners" and generally treated them with hostility and even brutality. Everyone on the mining frontier knew the odds facing a person who did not have more than "a Chinaman's chance."

By 1882, widespread resentment of the Orientals caused Congress to pass the Chinese Exclusion Act. Immigration from China was suspended for 10 years, and the Act was later extended indefinitely. Anti-Chinese riots and lynchings took place in California, Washington, Wyoming and Idaho.

At the height of this agitation, Chinese miners began to appear in appreciable numbers along the Salmon and Snake Rivers. A party was reported coming up through Hells Canyon as early as 1877, and several groups came through Lewiston in 1886-87, on their way to the Snake River diggins. One such group pulled supply boats upriver in October, 1886, and the members divided in two contingents — one worked the winter at Salt Creek, the other placered in the Robinson Gulch — Deep

Creek vicinity. Most of their mining was done with dipper sticks and wooden rockers.

In May of 1887, a gang of horse thieves was using the old Douglass cabin at Dug Bar, about two and a half miles below the Deep Creek camp. The outlaws were operating on both sides of the river, stealing horses in one state and selling them in the other. Chinese in the area must have been welcome as polecats at a picnic. The horse thieves suspected the Orientals had collected considerable gold through the winter, and decided to rob them.

One morning in the last week of May, rifle fire errupted on both sides of the Deep Creek ravine, catching the unsuspecting miners at their labor. Most of them were murdered within a few minutes, but a few were spared in an effort to learn where the gold was hidden. The outlaws knew the dust was there, but like the devil's ice cream, they had no idea where it was kept. The surviving Chinese apparently spoke no English, and though mutilated by the gunmen, were unable in their terror to disclose the location of their stash. When the rustlers' efforts proved futile, they shot the rest of the miners, threw their bodies in the river, took the provisions they could use, burned the camp and returned downriver to Dug Bar.

Bullet-riddled bodies began appearing in the river above and below Lewiston. In early June, the Chinese miners at Salt Creek boated down to visit their countrymen at Robinson Gulch and Deep Creek. Amid evidence of the atrocity, they found the bodies of three of their friends. Overcome with fear, they returned to their boats and floated to Lewiston, where they reported the crime to the authorities. Learning of the murders from newspaper reports, the Chinese consul general in San Francisco requested the Sam Yup Company (one of the Six Companies of California which controlled indentured Chinese emigrants) to pursue the case. The company dispatched Lee Loi to Lewiston, where he hired U.S. Commissioner J. K. Vincent as an investigator and offered a $1,000 reward for apprehension of the murderers.

Vincent wasn't raised on the short grass. He headed upriver with a Chinese guide and Jim McCormick, disguising himself as a miner. He left his companions pastured out of sight on a river bar a few miles below the Chinese camp with instructions to return to Lewiston if he wasn't back within 10 days.

As he worked his way up the Oregon shore, the detective encountered a group of drifters near the Douglass cabin, without visible means of support. He allayed their suspicions with stories of his mining endeavors, and elicited information with innocent questions. He learned the leaders of the group were Canfield, Evans and LaRue, and he noticed sacks of flour with Chinese markings. Vincent panned along the river while keeping the camp under discreet observation for several days. He estimated the strength of the gang at close to 30 men. At that point he rejoined his companions downriver and they returned to Lewiston.

Vincent made a trip to the Salmon River country to check on the activities of the outlaws in that area and then went back to Lewiston again. There he received a letter from Liang Ting Tsan, Consul-General, and F. A. Bee, Consul, of San Francisco, asking for details regarding the killing of the miners.

Vincent answered their inquiry July 19:

I have been and am still in the employ of the Chinese company, ferreting out the matter. From what I have so far found, things seem to show that white men were the murderers, as some of the provisions 'flour' I have traced directly to them. I have been following up, for six days, a white man who was at their camp and one who is the last one known to have been there. He has told some very curious stories about the matter, and some circumstances look very suspicious. But there is in that vicinity some twenty or thirty bad men and I was watched very closely for nine days. I expect to start again up Snake River on the east side and will get into their camp by some means and know what has been done with their property, if the agent here thinks best.

It was the most cold-blooded, cowardly treachery I have ever heard tell of on this coast, and I am a '49er. Every one was shot, cut up, and stripped and thrown in the river.

The Chinese here have paid me for what I have done so far, but Government ought to take it in hand, for with actions like this none are safe.

Vincent then checked some Idaho towns along Salmon River in an attempt to learn whether the gold dust and nuggets had been sold by members of the gang. Failing to uncover such a transaction, he returned to the Snake River by way of White Bird, Idaho. With assistance from a rancher who loaned him a boat, Vincent collected information about the outlaws by approaching their camp at night and eavesdropping on their conversations. He knew that if his presence was discovered his life wouldn't be worth a holler in a box canyon. Nonetheless, in this manner he was able to ascertain that some gold had been found and was to be converted to cash at a distant point, that the outlaws were aware an investigator was working on the case, and that the gang intended to disband — at least temporarily.

The detective returned to Lewiston once more, but knew he lacked sufficient evidence for an arrest. Repeated letters to him from the Chinese consul general requesting information went unanswered. The consul ordered Lee Loi and Chea Ke, another Chinese at Lewiston, to continue their inquiries, but they were unable to learn the names of the guilty parties.

In February of 1888, the Chinese minister to the United States, Chang Yen Hoon, sent a detailed report of the crime to Secretary of State Thomas Bayard. The minister did so, he wrote, "to the end that the local authorities may be communicated with so that justice may be secured by having the murderers arrested and punished, and that the Chinese during their sojourn here may be protected."

Vincent went to Wallowa County, Oregon, in the spring of 1888 and talked with two young men who had been members of the ring: Hezikiah Hughs and Frank Vaughn. He apparently persuaded them to turn state's evidence, and Vaughn testified before the grand jury. As a result of this testimony and Vincent's evidence, an indictment was issued against six men: Hiram Maynard, Carl Hughs, Robert McMillian, J. T. Canfield, Bruce Evans, and C. O. LaRue.

In April of that year, James Slater, a former U.S. Senator from Oregon, then living in Joseph, wrote Lewis McArthur, U.S. District Attorney in Portland:

> ... (McMillian, Hughs and Maynard) ... are in jail, the other three, who are regarded as ring leaders, are at large and out of the State and their exact whereabouts not definitely known, but it is believed that with proper effort they can be secured.
>
> Detectives will have to be employed to hunt down the three out of State. I believe there is no power vested in the Court or County to employ detectives for the purpose named.
>
> I feel sure that in such a case the Department of Justice can find some way to aid in the hunting down of these men.

A month later, Minister Chang Yen Hoon received a reply to the request he had addressed to the Secretary of State, signed by the Acting

Secretary. In part, it said:

> The crime having been committed against the laws and peace of Oregon, and the Indictment against certain of the alleged murderers having been found by the Criminal Courts of that State, there is no present occasion for Federal jurisdiction in the premises, or for interference to procure testimony on the part of the judicial officers of the United States.

The Wallowa County Circuit Court held a brief trial in August, 1888. The record shows:

> Hiram Maynard
>
> Carl Hughs (Hezikiah Hughs true name)
>
> Robert McMillian
>
> Arraigned for murder August 28, 1888.
>
> Plea entered of not guilty on August 29, 1888.
>
> Sept. 1, 1888 Verdict of Not Guilty was to each of the defendants above named and the case continued as to J. T. Canfield, Bruce Evans and C. O. La Rue.
>
> Sept. 1, 1888 Frank Vaughn, Grand Jury returned not a true bill. Defendant released and his bond ties discharged from all and any future liability therein.
>
> J. L. Rand, District Attorney, Ivanhoe and M. L. Olmstead Attorneys for the men acquitted. Piper and McGowan assisting in defense of M. & H.

So no one was ever convicted and punished for the Deep Creek massacre. Nor did the relatives of the murdered Orientals receive nities. In October, 1888, the United States agreed to pay the Chinese government $276,619.75 "for all losses and injuries" suffered by Chinese nationals in this country. But complete information about the Snake River deaths was not available when the negotiations took place, and the amount paid did not include compensation for the lives and property lost here.

Two stone walls against the rock outcrop on the downstream side of Deep Creek are all that remain of the Oriental camp. The marks painted on the outcrop are Indian pictographs, not Chinese ideograms.

Walt Beith and Frank Winters were involved in a cattle drive on Deep Creek in the fall of 1893. Beith's recollection of the event is interesting in its own right, but it is quoted here because it conveys a sense of how difficult it was to move a small herd of cows through this type of terrain — even when things went well.

Among the suggestions made by W. H. Winters in the letter I carried to his son, Frank, in April, one had to do with a small bunch of cattle which was reported off the range and running on lower Deep Creek. Prospectors and trappers reported both to Mr. Winters in the valley and to the boys on the river having seen cattle on Deep Creek. The number varied from 7 to 25 head.

Deep Creek was unoccupied and at that time was supposed to be too rough for any kind of stock. Mr. Winters wrote to Frank that he was sure there was a lost bunch of Anchor cattle somewhere on that creek and if we could find the time we should make an attempt to recover them.

Frank and I had talked about it all summer. We were both very anxious for the trip. I had asked Alex Warnock what he thought of our chances of success in attempting their recapture. Alex said, "You two lads have no more chance than a snowfall in —— (naming some hot country, I forget where.) Those cattle have been in there for three years. You could just as easy go up to the head of Granite Creek and round up a head of mountain sheep as to drive out that Deep·Creek bunch of cattle."

I told him we had some good tough and sure-footed mules. I asked him if the cattle could climb any place the mules couldn't follow. He admitted, perhaps not. Then I asked him why we could not follow the cattle until we wore them out and finally in the course of days or weeks break them to drive. He admitted that might be possible if we spent unlimited time on it; that all this might be done; but he still insisted that we could never drive them away from their home so long. They would have become so attached to their own locality that one had as well try to drive a squirrel away from his hole, as to try to drive them away from it.

Well, I did not feel so optimistic but still wanted to go and this seemed the time. Frank and I proceeded to get ready. We got two of George's best mules and one little buckskin horse that would follow like a dog. We took two weeks grub and a good bed.

It required a day to get into Deep Creek, another to locate the cattle. We sighted them late in the afternoon of the second day. While we were half mile away they broke cover and ran like deer. We calmly followed their tracks without hurrying and without stopping. At dark we camped and at daylight we took the trail. We sighted the cattle about three times and were within a quarter of a mile of them.

Never before or since have I seen cattle take such rough ground. They tore along over shale rock slides, up and down thru the rimrocks, they climbed ledges till several tore their dew claws off on the rocks, and left a bloody trail. We expected them to kill themselves in their mad flight, but only one, a yearling heifer, fell. We came up with her and put her out of her misery.

The third day they were more quiet. We were often within a hundred yards of them and so got a count. There proved to be 18 head after the death of the yearling. There were four cows and one steer that wore the Anchor brand. All the rest were slick ears, ranging from calves to three-year-olds.

The fourth day they could be turned at will. Our mules learned to follow the trail of those cattle like hounds would follow a trail. After the first day we did not have to bother, the mules would stick to the tracks, the little buckskin pack-horse right behind.

The fifth day we drove the cattle to the smoothest benches and really broke them to drive. Some of them would turn and fight every little while. Whenever they were pressed a little too hard and felt unable to escape by running they would turn on us. Our mules got to be expert in escaping a charge. We would have to stop and let the cattle cool off. By the evening of that day we could drive them wherever we wanted within the limits of their little range. We decided to make the attempt to force them beyond the limits of their territory on the seventh day. This was the job about which had our doubts. We spent the sixth day training our cattle to drive.

In the afternoon Frank asked me to go and pick out a route out of Deep Creek on which to take them over the ridge. I rode all afternoon and finally selected a route. There were two long lines of rimrock around the hill for three-

310

quarters of a mile. These were a hundred yards apart and were practically unbroken. They really made a lane for that distance, one end in the canyon and the other reaching the backbone of the ridge. Here there was one notch in the otherwise unbroken ledge down the ridge. If we could ever get the cattle between these two rimrocks I thought we could hold them and force them thru this notch. There they would be on smoother ground and headed for our home range.

Much to our surprise we had little trouble. We started the cattle at daylight the morning of the seventh day. In two hours we had them in the mouth of that rimrock fenced lane. We worked them very gingerly from there. In another hour they were thru the gap. We kept our advantage and soon had them on the smooth benches of Somers creek. That night we corraled them on Cougar Creek. The next day we branded 13 head. It took us all day and was ticklish work. Any of them would fight and we dare not get off our horses in the corral with them. If we had not had twin corrals we could not have handled them. No wild animal was ever more terrified or desperate than those cattle when caught. We would get them all in the back corral, shut the front gate, open the middle gate and ride in carefully to edge out one animal. Our mules were about as afraid of the cattle as the cattle were of us. We would get our slick ear out in the front corral by itself. Frank would tie onto it by the head and keep it tight snubbed. I would venture on the ground with a heel rope. The first big eight-months-old calf failed to give me time to get on my mule. In fact the mule was so scared it dodged me when I jumped for the saddle, after slipping the rope off the calf. The calf cut me off from the mule and finally poked me out thru a very narrow crack in the corral fence. After the first one we quit our mules and went and caught some cow horses that were not so afraid.

That night we had them all branded and turned out. We drove them to the extreme upper limit of the range with a view to keeping them from going back to Deep Creek. We felt pretty good about this trip. It came the nearest to being a complete success of any stunt we pulled. These 18 head of cattle stayed together for a month and did not mix with other cattle. Finally they broke up and formed new friendships with the rabble.

In all we were 11 days. Outside of the tediousness it was not a hard trip.

◆

Olin Reel used the mouth of Deep Creek as his shearing crew quarters in the 1920's. He tried to swim the river one afternoon when his boat was on the opposite shore. Impatience cost him his life. Art Spivy and Saxby Boles recovered Reel's body.

The campsite at Deep Creek will accommodate a small party; larger groups prefer **Robinson Gulch,** a quarter mile downriver.

Daisy Spivy with her children, Fred and Avo, about 1920 at Olin Reel's sheep camp at the mouth of Deep Creek. Daisy did all of the cooking and baking for the crew on a wood stove.

Mile 50.8 **Dug Creek** on the left shore.

Mile 51.2 **Little Sulphur Creek** on the right. The location for Appaloosa Dam, proposed by the Department of Interior, is just below this drainage. The dam would have been a 600-foot concrete arch with a 1,500,00 KW capability. It also would have entailed 32 miles of roads, inundation of 17,000 acres, and steel towers with transmission lines on the Oregon side clear across the Imnaha River.

Mile 51.7 **Fence Gulch** on the left bank. Named because of a pole fence built here by T. J. Douglass to hold his horses upriver.

The bar wears a contracted version of the name Douglass. Thomas J. Douglass built a cabin here about 1880, Horner relates, and used the area for winter range. Horner also indicates Douglass was shot from ambush near his place in 1883. The Porter brothers, who found his remains several months later, buried the stockman between Robinson and Dug Creeks.

The site was being used by George Craig at the time of the Deep Creek massacre. The range supported his cattle during winter months.

In more recent times, the Dug Bar ranch was part of Leonard Johnson's sheep operation. At the time this was written, the place was owned by Doug Tippett, son of Jidge Tippett, — a well-known Wallowa County stockman.

Nez Perce Crossing sign at Dug Bar.

Mile 52.5 **Dug Bar** and the **Nez Perce Crossing** on the Oregon side.

Along the backeddy at the head of the Dug Bar ranch hayfield stands a sign which marks for many the most poignant historical site in the canyon: the Nez Perce Crossing.

It is not the purpose of this guide to chronicle the Nez Perce or their flight, but river travelers unfamiliar with the incredible journey that began here might find a succinct version of the events which preceded and followed this epic crossing helpful in appreciating what otherwise appears an unremarkable location. (A more complete understanding may be had from titles listed in the bibliography.)

Early photograph of a Nez Perce woman.

Ancestors of the Nez Perce occupied portions of Hells Canyon and the Middle Snake River 6,000-8,000 years ago. Theirs was a stone, bone and horn culture and food consisted of camas, kouse, berries, fish and game.

The Nez Perce tribe was comprised of villages and bands ruled by war and peace chiefs who were elected, rather than hereditary. Each could speak only for his own village.

Rabbit Leggings, Nez Perce Indian.

The Nez Perce, or "Nimapu" as they called themselves, acquired horses in about 1730, discovered selective breeding, and developed herds which contained thousands of animals. With the acquisition of this new mobility they obtained materials from coastal and Great Plains tribes. Their mat-covered lodges gave way to buffalo hide tipis.

Physically the Nez Perce were above average height and had features of the finest Indian type. In temperament they were brave, trustworthy, hospitable, and unlike Plains Indians, refrained from torture.

From the time of Lewis and Clark, they had a tradition of friendship with whites. Nez Perce were a favorite with the mountain men. Several bands embraced Christianity as early as 1831, though missionaries from rival sects eventually alienated chiefs like Old Joseph: "White man's religion teaches him to quarrel about God."

With the discovery of gold at Pierce, Idaho, in 1860 and the establishment of Idaho Territory in 1863, the Nez Perce were pressured to revise an 1855 treaty by reducing reservation lands from 10,000 square miles to 1, 200. A council was held in May, 1863, at Fort Lapwai with government and military leaders. Chief Lawyer and most of the Chris tian chiefs such as Timothy, Jason, and Levi, agreed to the reduction because scarcely any of their own lands were affected. But Old Joseph, Toohoolhoolzote, and other headmen whose holdings would be confiscated under the new treaty angrily refused to sign it, and returned to their villages.

The government then maintained that Lawyer's signature and those of the other Clearwater chiefs bound *all* members of the Nez Perce tribe.

How specious that argument was is best revealed by two comments. Captain Curry, who observed the council, wrote in his journal:

Although the treaty goes out to the world as the concurrent agreement of the tribe, it is in reality nothing more than the agreement of Lawyer and his band, numbering in the aggregate not a third of the Nez Perce's tribe.

I withdrew my detachment, having accomplished nothing but that of witnessing the extinguishment of the last council fires of the most powerful Indian nation on the sunset side of the Rocky Mountains.

The second statement is that of Major Wood, Adjutant General who investigated the situation for General Howard six months before the outbreak of fighting. Wood wrote:

The non-treaty Nez Perces cannot in law be regarded as bound by the treaty of 1863, and insofar as it attempts to deprive them of the right to occupancy of any land, its provisions are null and void.

For five years the treaty went unratified, promises were broken and payments forgotten. Old Joseph died, and his son, Young Joseph (Thunder Rolling from Mountain Heights) took his place with the Wallowa band. He had promised his father that he would never sell the land of his people.

Wallowa Lake as it looked when the Nez Perce camped there.

Gradually farmers and ranchers encroached on the Indian portions of the Wallowa country. Missionaries were uneasy about the effect free Indians were having on reservation Indians who practiced subsistence farming and Christianity.

Influence was exerted to confine the non-treaty Indians to the Lapwai reservation so that the treaty Nez Perce would no longer be ridiculed for having sold their freedom for an empty promise. Once all the Nez Perce were corralled at Lapwai, farmers in the Wallowa could usurp their lands with unconcern.

But the Bureau of Indian Affairs had some doubts. A commission of the Department of the Interior and the War Department both indicated Joseph's band was not bound by the treaty. The Secretary of Interior obtained an Executive Order from President Grant in 1873 reserving the mountain and lake country of the Wallowa to the Indians and the lowland prairie, with 87 farms worth $67,000, to the settlers.

Unfortunately, the B.I.A. in Washington, D.C., mistakenly reversed the provisions of the division, thereby upsetting both factions. Eighteen seventy-four was an election year, and the Governor of Oregon, along with his delegates, was able to effect a recision of the Executive Order. Chief Joseph was not even informed of this action for nearly a year.

Nez Perce tipi, a pre-war photograph.

General Oliver Otis Howard was appointed commander of the Department of Columbia, which at the time included Idaho Territory. Howard had fought in the Civil War, at Fair Oaks where he lost an arm, at Gettysburg, and with Sherman in Georgia. He had also been on campaigns against Cochise and the Apaches.

Chief Joseph: Thunder Rolling From Mountain Tops.

After listening to the complaints of settlers and missionaries, he ordered Joseph's band onto the Lapwai reservation. The Indians were given one month to make the move. Joseph replied:

> War can and ought to be avoided. I want no war. My people have always been friends of the white men. Why are you in such a hurry? I can not get ready to move in thirty days. Our stock is scattered and the Snake River is very high. Let us wait till fall, then the river will be low. We want time to hunt up our stock and gather supplies for the winter.

General Howard was unmoved by the plea. "If you let the time run over one day, the soldiers will be there to drive you on the reservation and cattle outside the reservation at that time will fall into the hands of the white men."

The Indians went into the canyons and draws to gather their horses and cattle with heavy-hearted haste.

When the Indians arrived on the bank with their stock they found the river in full spring flood. They made rafts from tightly rolled skins lashed together and loaded with packs. Riders used horses to tow the rafts across the powerful current. The skilled horsemen and range-wise horses accomplished the crossing without loss of life. While most of the Nez Perce are believed to have crossed at Dug Bar, a few may have crossed upriver at Pittsburg Landing. They trailed their stock up Divide Creek, crossed the ridge, went down across the turbulent Salmon.

While these non-treaty Nez Perce were enjoying their last day of freedom before entering the Lapwai reservation, three young braves from White Bird's band went up Salmon River and killed several white men for past grievances. They returned boasting of their deeds.

When Joseph and White Bird learned what had occurred, they knew there would be trouble. They moved with their people to the bottom of Lahmotta (White Bird Canyon) and braced themselves for repercussions.

General Howard got word of the murders and promptly dispatched Captain Perry with 99 men to Grangeville to protect the settlers. The General also fired off a telegram to his commander in San Francisco: "Think we will make short work of it" — perhaps the most erroneous surmise in the history of western Indian warfare.

It was June 17, 1877, a year since Custer's debacle at Little Big Horn, when Captain Perry and his men went down the slopes of White Bird Canyon to meet 70 poorly armed Indians who were accompanied by 2,500 horses.

The Nez Perce hoped that explanatory discussions might allow a peaceful resolution of the situation — they rode out to meet Perry with a white flag. Several soldiers opened fire. The Indians replied in kind, and routed F and H Companies of the First Calvary, killing a third of the command without loss to themselves. In addition, they gathered a windfall of Army rifles.

Howard was stunned by the news. Fearing a general uprising, he summoned units from Alaska, Washington, Oregon, California and Georgia. Five days later he arrived at the canyon with 227 soldiers, 20 volunteers, and 175 non-soldiers, including packers and guides. The Indians simply crossed to the Salmon's south shore and awaited whatever movement the troops would make. With the help of a cable and boats, Howard began transporting his men across the river. The Nez Perce moved downriver 25 miles in 36 hours, and recrossed to the Salmon's north bank.

Major-General Oliver Otis Howard.

When General Howard reached the second ford, he realized his men were incapable of accomplishing the same feat without boats and began a reluctant withdrawal to White Bird Canyon and Grangeville. It is interesting to speculate what his thoughts were as he stared at the river, now crossed three times on his account by the Indians, without aid. Did he recall his ultimatum, which only a week earlier had forced the Wallowa band to risk their lives and property swimming the even more treacherous Snake? There was a certain justice in Howard's five-day trudge back to Grangeville, and the nettles of remorse would sting him frequently in the days ahead.

Looking Glass, Nez Perce war chief.

While General Howard made his ignominious withdrawal, Lieutenant Whipple with two companies and a Gatling gun attacked Looking Glass's village on the Middle Fork of the Clearwater River. That band desired neutrality, and rode out to meet the troops with a white flag. Bullets were their welcome. Converted to the non-treaty cause, Looking Glass and his people joined Joseph and White Bird. Looking Glass was soon recognized as war chief.

Whipple sent scouts to locate the Nez Perce camp; an encounter on the prairie near Cottonwood cost the Army 13 additional soldiers, while the Indians escaped unscathed.

The band now moved to the Clearwater River and camped. On the first of July, McConnville's Volunteers with 80 men from Mount Idaho attacked the Indians, and were swiftly counterattacked. Howard joined with another 550 soldiers. When the Nez Perce withdrew from the battleground they left four dead and carried half a dozen wounded. Howard lost 15 men and suffered 25 casualties.

At this point, the Nez Perce warriors decided to leave the hostilities behind by taking the buffalo-hunting trail to Montana where they could stay with their friends the Crows, returning to Idaho when feelings subsided.

With women, children, family possessions and a huge horse herd, the Indians traveled through the thickly forested slopes along the Lochsa River and over Lolo Pass.

Below the pass, Captain Rawn with 50 soldiers and 200 volunteers had erected a log barricade to intercept the band. The Indians asked to pass, and on being refused, simply flanked the soldiers and filed down the Bitterroot Valley. From that time, the log corral was known as "Fort Fizzle."

Nez Perce behavior in the Valley was exemplary. They purchased some supplies and avoided any unpleasantness. Though some of the warriors experienced dream-premonitions of danger, knowing Howard (now referred to as "Two Sleeps Back") was well behind, Looking Glass instructed the camp to pitch their tipis at Big Hole on the north fork of that river.

Unknown to the Indians, Captain Perry had gone to Fort Missoula, joined Captain Rawn's men, acquired a howitzer, and then met Colonel Gibbons, a West Point graduate whose company was known as the "Iron Brigade."

Scouts informed Gibbons of the Big Hole encampment. Seventeen officers, 196 enlisted men and volunteers from the Bitterroot Valley infiltrated the wooded slope above the tipis under cover of darkness. At first hint of dawn they attacked with the advantages of time, place, and momentum. The Nez Perce were taken by surprise. The soldiers quickly killed 50 women and children (including Joseph's wife) and nearly 30 of the bravest warriors.

But as the Indians regrouped, and retrieved rifles from their dew-drenched lodges, they began to drive the Army from their camp. The ferocity of the counterattack pushed the soldiers across the North Fork of the Big Hole and back to their rifle pits on the slope, where they were pinned without water. Daylong the battle continued, as the warriors fought a covering action which allowed their women and children to escape. They captured an Army cannon and disabled it. Evening brought a finish to the fighting — the braves rode away to join their shattered families.

Six medals of honor were awarded to soldiers for actions at Big Hole. Each side could claim a victory. Volunteer Captain John B. Catlin said, "We were whipped to a frazzle . . . but we broke the backbone of the Nez Perce nation. They never rallied again, so to speak." Yet the war was to continue another 55 days across an additional thousand miles.

The Indians now realized every white man could be counted their enemy. They decided to seek refuge with Sitting Bull in Canada. Looking Glass was in disgrace and the duties of war chief fell upon Lean Elk.

With 29 dead and 40 wounded, Gibbon's command was not in condition to renew the pursuit immediately.

The flight had become a national drama. Howard began getting criticism from General Sherman. He replied to Sherman's message:

Yours of the 26th (24th) received. You misunderstood me. I never flag. It was the command, including the most energetic young officers, that were worn out and weary by a most extraordinary march. You need not fear for the campaign. Neither you nor General McDowell can doubt my pluck and energy. My Indian scouts are on the heels of the enemy. My supplies have just come, we move in the morning and will continue till the end.

The Indians moved south through Bannock Pass into Idaho again.

At Camas Meadows, Joseph's younger brother, Ollikot, led a small band of warriors in a night attack designed to unseat General Howard's cavalry. They got away with 200 head of stock, but dawn revealed mules had been captured instead of horses. Chagrined, the Indians (who had no use for mules) released the animals, though their loss could have

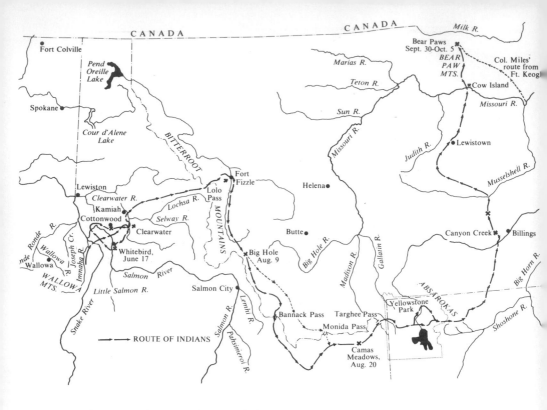

hampered Howard's supply line seriously.

At this time, Bannocks, and their chief, Buffalo Horn, together with numerous Crows, were serving as scouts for Howard's troops. As Edward Abbey remarked, "The trouble with the Indian is that he's no better than the white man." In one of the ironies of history, Buffalo Horn and his tribe would be engaged in an unsuccessful war with General Howard and his soldiers only a year later.

The Nez Perce now crossed Targhee Pass and entered Yellowstone, a National Park created five years earlier. The U.S. Army promptly assembled what has become known as the "Absaroka Blockade."

Lieutenant Bacon and 40 men were left at Targee Pass. Lieutenant Doane and two companies blocked the northern pass at Mammoth Hot Springs. Colonel Sturgis with six companies (360 men) guarded the exit at Clark's Fork on the east. Major Hart with five companies of Crook's Fifth Calvary and a hundred scouts were stationed on the Shoshone River exit near present-day Cody, Wyoming. Colonel Merritt with ten companies was positioned on the Wind River, and Colonel Miles had been alerted at Fort Keogh, Montana.

With Spurgin's Idaho axemen clearing the way, General Howard pushed in from the west. It was the first week of September, and he was confident of closing the trap.

A Nez Perce encampment near Yellowstone prior to 1877.

A northwest newspaper exulted over the promise of victory:

In view of the bad effect their success and escape would have on other Indians, and in view of the evil they would probably hereafter do Montana, this concentration of forces, and the determination to destroy them, is in the highest degree gratifying. We are largely indebted for it to the presence of General Sherman in Montana, who has had the lion in him roused by the defiant progress of the Nez Perce, and by personal attention to the movement of troops has raised up an army on the four sides of Joseph just when it seemed most probable that he was about to escape, scot free, except for the blow Gibbon struck him, and laden with booty, into the great open country of the hostiles. We wait now hopefully for news that the Nez Perce have been struck hard and fatally. They are too brave and dangerous a foe to escape, for their escape unscathed means still darker days for the border.

Colonel Samuel Sturgis had lost a son at Little Big Horn. His Seventh Cavalry had inherited Custer's tarnished guidon. Sturgis wanted the Nez Perce to pay for the deeds of Sitting Bull and Crazy Horse.

327

In his eagerness for confrontation, he read the sighting of Indians on a ridge and the death of a messenger as evidence the Nez Perce were coming down the Shoshone River. He abandoned his position at the mouth of Clarks Fork Canyon and moved south to the Shoshone, heading up into the mountains.

In fact, the Indians had feinted toward the Shoshone, milled their herd of ponies to leave confounding tracks, then turned abruptly north down the Clarks Fork defile, doubling back past Sturgis without being detected, even by his Crow scouts. They poured past the point recently vacated and were on the plains of Montana, free of the web.

General Howard continued to push east. Sturgis and the Seventh arrived behind the General. Consternation! The Indians were already 50 miles way.

Sam Sturgis was infuriated by the deception. He promised Howard he would catch the band before it reached the Missouri, even if he had to go on foot and alone. The General gave him fresh men and horses for the chase.

Sturgis covered 50 to 60 miles a day. With Crow and Bannock scouts, he managed to trail the Nez Perce to Canyon Creek. But the Nimapu sharp-shooters took refuge behind clumps of sage and with deadly rifle fire forced the pursuers to dismount and hunt cover. Women, children and horses escaped up the canyon.

Colonel Sturgis abandoned the chase, explaining in a letter to Howard:

> I find it impossible for my command to gain upon them, and their direction is taking further and further from supplies. I have . . . reluctantly determined to abandon a hopeless pursuit before my horses are completely destroyed or placed beyond recuperation . . .

It had only taken a week to teach him what Howard had known for two months.

Looking Glass was now back in command, and knowing how far behind were Howard's troops, he again slackened the pace. He did not know that Howard had telegraphed Colonel Miles to strike northwestward from Fort Keogh and intercept the Nez Perce in route.

Nelson Miles was an unusual man. Not a West Pointer, he was something of a glory-chaser and eager for exploits which might advance his reputation and rank. A veteran, he had fought against Geronimo and the Apaches, as well as the Sioux. He was anxious to reach the Nez Perce ahead of Howard, certain it would assist his career.

Colonel Nelson A. Miles of the Fifth United States Infantry at Fort Keogh.

Assembling 383 men, a Hotchkiss gun, a Napoleon cannon, and supply wagons, he moved rapidly westward.

The Nez Perce had reached Cow Island crossing on the Missouri, and after a brief military scuffle, helped themselves to some supplies found there.

An amusing message from soldiers guarding the cache survives:

Rifle Pit, at Cow Island

September 23, 1877 10AM

Colonel:

Chief Joseph is here, and says he will surrender for two hundred bags of sugar. I told him to surrender without the sugar. He took the sugar and will not surrender. What will I do?

Michael Foley

329

Colonel Miles arrived on the Missouri and had the last steamboat of the season ferry his troops and supplies to the south shore. As the ship headed downriver, he was astonished to learn from three men in a mackinaw boat that the Indians had already crossed the Missouri 60 miles west on their way north. In dismay he watched his only means of crossing troops disappearing downstream. One of Miles' officers made a historically fateful suggestion: try firing the cannon at the steamboat. The ploy attracted the necessary attention and soldiers were soon north of the river again.

By now it was almost October. The Indians had paused at the Bear Paws. Knowing Howard was more than "two sleeps back," and that refuge in Canada lay only 40 miles north, the band took shelter in a crescent-shaped hollow along a creek. There were no trees, but ravines and coulees below the bluffs afforded some relief from the wind's cold edge.

There Mile's thundering charge took them with a minute's warning and drove off the essential herd of horses. The last battle began.

Miles had planned to overrun the encampment with a three-pronged calvary charge. He had, however, never experienced the accuracy of Nez Perce rifle fire and his baptism made him a believer. Captain Carter's charge on the edge of the village was repulsed with the loss of a third of his command. Captain Hale was killed instantly, and his comrades remembered his recent response to Miles' order to advance: "My God, have I got to go out and get killed in such cold weather?" Hale's K Troop was almost annihilated. When Lieutentant Eckerson rushed back to Miles and yelled, "I am the only damned man of the Seventh Cavalry who wears shoulder straps alive!", the Colonel switched tactics from charge to siege. Soldiers took shelter in depressions above the Indian camp.

One of the soldiers, Louis Shambow, said later, "Those Indians were the best shots I ever saw. I would put a small stone on the top of my rock and they would get it everytime."

Battlesmoke and snow swirled for five days. Indian messengers slipped away in darkness to seek help from Sitting Bull. In another of fate's capricious turns, the sign language of messengers was misinterpreted by the Sioux chief and aid was withheld initially in the belief that the battle was too far away. Then help was sent, but it didn't arrive in time.

A tragic misidentity caused Lean Elk to be shot as a Crow. In another, Looking Glass, anguished by his lack of vigilance, imagined distant shapes glimpsed through a net of snow to be Sitting Bull's warriors. He stood and was shot through the head. On drawing closer the shapes were those of buffalo.

Miles began to fear the battle's duration would allow General Howard time to arrive for the Nez Perce surrender. Under a flag of truce, Colonel Miles persuaded Joseph to parley. In a shameful betrayal, the chief was taken captive, bound, and rolled in a blanket.

Later, the Indians captured an army officer and managed to obtain Joseph in trade.

Yellow Wolf, a Nez Perce warrior at the Bear Paw battlefield, left this moving Indian version of the fighting:

But now, when I saw our remaining warriors gone, my heart grew choked and heavy. Yet the warriors and no-fighting men killed were not all. I look around.

Some were burying their dead.

A young warrior, wounded, lay on a buffalo robe dying without complaint. Children crying with cold. No fire. There could be no light. Everywhere the crying, the death wail.

My heart became fire. I joined the warriors digging rifle pits. All the rest of night we worked. Just before dawn, I went down among the shelter pits. I looked around. Children no longer crying. In deep shelter pits they were sleeping. Wrapped in a blanket, a still form lay on the buffalo robe. The young warrior was dead. I went back to my rifle pit, my blood hot for war. I felt not the cold.

Morning came, bringing the battle anew. Bullets from everywhere! A big gun throwing bursting shells. From rifle pits, warriors returned shot for shot. Wild and stormy, the cold wind was thick with snow. Air filled with smoke of powder. Flash of guns through it all. As the hidden sun traveled upward, the war did not weaken.

I felt the coming end. All for which we had suffered lost!

Thoughts came of the Wallowa where I grew up. Of tipis along the bending river. Of the blue, clear lake, wide meadows with horse and cattle herds. From the mountain forests, voices seemed calling. I felt as dreaming. Not my living self.

Howard and his troops arrived. Shelling from the cannon continued. Chief Toohoolhoolzote and Joseph's brother, Ollikot, were killed. Reluctantly, Joseph decided further resistance meant only death for the rest of his people. He decided to surrender his band. General Howard told Colonel Miles that he could have the honor of accepting Joseph's surrender.

The chief's words were delivered by one of his men, who with tear-filled eyes uttered perhaps the most memorable speech in native-American oratory:

Tell General Howard I know his heart. What he told me before, I have in my heart. I am tired of fighting. Our chiefs are killed. Looking Glass is dead. Toohoolhoolzote is dead. The old men are all dead. It is the young men who say yes and no. He who led on the young men is dead (Ollikot). It is cold and we have no blankets. The little children are freezing to death. My people, some of them, have run away to the hills and have no blankets, no food; no one knows where they are — perhaps freezing to death. I want to have time to look for my children and see how many I can find. Maybe I shall find them among the dead. Hear me, my chiefs. I am tired; my heart is sick and sad. From where the sun now stands I will fight no more forever.

During the night, 70-year-old Chief White Bird, who was not bound by Joseph's surrender, escaped to Canada with 233 of his people.

There were 418 prisoners: 87 men, 184 women, 147 children. A large portion of the men were elderly and 40 were wounded.

At the request of the Senate, General Sherman wrote a summary of this campaign which covered 1500 miles, involving 2000 soldiers in 18 engagements at a cost of nearly $2 million. He concluded:

Thus has terminated one of the most extraordinary Indian wars of which there is any record. The Indians throughout displayed a courage and skill that elicited universal praise. They abstained from scalping; let captive women go free; did not commit indiscriminate murder of peaceful families, which is usual, and fought with almost scientific skill, using advance and rear guards, skirmish lines and field fortifications. Nevertheless, they would not settle down on lands set apart for them ample for their maintainance; and, when commanded by proper authority, they began resistance by murdering persons in no manner connected with their alleged grievances. With your approval, these prisoners are now en route by the most economical way to Fort Leavenworth, to be there held as prisoners of war until spring, when, I trust, the Indian Bureau will provide them homes on the Indian reservations near the Modocs, where, by moderate labor, they can soon be able to support themselves in peace. They should never again be allowed to return to Oregon or to Lapwai.

When Chief Joseph surrendered his band, it was with the understanding that his people would be returned to the Idaho reservation in the spring. This belief was unfounded. They were taken to Fort Leavenworth to live along the bottomlands of the Missouri River. The Nez Perce never became acclimated to this area — nearly half suffered malaria, and 21 died.

They were moved again; this time to 7,000 acres of sand and sage in the Oklahoma Indian Territory. Nearly fifty of them died there. Relocated a third time within the Oklahoma reservation, the death rate continued to grow. Over a hundred children died, including Joseph's daughter.

It was scarcely their fault. In 1881, Indian Agent Thomas Jordan reported there were only 328 survivors. He said the death rate continued to be so high that "the tribe, unless something is done for them, will soon be extinct." He absolved the Nez Perce from carelessness in regard to health. "They are cleanly to a fault . . . they keep their stock in good order, and are hard working, painstaking people."

Joseph was taken to Washington where he pleaded the case of his people to President Hayes. Nothing changed. To his credit, General Miles, who eventually became Secretary of the Army, tried to correct the governmental injustices against the Nez Perce, but all his letters were ignored by Generals Sherman and Sheridan.

Chief White Bird died in Canada in 1882; his followers drifted back; some were killed and some were captured and deported to Oklahoma.

Public sympathy was aroused, and by 1885 caused the return of Joseph and 150 of his people to the Yakima Indian's Colville Reservation in northeast Washington. Two hundred sixty-eight Nez Perce were sent to Lapwai.

Chief Joseph was allowed to visit his father's grave in the Wallowa valley five years later. Now there were four towns in the valley. While there, he asked that a small tract be set aside for his people. The settlers replied that Joseph and his band would never be welcome there.

Fifteen years later, in 1905, while sitting before his tipi on the Colville Reservation, Chief Joseph died of what the examining doctor said was "a broken heart."

It is fitting that the site which marks the start of these events is signed, so that those who pass may pause, regarding the sweep of water between brown banks, and with imagination, people the river at a time now some hundred years distant, when bodies human and animal strained against the current, beginning an odyssey longer than the river itself.

Chief Joseph after his request for a small tract in the Wallowa country for his people had been denied.

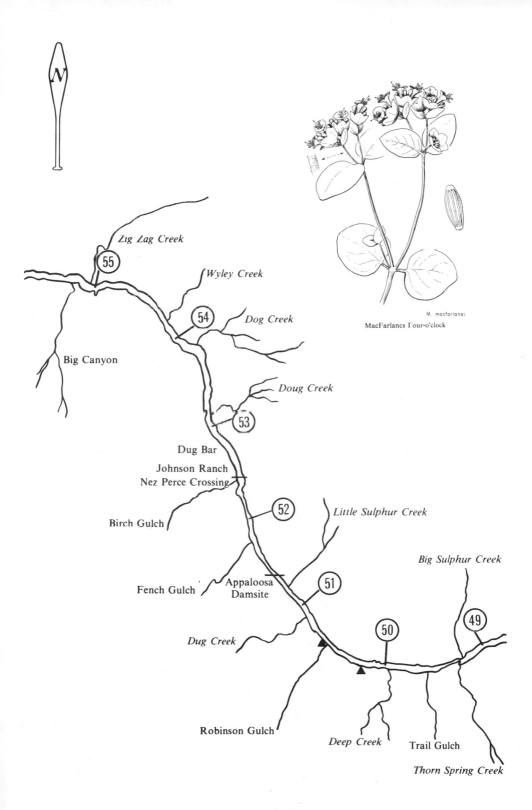

M. macfarlanei
MacFarlanes Four-o'clock

Zig Zag Creek
55
Wyley Creek
54
Dog Creek
Big Canyon
Doug Creek
53
Dug Bar
Johnson Ranch
Nez Perce Crossing
Little Sulphur Creek
52
Birch Gulch
Big Sulphur Creek
Fench Gulch
Appaloosa
Damsite
51
49
Dug Creek
50
Robinson Gulch
Deep Creek
Trail Gulch
Thorn Spring Creek

Mile 53.1 **Doug Creek** on the Idaho side is also named for T. J. Douglass.

Art and Daisy Spivy took homesteads on Doug Creek, about a quarter mile from the river, in 1914. Under Desert Entry they were able to expand their holdings to a full section — 640 acres.

The Spivys were from the Lewiston-Spaulding area and had known each other from childhood — they went to school together. They lived on Art's ranch at Gifford after they were married and moved from there to the Snake River.

The Spivy's tent cabin up Doug Creek.
The mules have just arrived with
another load of lumber. At night, the
spring around the side of the hill would
run enough water to irrigate the garden.

Avo Spivy on a horse in front of the Spivy house in 1917. The house was located on a flat about a quarter-mile from the river just below Doug Creek. It had two bedrooms, a kitchen and living room. The lumber was hauled from a mill at the head of Wolf Creek down to Sugar Loaf, skidded down a grassy north hillside, then bundled on mules for the trip to Doug Creek.

Avo Spivy milking "Old Skunkface" at their Dug Creek homestead.

When the Spivys settled on Doug Creek they brought their two children, Avo and Fred, with them. Avo was almost two years old and Fred was seven months.

The couple bought Jim Bond's and Della Smede's cattle. They used Divide Creek as a winter camp downriver and Warm Springs across from Dug Bar as another camp. The cows were summered on the Joseph Plains near Boles and stock was sold and shipped at Cottonwood in the fall. Supplies were trucked from Grangeville to the road end or boated up the river from Lewiston.

The Spivys sold out to John Spencer in 1937; he owns the land at this writing. They moved to Boise Valley and ran a herd of dairy cows there and subsequently purchased a cattle ranch in the Owyhee country. Art died in 1957. Daisy lives in Riggins at this time, near her daughter. Mrs. Spivy has three grandsons, eight great grandsons, and one adopted granddaughter.

Mile 53.8 **Dog Creek** on the right. White Horse Rapid.

Mile 54.2 **Wyley Creek** on the right.

Mile 55 **Zig Zag Creek** on the Idaho shore and Big Canyon just below it on the opposite side. The Brownlee Sheep Company had its shearing sheds at the mouth of Zig Zag in the early 1920's.

Clara Humphries (left) and Eloise Hale (right) camped at the mouth of Zig Zag Creek in 1922. Their husbands owned a ranch on Flynn Creek of Salmon River and ran sheep along the Snake. There were three granaries which held shelled corn used as winter feed for the sheep. The corn was delivered by boat. This was Clara's honeymoon site.

Brownlee shearing shed at the mouth of Zig Zag.

Left to right: Art Spivy, Mack Hand, and Elmer Winds at the Brownlee Sheep Company sheds at Zig Zag Creek.

Mile 55.8 **Divide Creek** on the Idaho side. Jim Bond, and his cousin, Della Smead, built a cabin a mile up Divide Creek and grazed cattle in the drainage. They were squatters, and eventually sold their stock to the Spivys. Lawrence Spivy, Art's nephew, filed a homestead entry on the Bond-Smead location and proved up on it in the 1920's.

Indian sites at the mouth of Divide Creek were excavated by the Idaho State University archeology department under a grant from the Smithsonian Institute. Material from the pits was dated at about 6,000 years.

Art Spivy hauling wool at Zig Zag.

Wool sacks (300 pounds each) being loaded on the **Idaho** *at Zig Zag for transport to Lewiston.*

The power lines suspended across the river just below this point carry 220,000 KW from Brownlee and Oxbow Dams to the Lewiston supply station.

Mile 56.5 **China Gulch** is the draw on the left. The small wooden building was used as a shed for storage of rock cores drilled by crews doing preliminary work for Mountain Sheep Dam. The dam would have been located a short distance below the draw. Plans for Low Mountain Sheep called for a 275-foot concrete gravity-type dam and a road from the town of Imnaha, Oregon, down the Imnaha River, across Cactus

Scotty Hollingsworth's cabin was below the Bond house on Divide Creek. Scotty proved up on 320 acres; trapped, gardened, and worked for other ranchers. He died in Lewiston.

The Jim Bond and Della Smead cabin which was located about a mile up Divide Creek. Art and Daisy Spivy used it as a cow camp until 1937.

Mountain and along the Snake for eight miles to the top of the dam. This edifice would have acted as a regulator for peak releases from the Pleasant Valley Dam.

Mile 57.3 The **Imnaha River** flows into the Snake from the Oregon side. Imnaha is a Nez Perce word but the meaning is lost beyond certainty. The foremost linguist of the language, Dr. Haruo Aoki, was unable to find an etymological breakdown for the word. It appears on the Lewis and Clark map in the first edition of their journals as "Imnahar."

J. H. Horner says the name has some reference to root digging country. He also stated a traditional claim that a sub-chief Im-na always camped near the river with some of his tribe. The Nez Perce prized the stream for its salmon fishing.

This is the river which Captain Bonneville reached in 1834, after crossing from Kirby Creek to Post Office Saddle. He reached the Imnaha about four miles above its mouth.

The first settlers on this river arrived in the late 1870's and early 1880's. They had a school by 1884 and a post office a couple of years later.

Mile 57.5 **Imnaha Rapid.** This innocuous-looking stretch of choppy water sank a jet boat in the spring of 1974. Seven people were aboard without life-jackets and two of them drowned. One girl, who managed to clutch a flotation cushion, was fished out of the river miles downstream.

Mile 58. **Eureka Creek** and **Eureka Bar** on the Oregon shore. This stream was called Deer Creek until the Eureka Mining Company moved onto the site. Eureka Bar experienced more mining activity than any area on the river between Hells Canyon Dam and Lewiston. The gravel bar between the Imnaha and Eureka Creek was busy as a honey hive for a few years.

Mart Hibbs, (whom the reader met at Granite Creek) lived at the mouth of Horse Creek on the Imnaha in the 1890's. He ran cattle downstream toward the confluence of the Imnaha and Snake Rivers. Mart was in the habit of picking up rocks whose composition intrigued him and often deposited them on the window ledge of his blacksmith shop at Horse Creek.

In June, 1898, a mining engineer paused at Hibbs' place and noticed one of the ore samples. He remarked that if Mart knew where it came from he'd have it made. Of course, the cowman couldn't recollect its origin.

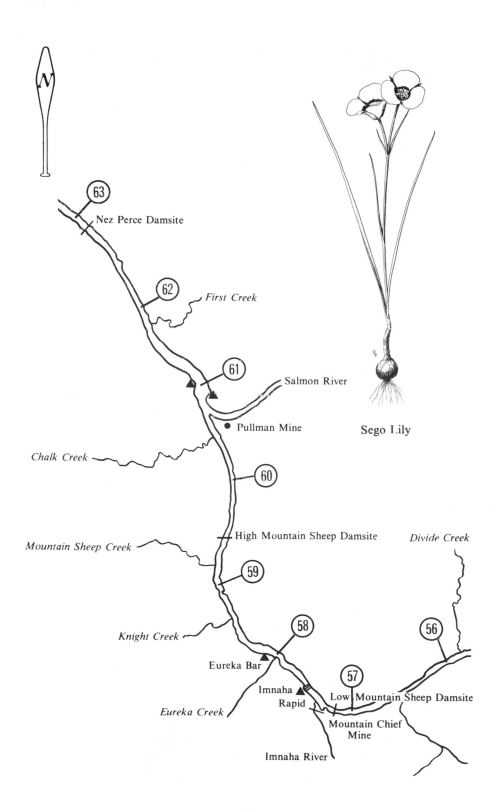

Nez Perce Damsite

First Creek

Salmon River

Pullman Mine

Chalk Creek

High Mountain Sheep Damsite

Divide Creek

Mountain Sheep Creek

Knight Creek

Eureka Bar

Imnaha Rapid

Low Mountain Sheep Damsite

Eureka Creek

Mountain Chief Mine

Imnaha River

Sego Lily

½

As soon as the fellow left, the eggs hit the fan. Hibbs, and Elmer Barton, who was working there, threw some grub together and burned a hole in the wind heading for the mouth of the Imnaha. They rode all night, staked their claims and some for their brothers. Elmer stayed to guard the claims while Mart rode to Joseph to record them. The boom was underway.

The Hibbs and Barton claims were bonded to the Idaho Exploration and Copper Company for $100,000. As usual in the canyon, access was the perennial, formidable problem. The closest road of sorts came from Enterprise to Buckhorn Springs, six miles from the river. Development money was needed and it wasn't long in arriving. The Eureka Mining, Smelting and Power Company was organized in Clarkston in 1902.

It has been said that the man who reads nothing at all is better informed than the man who reads nothing but newspapers. Nevertheless, newspaper accounts of the period contain information which probably has more substance than the speculation and oral tradition parroted at present. A *Lewiston Tribune* report on Eureka Bar was carried by the *Wallowa County Chieftain*, February 20, 1902:

New Smelter Company

Company has been Organized with Capital of $2,000,000.

A Company has been organized with a capital of $2,000,000 for the purpose of erecting a smelter at some point on the upper Snake river to reduce the copper ores of that district. For some time past reports have been in circulation regarding the project, but no definite action in the matter became public until a few days ago when articles of incorporation for the Eureka Mining, Smelting & Power Company were filed at the county auditor's office in Asotin county. These articles showed the directors to be H. G. Johnson and G. A. Nehrhood, of Waukon, Iowa; C. O. Howard and M. S. Howard, of Omaha; Wm. J. Wilkinson, of Sterling, Illinois; J. T. Miller of Chicago; O. E. Guernsey, of Dubuque, Iowa; J. E. Hubbell, of Lansing, Mich.; H. M. Peterson, of Fargo, N. D. and L. D. Lively, of Lewiston.

When seen yesterday and questioned regarding the plans of the smelter company, Mr. Lively said: "The smelter project is indirectly, or it might be said, directly the result of the operations of the Fargo Company in the Snake river copper belt. The copper company is composed of capitalists and well-known smelter men, and the organization of the company has resulted after a personal investigation of the belt made by them last November. The immediate plans provide for the installation of an electric smelter with a capacity of 200 tons daily, but the large capitalization of the company has been made with a view of increasing the plant to such capacity as may be demanded. I cannot at this time speak definitely as to the location of the smelter. It, however, will be located at some point between the mouth of the Grande Ronde river and Imnaha. The providing of transportation facilities by water will be a necessary preliminary step in our plans, and we expect to have that feature provided within three months."

A year later, an article which ran in the *Chieftain* brought the story up to date:

> *Chieftain,* March 12, 1903
> Town of Eureka
> G. A. Neluhood and J A. Huseby have returned from a 10 days trip to the Imnaha, where they inspected the work that is being done on the properties of the Eureka and Fargo companies. These companies have conducted their operations so quietly and unostentatiously that the public has but little conception of the magnitude of their undertakings. They are not only opening a vast mineral belt but are putting in a smelter to reduce their ores, a telephone system from their properties to Lewiston, laying out a townsite near the smelter building, a wagon road and a sawmill, but greatest of all, and especially as to its bearing on Lewiston, and each development will rebound to the benefit of Lewiston, is the opening up of river transportation to that country by the construction of the steamer *Imnaha,* which is now only awaiting the arrival of its machinery when regular trips will be made between Imnaha and Lewiston three times a week and perhaps oftener.
>
> At their Imnaha camp a force of 30 men are now driving extensive tunnels to the bowels of the mountains making mother earth give up her precious metals. Chas. Wallace the contractor has a force of 40 men at work on the construction of the wagon road from the mouth of Deer creek to the

timber belt a distance of eight miles. Almost half of the road is completed including the heaviest rock wall and it is expected by the first of April the entire road will be completed.

Arrangements have been made for a sawmill at the top of the mountain and a contract will be let for 1,000 cords of wood for the use of the smelter. W. E. Adams, the engineer, is now engaged in surveying a townsite at the mouth of Deer Creek about a mile from the smelter.

Eureka has been selected as the name of the new town which ought to become a place of considerable importance in the near future.

A *Tribune* reporter called on Messrs. Nehrhood and Husebye yesterday and asked for a statement of the conditions now existing at Imnaha. "While we are actively engaged at present on developing six of our claims," said Mr. Nehrhood, "we have ore now blocked out in two of them to keep the smelter running day and night for an indefinite period. On the Mountain Chief we are driving the tunnel from both the Snake and Imnaha sides and when connected it will be 740 feet in length. We are now on the Snake river side 190 feet and the Imnaha end 65 feet, all of it being through good smelting ore. We will sink and drift both ways under the water level. The Mountain Chief has from eight to 15 feet of good pay ore and can alone furnish the smelter with 100 tons a day. The tunnel through this property will be 7x8 feet and will form a part of the surface tram, connecting our various properties with the smelter. The tunnel is on the Delta 120 feet in good ore and we are working two shifts on this property. On the Headlight we have cross cut the pay streak on the hanging walls in six different places. It has an average of seven feet of good ore and in six weeks more work, it can furnish the smelter 100 tons of ore every 24 hours. On the Mother Lode we are drifting on the ore body and it is showing up well. The Eureka camp is being moved to the new townsite location from the Fargo's property where there has been a joint camp.

"What about the smelter? Well a crew will start Monday excavating for the foundation and cutting the stone so that by the time the machinery can be gotten there everything will be ready for its quick installation. Some of the electrical parts of the smelter are now here in our warehouse and bills of lading have been received for all of the machinery. It should all be here within a week or ten days. The Allis-Chalmers company of Chicago have furnished the machinery and a Denver company have the contact for the smelter. They will operate it for us for 60 days, and when tested and accepted by us we will expect to have as complete a smelter as can be had. It should be in operation not later than 90 days. This will be only the first section of the smelter and as we desire to do custom work we expect to largely increase its capacity. By May 1st we can anticipate having a payroll of 125 men."

The Fargo is an allied company with the Eureka and owns a number of claims adjoining and on the same veins. M. Huseby states that on the Last Chance the tunnel is in 130 feet and on the Snake River Chief 160 feet, both in splendid ore. He expects to return to the camp next week and start another tunnel on the Snake River Chief.

The steamer *Imnaha* which is being constructed by one of the allied companies is now practically completed, the painters are about through and the carpenters are putting the finishing touches to the staterooms. The machinery arrived from the east last night and will all be in readiness by the time the boiler gets here. L. H. Cambell, who has been secured as Chief engineer, as navigated the western rivers for a number of years. He has just returned from Laky City, Minn., where he has been for two months superintending the construction of the machinery, especially the boiler. The boiler has a locomotive fire box with a pressure of 225 pounds to the square inch, and Mr. Cambell says will carry the *Imnaha* over any rapids in the Snake river or any other river out here. The shaft is of Bethlehem nickel steel, 7¼ inches in diameter and 21¼ feet long. The boat will be equipped with its own electric light plant and will carry a 2,000 candle power searchlight. Captain Harry Baughman, who resigned his position as captain on one of the boats on the Yukon to take command of the *Imnaha,* is very proud of his craft and says nothing in the northwest can be compared to her. The capacity of the boat will be 125 tons on the down trip and she can carry 50 tons up the river. On account of the delay in

347

receiving the boiler it is not expected to be able to make the first trip before the first of April. The company's warehouse 32x48 feet has been completed and it is already being used for the reception of the smelting machinery.

The mill at Eureka Bar. Only the stone foundations remain.

Hibbs and Barton reportedly received $15,000 for their claims from the Fargo Company. Billy Rankin and his friend Bidwell sold 13 claims to the Eureka Company for the same amount — though all but $1000 was taken in the previously mentioned "shipping credit" for the Copper Mountain lode.

Rankin asserted that the Eureka and Fargo companies were interlocked, with each owning nearly half of the other's stock. Together they formed the Lewiston Southern Company, a subsidiary that built the steamship *Imnaha*. Rankin also believed that G. A. Nehrhood was buying mining equipment and reselling it to the company at a substantial mark-up.

J. H. Horner recalled that the business men of Joseph and Enterprise subscribed $1500 for the road from Buckhorn to Eureka Bar and that the County Court gave $3000 more. The road was completed in 1903. Electric mining drills were shipped from Denver to Elgin, Oregon, and freighted with team to Dobbin's cabin, then dragged down the mountain to the mines.

The hotel at Eureka Bar; the river is off to the right. Photograph reproduced from an old newspaper.

The hotel as it looked in 1916. The stone cellar can still be seen by visitors to the site.

The sawmill, purchased in Portland, was set up and cut a reported 350,000 board feet of lumber for the smelter and other camp buildings. A two-story hotel opened, a grocery store, and a post office with Thomas Alyea as postmaster. It is estimated that about 150 men were employed on the bar when the stir reached its zenith. The mill building was finished and the *Imnaha* began hauling equipment on a regular basis. She made 13 trips without problems.

There was a saloon a short way up Eureka Creek which served the miners in a dubious fashion with bronco whiskey. It has been the source of several apocryphal stories, so again, the contemporary newspaper account might inhibit exaggeration:

Chieftain, July 16, 1903
BLEW UP SALOON
Mr. Shorty at Eureka Peddled
Out Bad Booze.

Lewiston Tribune — A report reached here last night stating that the tent saloon on Deer Creek about one and a half miles from Eureka in the Imnaha district, had been blown up with dynamite by some cowboys, who believed they had a grievance against the proprietor, who is known amongst the miners as "Shorty". The place was first established at Imnaha, but the boys became tired of it last fall and placing a box of dynamite under the joint suddenly started it skyward.

This was enough to convince "Shorty" that he was not wanted there so he moved to Deer Creek, where he has since been running his place. The men who have patronized the place say that only the vilest kind of liquor was handled and that it was the custom to fill a man up on the poison and then take his money away from him. The night the place was blown up there was a miner there who had drawn his wages that day and when he returned to the mine that night he had neither money or watch, nor had he any recollection of what had become of his belongings.

As told by an eye witness the place was running as usual when, without warning, in walked two masked cowboys and ordered everybody to leave the tent. Soon after the tent was vacated there was a loud report that was heard for miles and there was not enough left of the joint to tell what it had been. Cigars, tobacco, broken bottles, and all kinds of canned

350

goods were scattered over the hillside, but the wiley booze seller had been so badly scared that he did not stop to see what he could save, but hurried to a place of safety and has not yet returned. It is understood that the miners will not tolerate any institution that will rob them of their wages and give them nothing in return.

In mid-November, 1903, the *Imnaha* sank — with machinery essential for the mill aboard. Her replacement, the *Mountain Gem,* made only a couple of trips. The sunken steamboat spawned unsinkable rumors. Quicker than you could spit and holler howdy, the bubble popped. The mines closed abruptly. Explanations, theories, surmise and conjecture concerning the demise are now common as dirty socks in a bunkhouse.

The steamboat **Imnaha** *in 1903, arriving at Eureka Bar.*

It is a fact that a party of Oregon state geologists visited the site in 1942 looking for copper and tungsten that were needed for the war effort and concluded that the width of the veins should be "measured in inches rather than feet." This group's report also stated: "Development consists of tunnels, and is relatively extensive, considering the non-commercial character of the ore in general . . . The area is relatively inaccessible, and there seems to be little hope that any commercial mining operation would be warranted." Assays by the U.S. Bureau of Mines in 1968 failed to find more than a trace of copper.

The lumber from the mill and various buildings was salvaged by ranchers along the river. The Forest Service bought what timbers remained in 1931 and used them for trail bridge construction.

*The **Mountain Gem** moored at Eureka Bar in 1904.*

The tunnel for the Mountain Chief mine runs 600 feet through the point that separates the Imnaha from the Snake. With two portals and excellent ventilation, it is safe to explore with a flashlight. This site was part of the Fargo Group of mines, which included 41 patented claims covering 488 acres along this section of the river.

The walls of the blacksmith shop, the basement of a building, several abandoned adits, and the stone terraces of the mill foundation stepped against the hill can still be seen by those who visit the site. To wander the vacant bar is to remember a phrase from Loren Eiseley: "People are incalculable in their departures — it will be so with us."

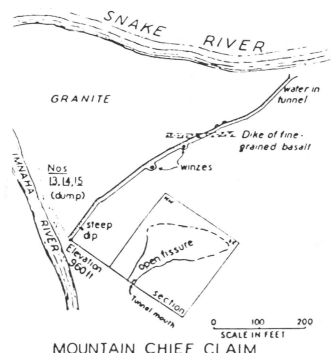

SNAKE RIVER

GRANITE

water in tunnel

Dike of fine-grained basalt

winzes

Nos 13, 14, 15 (dump)

steep dip

Elevation 960 ft

open fissure

section

Tunnel mouth

IMNAHA RIVER

0   100   200
SCALE IN FEET

MOUNTAIN CHIEF CLAIM
RIVER TO RIVER TUNNEL

An early photograph of the George Snell homestead up the Imnaha River. The picture conveys the appearance of the Imnaha Valley a few miles up from the Snake River.

353

There is a second story properly associated with Deer or Eureka Creek, which preceded the mining boom — but it is presented here because evidence of the endeavor is not as visible from the river. It is the story of the Dobbin and Huffman Sheep Company.

Jay Dobbin left the family's Illinois farm in 1889, at age 19, after selling his horse and borrowing some money from his father for a train ticket to Union, Oregon. In Union he went to work on his cousin's farm

Jay Dobbin in 1905 at the time he was serving in the Oregon legislature.

for $20 a month until he could lease a farm of his own. He raised barley, sheared sheep and bought half interest in 100 yearling cattle.

Eventually Dobbin sold the cattle and purchased 2,000 head of ewes and lambs. He took delivery in Umatilla County. The mild winter climate and quality forage of the Snake River had impressed him, so he drove his band 200 miles to the canyon country.

Jay took a homestead in 1896 on what was to become known as Eureka Creek. The site was about two miles from the river. Owning land entitled him to graze his sheep without charge on adjacent government land. He bought another homestead in the area, before building a one-room frame cabin with lumber and shingles hauled from a mill in upper Wallowa Valley. Two years later, his youngest sister arrived to take a homestead next to his Eureka Creek location.

The Dobbins could travel by wagon from Joseph to Buckhorn Springs, though referring to the access as a "road" was a form of hyperbole. The route from the springs to the river was a horse trail.

Though he didn't drink, smoke, chew or swear, Jay was a sociable person. He attended Union County picnics and dances and thereby met his wife, Mary Etta Huffman. She was a school teacher before they were married.

Their wedding took place in 1900, after a three-year engagement, and they lived in a house on Prairie Creek in upper Wallowa Valley. Then Jay founded the Dobbin Ranch with the purchase of 440 acres on lower Prairie Creek and they moved to the place.

Dobbin's sheep were wintered on the Snake River range and lambing occurred there as well. Lambing began in late March and was finished after about 20 days. Prior to 1907, range was on a "first come, first served" basis — after the Forest Reserve Act, grazing fees were established.

Shearing was done in late May or early June after the sheep were above the canyon, though once river boat transportation began some shearing was done on the river ranches. At first, wool had to be hauled by wagon to the railhead at La Grande, and later Elgin. Sometimes the wagon trains would be a quarter-mile long with fine teams and fancy wagons.

In 1909, when the railroad had been completed to Enterprise, Jay and some fellow sheepmen formed the Woolgrowers Warehouse Company and built a small warehouse in Enterprise where they could store their wool until the selling price seemed favorable.

In the fall, the herders would trail the flocks down to another Dobbin ranch at Crow Creek where the lambs were separated from the ewes and pastured for six weeks before being sold and shipped.

About the first of November the ewes were trailed from Crow Creek to the Snake River ranches and the grazing cycle was renewed.

Dobbin's first sheep were Spanish Merino. After 1900 he had Rambouillets and later crossed them with Hampshire, Shropshire and Lincoln rams.

In 1906 the Dobbin outfit consisted of 17 employees, six bands of sheep (about 1,200 ewes to the band), and 2,000 acres of land.

Jay and Etta began building a new house in 1908, "up on the hill" about a mile from the home they had occupied for nine years. The new house cost $10,000 and was designed by a Portland architect. It was paid for upon completion. The couple now had four children: one son and three daughters.

By 1913 Jay owned 28,000 sheep and at that point he chose a partner: Guy Huffman. Guy was Mary Etta's orphaned youngest brother. He had come to live with Jay and Etta two years after they were married. Guy had worked with the sheep on ranch and river, and at age 21 homesteaded on Cache Creek, a tributary of the Snake.

After the partnership was formed, Guy directed most of the activity on the river and in Idaho. As the operation expanded, they used summer range in the Idaho mountains. Sheep had to be ferried across the Snake before trailing them up canyons, across Camas Prairie and on to the Clearwater and Lolo National Forests. Dobbin and Huffman kept an office in Lewiston, with a bookkeeper who bought supplies for the camps upriver, and sent provisions and mail by boat when water levels allowed.

The partnership of Dobbin and Huffman was for the most part a fairly happy and prosperous combination until they decided to divide their interests in the 1930's. A few years later, Guy sold his share and moved to California where he supervised a feedlot until his death in 1958.

Jay was twice elected to the Oregon House of Representatives, served on the board of the National Woolgrowers Association, and was a two-term president of the Oregon Woolgrowers Association.

The Depression years of the 1920's and 30's hammered livestock and agricultural interests. Two businesses in Portland and a bank in Joseph in which Jay had invested his money all failed. Bank closures affected the sheepmen. Dobbin was one of the few who kept his business because the creditors trusted him to pay when it became possible — and they realized Jay could run the outfit better than any bank which might take it over.

Jay Dobbin practiced a Chinese proverb: "The footsteps of the master are the best fertilizer." Like all stockmen, he fought uphill: competition for range, ticks, foot rot, coyotes, grass and hay fires — even a flood on the river that soaked his bags of wool. And always he was at the mercy of the weather and market — one could delay shearing, affect crops and range — the other might make all the effort tally up to a cipher.

Jay and Etta Dobbin at the 1956 Jay Dobbin Day banquet in Joseph, Oregon. He is 86 and she is 79.

A full house divided wins no pots, and Jay's wife Etta was a complete partner in their accomplishments. She did what all ranch wives of that time did — cooking and canning, churning butter, gardening, caring for chickens, sewing clothes for herself and the children, washing and ironing. She also organized a Sunday school, belonged to a couple of women's organizations, and did accounting for the ranch and sheep business during the Depression. She even ran the Lewiston office for three winters. In addition, Mrs. Dobbin filled her house with books and read to her children before they went to sleep at night.

Jay had some health problems in 1937, and again in 1946. These two incidents persuaded him to ease up a bit. At the time he sold his Cherry Creek ranch to his Basque herders his holdings covered 10,000 acres.

Dobbin was voted "Father of the Year" in 1957, and the award was presented at the American National Cattlemen's convention. The couple's children all found successful careers outside of Oregon. Jack became president of the Wooden Box Institute, Annette earned a doctorate in Romance languages and taught at New York State College for 30 years, Margaret became a medical technologist and Catherine received a PhD. in zoology, teaching for a time at Smith College in Massachusetts.

Jay died two days after his 91st birthday, in 1961, and Etta passed away five years later. Both are buried in the Enterprise cemetery, overlooking the handsome Wallowa Valley and Mountains which they knew so well.

Mile 58.5 **Knight Creek** on the left.

Mile 59.2 **Mountain Sheep Creek** on the Oregon shore. There are iron rings set in the rocks on both sides of the river at this point. It was in the rapid just below the creek that the steamboat *Imnaha* turned before lodging crosswise in the current and breaking up.

Mile 59.5 **High Mountain Sheep Damsite.** HMPNP is painted on the rocks on the Oregon side of the river. White marks can be detected on the rocks showing the 670-foot height of the dam proposed by Pacific Northwest Power Company, Washington Public Power Supply System and the Department of Interior. Backing water almost to Hells Canyon Dam, this edifice would have cost $667 million at the time and would have taken seven years to construct. Most of the Imnaha River canyon was slated to be an arm of the reservoir, with a marina at its upper end.

Mile 60.6 **Chalk Creek** on the left.

Mile 60.8 **The Salmon — "River of No Return"** sweeps in from the Idaho side of the river. The confluence of these famous rivers forms a singular site and it should be left in its natural state — no government bureaucracy can improve upon it. Nonetheless, the Bureau of Land Management has insisted on explicatory signs; and the Idaho Fish and Game Commission, in a remarkable display of visual insensitivity, installed a cabin at the mouth of the Salmon — but the river erased those efforts in June, 1974, when its waters rose to a hundred-year flood crest. The unnecessary wooden shelter whose presence now mars the beauty of this confluence was erected by BLM in 1975.

Looking up the Salmon from the Snake, one can see mine tailings on the Salmon side of the rock point that divides the two rivers. The mine was called the "Pullman" because Mr. Baker, the principal investor, was from that Washington city. The copper lode was worked in the 1920's; a few loads of ore were shipped to Lewiston. Some equipment is still situated at the mouth of the mine.

Confluence of the Salmon (left) and the Snake (right).

Most of the range from the mouth of the Salmon up to Pittsburg Landing, and much of the same stretch on the Oregon side of the river, was for a period under the control of Frank "Bow" Wyatt. Wyatt's headquarters were on Deer Creek, a tributary of the Salmon, about 50 miles upriver. Since Wyatt's name is inextricably linked to Hells Canyon livestock operations some biographical information is added here.

As with many settlers along the Salmon and Snake, Wyatt was from Missouri, where he was born in 1849. As a young man he went to Kansas and hired on with an Army wagon train hauling provisions to Fort Union, New Mexico. The wagon was pulled by eight yoke of oxen and the journey required 45 days — the trip included a brush with a band of Cheyennes.

Two men attempting to salvage wool sacks from the river's spring floodwaters at Salmon Bar, on the Oregon side, across from the mouth of the Salmon River. The shearing sheds in the background belonged to Dobbin and Huffman. Photograph was dated 1919.

Doris Sigler, and her children, Gene, Don and Zoe, mining near the mouth of Salmon River, on the Oregon side of the Snake in 1937. Doris would teach at Orofino in the winter and mine during the summer. Sometimes their three month's labor would be rewarded with about $1600 in gold. Gold was worth $26 an ounce and the family worked 16 hours a day. She is modeling what her mother called "that thing you wear on your front."

Frank then tried hard-rock mining in Colorado, around Black Hawk and Central City, before turning buffalo hunter in eastern Colorado. He quit when hides wouldn't even fetch a dollar apiece. Texas cattle were being trailed into the territory and Wyatt became a cowboy. He bought a bunch of longhorns after a drive for $13 a head, and settled on the headwaters of the south fork of the Platte in 1871. Thus began the saga of the "Bow and Arrow" brand.

Mr. Ross, a Denver business man, went partners with Wyatt. They got along like wax and wick. Most of their cattle were in Colorado and Wyatt located in Greeley, where he married Margaret, and where Edward, the first of their four children, was born.

Wyatt and Ross trailed a herd of longhorns to the Snake River country and fattened them on the range in the Malad River region. "Bow" Wyatt moved this herd's cows to the Snake-Salmon country in the fall of 1883.

The company of Wyatt and Ross is credited with shipping the first cattle over the Northern Pacific — five trainloads of steers from Spokane Falls to Miles City, Montana. They grazed the cattle on the Montana plains for a year, then sold them to a Boston syndicate, and Wyatt returned to the cattle venture in Idaho.

In 1895, the outfit had 2,000 head in the forks of the Snake and Salmon. Their holdings expanded to include Wolf Creek, (run by Frank's son, Ed), Pittsburg Landing, Johnson Bar, Temperance Creek, and Deer Creek. Wyatt and Ross even had their own office building on a block in downtown Denver.

As mentioned earlier, the summer of 1919 was dry as a mud creek in drought and the winter was cold as a clay farm in March. It was this disastrous turn of weather that snapped the Bow and Arrow brand. Cattle died by the thousands and the market soured. Frank Wyatt was past 70 and he never rallied. He and his wife Margaret died within six months of each other, in 1936, and rest in the Prairie View Cemetery at Grangeville, Idaho. "Bow" Wyatt was a modest man, even though at one time his outfit was the largest in the area. Interviewed by a reporter late in life, he remarked, "I never had a dead man for breakfast any place I ever lived. Oh, I could handle a six-gun — but only one at a time."

*Idaho cattle king Frank "Bow" Wyatt, a
native of Salmon and Snake Rivers for 50
years. Frank is buried alongside his wife,
Margaret, in the Prairie View Cemetery
in Grangeville, Idaho.*

Mile 61.8 **First Creek** on the right.

Mile 62.9 **Nez Perce Damsite.** Washington Public Power Supply System advocated construction of a 700-foot dam at this location. The development would have been, at the very least, a calamity for the already troubled fishery of the Columbia, Snake and Salmon Rivers. Between 30 and 40 percent of all salmon and steelhead in the Columbia are spawned on the headwaters of the Salmon. Anyone with sense enough to spit downwind could recognize the myopic folly inherent in this damn proposal. Fortunately, the concrete plan was never set in any forms except paper ones.

Mile 63.7 **Cherry Creek** falls into the Snake on the Oregon side. When the Snake is high, the mouth of this creek is only a couple of feet above the river, but, in late summer one can enter the recess where the stream drops between a pair of large boulders and shower beneath its pour.

The tributary was named by William Duncan, Mike Thomason and Jud Basin because choke cherries grew profusely there. The men built a cabin on this creek in 1888 or '89 and wintered their horses nearby.

The Cherry Creek Ranch was part of Jay Dobbin's land until 1948, when he sold the extensive ranch to three of his Basque sheepherders: Seberino "Silver" Egana, Gus Malaxa and Toney Martiartu.

The "Bascos," as they were affectionately called by stockmen, had worked many years for Dobbin. When the livestock business was in serious trouble in the 1930's, the herders came to Jay and said, "You take our money for your business. If you go broke we won't have a job." Dobbin eventually returned their trust by selling them his canyon holdings.

Egana, Malaxa and Martiartu took Joe Onaindia into the partnership. His wife was a sister of Malaxa's wife. The Bascos sold out in 1973.

Mile 64 **Frenchy Creek** on the right.

Mile 64.4 **Geneva Bar** on the left. An extensive sandbar campsite, best in low water.

Mile 65.5 **Cook Creek** on the Oregon side. This stream was formerly called Deep Creek. The name change was suggested by a member of a Forest Service survey crew. John Cook was a prospector who settled on the creek in 1888.

Mile 65.6 **Lone Pine Creek** twists down from the right.

Mile 66.8 **Jim Creek** on the Oregon side. This stream memorializes Jim Gaillard, a French-American who homesteaded about two miles from the river, according to Gerald Tucker. This site was the location of the Treasure Group copper claims, active at the same time as Eureka Bar.

The brown board building on the downriver side of the creek is a grain and supply storage shed for the Jim Creek ranch. The road, which travels three miles to the ranch, can be seen on the hem of the hill beyond the creek.

Charlie Spain's homestead at the head of Jim Creek. He took the homestead with his wife Daina, and their first child, Barbara, was born there. The Spains held the place for 14 years, *before selling it to Jay Dobbin and moving to McGraw Creek near Homestead in 1917. Spain Saddle is named for the family.*

Mile 68 **Cottonwood Creek** flows out on the Idaho bank. A boiler which was on the steamboat *Imnaha* can be found embedded in the sandbank on the upriver side of this stream.

Boaters will find good campsites above and below the mouth of Cottonwood.

Mile 68.3 **Coon Creek** on the left.

Mile 69.7 **Big Cougar Creek** on the right.

Mile 70.5 **Cochran Islands** interrupt the river channel. When Kyle McGrady had problems with his boat engine in May, 1948, his son, Kenneth, jumped out on the large gravel bar above Cochran rocks. Unable to hold the craft, Ken was left stranded on the island while Kyle drifted on down to Lewiston. There he immediately asked Bert Zimmerly for help.

Doris Sigler's placer mining outfit on Snake River just above Wild Goose Rapid.

Bert Zimmerly hauling a load of calendars and mail to Snake River ranches in the winter of 1948.

Bert was the pioneer bush pilot of Snake River. He learned to fly in 1930 and came to Lewiston in 1934 as a commercial pilot. Utilizing single-engine planes, he organized the first airline in Idaho. Zimmerly flew countless search, rescue and mercy missions. When boats couldn't get through, his plane was the canyon rancher's only link to the outside world. If conditions made a landing impossible, Zim would parachute supplies or mail to the settlers below.

It was dark when Bert took off upriver with Kyle. They dropped flares to determine the distance to the water, then landed his float plane on the river and taxied to the island. Ken had disappeared. Apparently, during his dad's absence, the boy had decided to swim to shore. His body was recovered 300 miles downriver.

Zimmerly was killed in a plane crash near Pullman less than a year later. He is remembered with admiration and affection by all who knew him. J. V. Cunningham's couplet seems appropriate:

"Life flows to death like rivers to the sea,

And life is sweet and death is salt to me."

Mile 71. **Garden Creek** on the Oregon shore. We are indebted to J. Harley Horner and Grace Bartlett for the information about this location:

The stream was named for the fine garden and lovely flowers grown here by Fielding, who was the first squatter on the creek. He was a little eccentric. He received a remittance of money regularly from somewhere. Fielding settled on the site in the early 1890's, and built a driftwood cabin near the mouth of the creek. He also raised a sizeable patch of tobacco and would hunt for a tamarack, cut off a block, bore a deep hole in it, put tobacco in and with a peg drive it in tight till full. After a time, he would split the block and have his chewing tobacco in a long, hard plug.

Gene P. Baldwin settled here at a later date and also raised a fine garden on the bar. He made final proof on the place in 1912.

Garden Creek was part of the Dobbin and Huffman holdings. The long wooden shearing shed was used by their outfit to cut wool from several thousand ewes each spring.

Mile 72 **Cave Gulch** on the Idaho side. The following article appeared in a 1904 issue of the *Lewiston Tribune:*

Cave Gulch, on Snake River

Lewiston, Idaho, March 13. —

Herman Wundram, a well known miner arrived here tonight with three horses packed with gold ore from a strike

366

made 30 miles from Lewiston on Cave Gulch in the Snake river country. The ore weighs about 400 pounds and its estimated value is from $1,500 to $2,000. Wundram also brought out gold estimated at $400, which he panned from a hat full of ore taken from the strike. The strike was made on an abandoned prospect and a five-foot lead was opened. A five-inch streak is marvelously rich in free gold and carries estimated values of $5,000 to $6,000 a ton. The strike has caused much excitement and has resulted in a stampede to the new district.

Mile 72. **Cache Creek** on the Oregon side. Again, Horner's efforts are responsible for our knowledge of this area. He indicates the creek was named by A. C. Smith, who with others was scouting the country on his way to the 1876 council at Lapwai. He found some Indian caches on the bar near the mouth of the creek. The Indians often cached dried salmon in a chalky place where water wouldn't soak it. This bar was one of the main Indian crossings to Lapwai, according to Horner.

Shearing crew at Cache Creek waiting for Press Brewrink's boat to take them upriver to shear more Dobbin and Huffman sheep.

In the early 1880's John Shoemaker and Captain Forester settled here and worked placer claims. They ground wheat in a coffee mill for their bread.

Tom Humphreys, T. B. Day, and another man in 1883 tried whipsawing lumber for sluice boxes in order to mine the bar, but the gold was too fine to placer at a profit.

Sam Marks, who was trapping at Granite Creek in March, 1892, drowned when his boat upset while crossing the river near Saddle Creek. His body was found here later in the spring, identified from his boots. He was buried on this bar.

The Jim, Garden, and Cache Creek ranches were all owned by Jay Dobbin at one time.

Mrs. Hickenbottom cooked for the Dobbin and Huffman shearing crew. She was plump as a 40-pound robin. On one occasion she took a horse to the camp at Jim Creek. She met one of the crew on the trail and he said, "Why, Mrs. Hickenbottom, if I'd known you had to ride I'd have gotten you a saddle."

She stared at him with some indignation and replied, "I'll have you know I've *got* a saddle!"

Mile 72.6 An interesting stone house on the Idaho side, about 300 yards from the river. Several homesteaders built such cabins because wood was scarce along the river.

Mile 72.9 The **Oregon-Washington** state line is marked by a sign above the river.

Mile 73 **China Garden Creek** on the Idaho shore. This site was known as the Madden Ranch. They raised cattle and hogs on the bench-land.

Mile 73.5 **Corral Creek** on the Idaho side. This was the access road for Dick Rivers' logging operation.

Before the first World War, there was a serious proposal to drive a tunnel from the mouth of Corral Creek nine miles through to the Salmon River, just below John Day Creek. A reservoir on the Salmon would have dropped water 435 feet down through the tunnel to a similar impoundment on the Snake.

Mile 74. On the Idaho riverbank there are some pieces of granite stacked like tombstones close to the water's edge. They were quarried by **Arthur Garlinghouse** of Lewiston.

Arthur's father, Arza, came to Lewiston in 1903 to visit a friend's stepson. Arza had been trained in the family tradition of stone-cutting in Kansas. He wanted to start a monument shop in the west and Lewiston seemed a likely location. He opened Garlinghouse Memorials on Lewiston's Main Street in 1903 and the business has remained in family hands to this time.

Arthur Garlinghouse followed his father to Idaho. He, too, had the skills to quarry granite and marble. He got a job from a builder at Lewiston Normal School (now Lewis and Clark College) to go up the

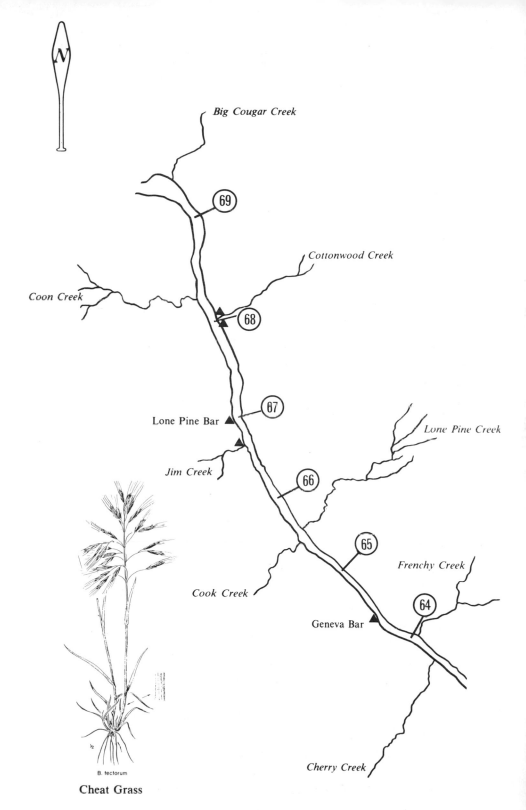

Big Cougar Creek

69

Cottonwood Creek

Coon Creek

68

Lone Pine Bar

67

Lone Pine Creek

Jim Creek

66

65

Frenchy Creek

Cook Creek

64

Geneva Bar

Cherry Creek

B. tectorum

Cheat Grass

Snake River and cut granite slabs that were to be used as window ledges and door sills at the school. The sills were quarried from the ledge (where some of them still lie) and hauled by steamboat to town.

After several ventures, including a homestead on Craig Mountain, Art finally bought Arza's business in Lewiston. He and his own son, Richard, opened a quarry at Corral Creek, just upriver from the pile of window ledges. They cut granite out of a wall about a quarter mile up the creek.

Granite ledges and sills quarried by the Garlinghouses from Lewiston. The pile can still be observed by boaters on the Idaho side of the river just below Corral Creek.

Garlinghouse and helper quarrying granite at Corral Creek.

The Corral Creek quarry was worked from 1925 to 1930. They used "plugs and feathers" (drills and wedges) to carve out the blocks. The granite was loaded on an iron-wheeled wagon and pulled to the river with a Fordson tractor where E. G. MacFarlane could load the rock on his boat. "Quite a little job," as Richard recalled.

The operation was discontinued because of the hauling expense and the waste involved. It was a fairly good grade of granite, but much time was lost removing checks and spots which couldn't be seen until the stone was polished.

Arza Garlinghouse in 1903 in front of his first monument shop in Lewiston.

Richard and his father worked together for 29 years. When Arthur died, Richard and his wife Eldora were joined in the business by their son, Jac. At this time, a fifth generation of Garlinghouses serves the Lewiston area as monument makers.

Mile 74.8 **Shovel Creek** on the left.

Mile 75 **Wild Goose Ranchos.** This subdivision, or rookery, is a good example of what might have happened in Hells Canyon had the area not received National Recreation Area status.

Mile 76. **Wild Goose Rapid.** H. W. McCurdy's *Marine History of the Pacific Northwest* indicates that the steamboat *Lewiston,* in charge of Captain E. W. Baughman, was dispatched by the O.S.N. to pick up a cargo of ore at the Great Eastern mine. The ship was unable to overcome this rapid, so the journey was a "wild goose chase" — hence the name. Others claim wild geese nested at this location.

There is a steamboat lining ring in the rock at the head of the rapid on the Washington side, not far from the water.

Steamboat cable ring at the head of Wild Goose Rapid. Ring was anchored with hot sulphur.

Jim Chapman's old cabin is the brown building on the Washington shore. He originally shingled the back of the cabin with the tops of evaporated milk cans, though shakes have since replaced them. Chapman had all the land from Chimney Creek to Wild Goose on the Idaho side. He sold his boat, the *Bryan,* to Press Brewrink. He later ran a grain warehouse on the river near Asotin.

The AA1 mine, whose tunnel and tailings can be seen on the Washington bench, was the lode that brought Brewrink to the river.

Just below the rapid is the China Gardens Dam site. This was to be a concrete dam 168 feet high and 1,000 feet long at its crest. Plans called for a 500-foot bridge across the Snake below the Grande Ronde to bring the road along the Idaho shore to the construction site. The dam would have been built at the same time as High Mountain Sheep.

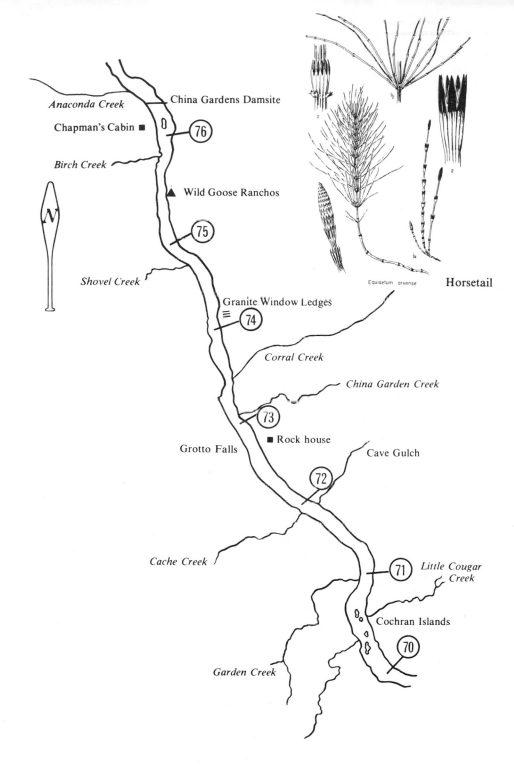

Anaconda Creek

China Gardens Damsite

Chapman's Cabin ■

76

Birch Creek

▲ Wild Goose Ranchos

75

Shovel Creek

Granite Window Ledges

74

Corral Creek

China Garden Creek

73

■ Rock house

Grotto Falls

Cave Gulch

72

Cache Creek

71   Little Cougar
          Creek

Cochran Islands

70

Garden Creek

Equisetum arvense   **Horsetail**

The Jim Chapmans camped at Chimney Creek. Jim's galvanized motor boat allowed them to get up and down river.

The mayor of Rogersburg.

Doris Stgler Babcock's house (loft) and post office/store at Rogersburg.

Mile 76.5 **Anaconda Creek** on the left.

Mile 77.2 **Middle Creek** on the right.

Mile 78.1 **Chimney Creek** on the Idaho side. There is a cave and Indian petroglyphs near the mouth of this stream. A marble quarry was developed a mile up this creek in 1904. George Koster, cashier of the Lewiston National Bank, was one of the owner-developers. A marble sawmill was built at the Lewiston Foundry and Machine Works with a gang of six saws which could cut 50 cubic feet of marble a day. It was shipped to the quarry and a wagon road was cut down to the river so that the blue-white stone could be shipped on the *Mountain Gem*. The limited extent of the deposit and transportation difficulties closed the quarry. Most of the workings were covered by a waterspout.

Mile 79 **Lime Point** on the Idaho shore. West Coast Portland Cement Company had a tunnel at Lime Point and there were several buildings here at one time. The point contains over 500 acres of cement materials. A U.S.G.S. report stated "analysis of the average sample shows it to be of exceptional purity and all that could be desired in the production of Portland Cement." The company installed the first unit of a plant intended to have a production capacity of a million barrels a day. Once again, transportation proved the limiting factor.

Mile 80 **Rogersburg** and the **Grande Ronde** on the Washington shoreline. "Ronde" is French for circle or roundness. Taken together, the words mean large valley and the name was bestowed by French Canadian trappers.

375

An oral tradition claims Chief Joseph was born in the cave on Joseph Creek, a tributary of the Ronde, that enters the river two miles above its mouth. Joseph's band wintered along the creek.

J. H. Horner relates the story of Albert Hester: Grande Ronde River recluse, found dead in his cabin in mid-November, 1927. Hester was a German and a geologist. If anyone expressed an interest, he would talk all day about the formation of rocks — in a squeaky voice. He lived alone in his cabin on the Ronde for 40 years. In deference to his mother's wishes, he always wore women's clothing and braided his long hair down his back. Hester kept several clean dresses and wore one, along with a sunbonnet and women's shoes, when he went visiting. On such calls he conversed with the women of the house, rather than the men. Albert survived by prospecting and is reportedly buried on his place.

The Rogers brothers filed mining claims on the bar on the upriver side of the Grande Ronde. They laid out a townsite and planned to sell lots, but business was slower than a snail on a slick log. There was a road from Enterprise and Joseph to the Grande Ronde, and another up the Snake to Captain John Creek (six miles downriver) but none to Rogersburg.

Eventually, there were three houses and a store with a post office. Mail was boated up from Asotin twice a week. Until a ferry was installed, it was necessary to cross the river with rowboat or horse.

Neil Smith, who was on Joseph Creek working cattle in 1913, recalled that the road from there to Rogersburg was completed in 1937. He said the first car to arrive in the community came over that route and "gentle saddle horses jumped fences and gates and just took off; they had never seen a benzine devil wagon before." The road from Captain John Creek was finished in 1938, but a bridge was not built until a later time.

Doris Sigler Babcock bought a house and the store at Rogersburg in 1934 and lived there for five years. She ran the post office and her children went five miles each day to school on Joseph Creek. When she sold the place, she made a living by sluicing for gold up the Snake River as far as Half Moon Bar.

Mile 81 **Heller Bar,** take-out point for boat trips. Lewiston is reached after a 32 mile drive from Heller Bar.

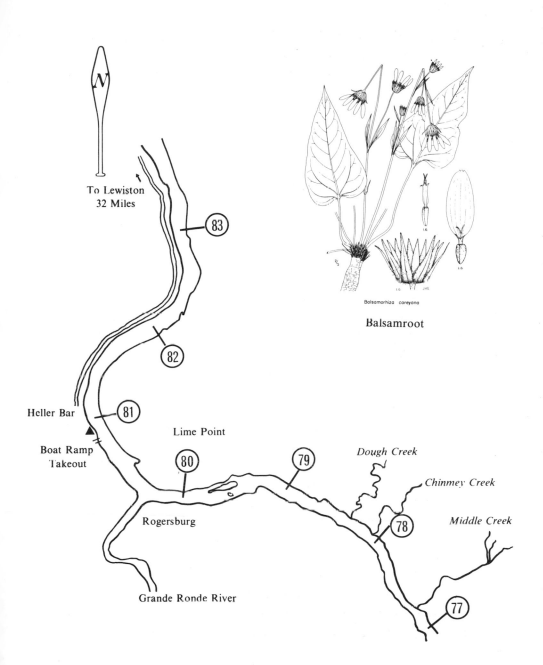

To Lewiston
32 Miles

83

82

Heller Bar

81

Boat Ramp
Takeout

Lime Point

80

79

Dough Creek

Chinmey Creek

78

Middle Creek

Rogersburg

Grande Ronde River

77

Balsamorhiza careyana

Balsamroot

Lewiston was established at the confluence of the Snake and the Clearwater Rivers as a result of Captain E. D. Pierce's gold discovery about 75 miles east of the present city in 1860. Portland newspapers promoted the strike and the easiest route to the Pierce placer mines from the coast was up the Columbia, Snake and Clearwater Rivers. The shallow bed of the Clearwater was an obstacle to steamboat traffic, so Lewiston was the natural choice for a supply center at the head of navigation.

At the time of the gold discovery the land where Pierce and Lewiston would be located was still part of the Nez Perce reservation. Indian agent, A. J. Cain, warned the settlers that he would tear down any permanent buildings, so framed canvas tents were used as dwellings. This worked a hardship on the early fortune seekers as the winter of 1861-62 was the most severe recorded in Idaho. Spring floodwaters followed.

Lewiston, Idaho Territory, circa 1863.

Fort Lapwai Army wagon master Tom Beall gave this account of how the town was named:

The way we came to name it Lewiston was when on May 19, 1861, there were five or six of us sitting on a log where Trevitt had his tent (Lewiston's first merchantile establishment). Several names were suggested by our party (The others present were Mr. Dutro, Mr. Carr and Dr. Buker) John (Silcott) suggested we name it after some Indian Chief. During our talk about the matter, Trevitt came out of the tent and said: 'Gentlemen,' why not name this place Lewiston after Lewis and Clark' and the suggestion was accepted by us at once. It turned out later that Trevitt didn't have Lewis so much in mind as Lewiston, Maine, his former place of residence.

A western view of Lewiston's Main Street in 1882.

Fifth Street in the 1880's.

Main Street of Lewiston, 1890.

Fifth and Main Streets in Lewiston about 1915. (Looking east)

Looking east in Lewiston, about 1899 at Third and Main.

Sternwheel steamers moored along the Lewiston waterfront.

Steamboats docked at Lewiston.

Steamboats moored at Lewiston during the winter: Front to rear: **Lewiston, Spokane,** *and* **Hannaford.**

Lewiston in 1900. Clearwater River on the left, Snake River on the right. The islands are now submerged by the backwaters from Granite Dam. The Interstate bridge links Lewiston with Clarkston.

Most of the Indians agreed to a new treaty in 1863 and the site of Lewiston was ceded to the United States. However, Congress did not ratify the treaty for four years.

The same year the new treaty was accepted by the Nez Perce, Congress organized the Territory of Idaho, which until that time had been part of Washington Territory. President Lincoln appointed William Wallace as first governor and Wallace selected Lewiston as the territorial capital. Within a month the governor had himself elected territorial delegate, resigned his position and departed for the nation's capital.

Fresh gold discoveries in the Boise Basin in 1862 had caused a wild exodus from the Clearwater camps for southern Idaho. Lewiston's population had plummeted from 10,000 to about 375 by the time the first legislature met there. Southern Idaho residents outnumbered those in the north nearly seven to one. Caleb Lyon, of New York, was appointed as the second governor in 1864. It was eight months before he arrived to fill his post. At the first meeting of the legislature under his tenure, southern legislators succeeded in passing a bill which moved the capital to Boise City. Furious Lewiston residents responded by placing the Territorial Seal and Archives under 24-hour guard to prevent their removal and kept a watchful eye on the new governor. Lyons decided to

go duck hunting on the Snake River. Southern Idaho friends rowed him across the river and put him on a stage that would eventually take him to Boise. Instead, the governor went to San Francisco and then East for 10 months. He visited Idaho once for a short spell, then went East again. You can't keep a squirrel on the ground in timber country. In Washington, D.C. he complained that $47,000 had been stolen from his money belt while he slept on the train. The sum was apparently federal money, and under suspicion he retired to New York, where he died. The state capital was never restored to Lewiston.

Gradually the city turned to farming and timber harvest. The Palouse Country, on the plateau north and west of the Lewiston North Hills became one of the best dry land wheat growing areas in the United States. Steamboats hauled harvests to Portland.

In the late 1920's, lumber mills began to operate in the city and eventually became the mainstay of the community. Potlach Forest Products on the Clearwater River at the edge of Lewiston employs about 2700 persons.

Though it is 470 miles inland from the sea, with the completion of eight dams and navigation locks on the lower Snake, Lewiston became a seaport. Any vessel drawing less than 14 feet may travel from the mouth of the Columbia to the mouth of the Clearwater. The grain and forest products of the Inland Empire now move to the Pacific coast on barges towed by efficient and economical tugboats.

Epilogue

Hear the wind
Blow through the bunchgrass,
Blow over wild grape and brier.
This was frontier, and this,
And this, your house, was frontier.
There were footprints upon the hill
And men lie buried under,
Tamers of earth and rivers.
They died at the end of labor. . . .
You shall remember them. You shall not see
Water or wheat or axe-mark on the tree
And not remember them.

Steven Vincent Benet
Western Star

Bibliography

Aoki, Haruo. *Nez Perce Texts*. Berkeley: University of California Press, 1979.

Ashworth, William. *Hells Canyon: The Deepest Gorge on Earth*. New York: Hawthorne Books, 1977.

Bailey, Robert G. *Hells Canyon*. Lewiston, Idaho: privately printed, 1943.

Beal, Merril D. *"I Will Fight No More Forever": Chief Joseph and the Nez Perce War*. Washington Paperbacks ed., Seattle: University of Washington Press, 1966.

Brown, Mark H. *The Flight of the Nez Perce*. New York: Capricorn, 1967.

Elsensohn, M. Alfreda. *Pioneer Days in Idaho County*, 2 vols. Caldwell, Idaho: Caxton Printers, 1951.

Gulick, Bill. *Snake River Country*. Caldwell, Idaho: Caxton Printers, 1971.

Haines, Francis. *The Nez Perces: Tribesmen of the Columbia Plateau*. Norman, Oklahoma: University of Oklahoma Press, 1955.

Horner, J. H. *"Origin of Wallowa County Place Names"* ed. Grace Bartlett, mimeographed manuscript, Historical Files, Wallowa Whitman National Forest, Baker, Oregon.

Howard, O. O. *Nez Perce Joseph*. 1881, reprinted. New York: Da Capo Press, 1972.

Huntley, James. *Ferryboats in Idaho*. Caldwell, Idaho: Caxton Printers, 1979.

Irving, Washington. *The Adventures of Captain Bonneville, U.S.A., in the Rocky Mountains and the Far West*. Norman, Oklahoma: University of Oklahoma Press, 1961.

—————— *Astoria, or Anecdotes of an Enterprise Beyond the Rocky Mountains*. Norman, Oklahoma: University of Oklahoma Press, 1964.

Jordan, Grace. *Home Below Hells Canyon*. New York: Thomas Y. Crowell, 1954.

Josephy, Alvin M., Jr. *The Nez Perce Indians and the Opening of the Northwest*. New Haven: Yale University Press, 1965.

Lockley, Fred, ed. *"Reminiscences of Captain William P. Gray"* Oregon Historical Quarterly 14 (December 1913): 321-54.

McArthur, Lewis A. *Oregon Geographic Names*. 4th ed. rev. by Lewis L. McArthur. Portland: Oregon Historical Society, 1974.

Mackenzie, Cecil W. *Donald Mackenzie: "King of the Northwest."* Los Angeles: Ivan Beach, Jr. Publisher, 1937.

McWhorter, L. V. *Hear Me, My Chiefs!: Nez Perce History and Legend*. Caldwell, Idaho: Caxton Printers. 1940

──────── *Yellow Wolf: His Own Story*. Caldwell, Idaho: Caxton Printers, 1940.

Moser, Don. *The Snake River Country*. New York: Time-Life Books, 1974.

Norton, Boyd. *Snake Wilderness*. San Francisco: Sierra Club, 1972.

Sincock, Robert. *"Case Is Closed"* Oregon Journal (Portland) September 18, 1938.

Stratton, David H. and Lindeman, Glen W. *A Study of Historical Resources of the Hells Canyon National Recreation Area*. 2 vols. United States Department of Agriculture, Forest Service, Baker, Oregon. Mimeographed. 1978

Stuart, Robert. *Discovery of the Oregon Trail*. New York, Scribners, 1935.

Thwaites, Reuben Gold, Ed. *Original Journals of the Lewis and Clark Expeditions, 1804 - 1806*, 8 vols. 1904. reprint., New York: Antiquarian Press, 1959.

Tucker, Gerald J. *"Massacre for Gold."* Old West, Fall 1967, pp. 26-28, 48.

──────── *The Story of Hells Canyon*. Privately printed 1977.

Vallier, Tracy L. *Geologic Guide to Hells Canyon, Snake River*. Geologic Society of America Field Guide #5, 1976.

Wells, Merle W. *"She will strike about there . . . : Steamboating in Hells Canyon."* Idaho Yesterdays 1 (Summer 1957): 2 - 9.

──────── *Steamboat down the Snake: The Early Story of the 'Shoshone'."* Idaho Yesterdays 5 (Winter 1961 - 62): 22 - 23.

Wilson, Fred W. and Stewart, Earle K. *Steamboat Days on the Rivers*. Portland: Oregon Historical Society, 1969.

Wright, E. W., ed. *Lewis and Dryden's Marine History of the Pacific Northwest*. Portland, 1895.

Maps

Index

Weinheimer, Bert 201, 208
Weiser, town of 5, 24, 84, 87, 92, 101,
    106, 139, 153, 161
Wenaha 93
West Creek 284
West, Oswald 124
White, Georgie 93
White Bird, town of 188, 218
White Swan Lumber Co. 301
Whittier, Nancy 292
Wild Goose Rapid 57, 62, 65, 372
Wild Goose Ranchos 371
Wildhorse Creek 117
Wild Sheep Rapid 75, 166
Willamette River 28, 40, 42
Willow Creek 223
Wilson, Allen and Hazel 164, 183, 185
Wilson, Bud 99, 183, 201, 222, 225, 230
Wilson, Ethel 177, 188-93
Wilson, Frank and Minnie 289
Wilson, Jimmy 192
Wilson, Lem 244, 277, 298
Wilson, Murrielle 202, 219
Wilson, Pete 188-194
Winchester, Sherm 157

Winehammer Gulch 208
Winniford, John 210
Winniford, Walter 210
Winniford, William 210
Winters, Frank 266, 308
Wisenor, Jim and Stella 245
Wisenor, William 248
Wolf Creek 298
Wood, George and Martha 279
Wood, Robert 87
Woolridge, Glenn 92
Wyatt, Mattie 298, 300
Wyatt, Frank 241, 280, 359-60
Wyley Creek 338

Y

Yamhill River 42
Yellowstone Park 1, 73
Yreka Creek 222

Z

Zimmerly, Bert 364
Zig Zag Creek 338

Authors

Johnny Carrey, Idaho County historian, raconteur, rancher, poet and humorist lives with his wife, Pearl above the Little Salmon River, near the Hells Canyon breaks. He spends considerable time carving belt buckles from mountain sheep horn, though he favors a reduced or rescheduled Bighorn hunting season. Carrey can be found at ease wherever fiddle players congregate – listening to music that is always better than his own. Well ahead of the event, he has written his own epitaph: "Served the soil for 60 years/with horse and rope and plow/but never really got a rest/till now. P.S. I'd rather be on Little White Bird Ridge.

Ace Barton, grandson of Mart Hibbs, and son of Lenora Hibbs and Ralph Barton, was born on Summit Creek of the Imnaha River. He was three years old when his parents brought him by horse to Battle Creek in Hells Canyon. Ace began fighting fire for the Forest Service when he was 13. He worked as a lookout on the Salmon River District and did trail and telephone line maintenance as well. While in the Army during World War II, Ace received a bronze star and the purple heart. Following the war, Ace returned to Hells Canyon where he labored on Lenora Barton's ranch holdings along the river until 1957. At present he is a fire control officer on the Nez Perce National Forest and lives with his wife, Hattie, and daughter, Adona, in Riggins, Idaho. Ace's ability as a master-of-ceremonies and his gift with amusing stories has made him the Salmon River cowman's answer to Johnny Carson.

Cort Conley is an Idaho river guide whose grub line always cuts through Cambridge, Idaho.

Colophon

Typeface: Century Schoolbook 10/14
Century Schoolbook Italic 8/10
Layout: Julie and Roger Sliker, Grand Rapids, Michigan
Front Cover: Philip Schofield
Rear Cover: Larry Hill
Typography: B & J Typesetting, Boise, Idaho
Binding: Smythsewn and Perfect, Caxton Printers
Printing: Joslyn/Morris, Inc., Boise, Idaho